CW01044359

RYAN MURPHY

You've got the Gig!

100'000 miles as a cycle courier in the gig economy.
The good, bad & the ugly.

To the best support team in the world, who taught me to ride a bike and how to get up every time I fall, time and time again, time and time again...

You may be an ambassador
to England or France.
You may like to gamble,
you might like to dance.
You may be the heavyweight cham-
pion of the world
You may be a socialite
with a long string of pearls
But you're gonna have to serve somebody

Bob Dylan - 'Serve Somebody'

Contents

Foreword

What if I told you there was a job that would pay you

To be happy,

To be healthy,

To lose weight,

To get much fitter,

To explore a city,

To sample free food,

To meet fellow enthusiasts,

To make other people happy,

To forget your stresses and strife,

To leave it all behind?

This aint no pyramid scheme amigos.

I left it all behind me.

I got the gig!

Preface

Who I am? It isn't that important. Why have I written this? Well, now seems as good a time as any, in the middle of a world pandemic like Covid-19, to share my story of giving up a very secure job while going back to university to study for a master's degree, and how that led to something I hadn't quite expected and certainly hadn't planned. I could never have predicted how the need to make a living while studying – by doing something I loved, cycling – would change my whole outlook on life, as I quickly became immersed in the little-known world of the gig economy.

With predictable negativity, news stories that focus on this growing economic sector have predominately depicted its business model as an exploitative way of eroding the rights and benefits workers have typically enjoyed as employees chained to a traditional company. While this may be the case, I won't be delving too deeply into the structural realities and adjustments faced by many, including myself, who work in this flexible and fast-moving (literally!) industry.

What I want to do is simply share my experiences of working in the gig economy as a cycle courier with Deliveroo, one of the most recognisable names among the new tech service delivery platforms and one of the fastest growing technology companies in Europe. A real peek behind the curtains at life in the saddle – with all the highs, lows, free food and random mishaps along the way, including one meal that ended up costing me a small fortune. The cold, harsh, busy winters, followed by the warm, laidback, quieter summers.

From working all day until your face was numb with pain from frost, to long summer days when only the sun going down makes you think of going home to get some much-needed rest. These everyday experiences often get overlooked when the media brings the magnifying glass down on this rapidly burgeoning way to work for millions of people in this country, and perhaps hundreds of millions around the world, shining what sometimes feels like a harsh, artificial light on the job, missing the many glaring positives and benefits that come from cycling for a living.

What started out as a part-time job while back at university for a year quickly became a near obsession of 55-hour weeks, as the gig economy took off across Britain and the rest of the world. From an initial and passionate love affair to a marriage made in hell, repeated several times over. Cycling to the brink of exhaustion, and trying to rein in the cycling when used for purposes other than paid work – the dark and depressing reality of simply overdoing it to extremes.

This is one man's bicycle journey – an adventure so epic that it would eventually stretch to more than a hundred thousand miles, the equivalent of four laps of planet Earth. It's a figure I can scarcely believe myself, mostly because it all took place within a small geographical area (well, two areas). But it's true, and here it all is: the good, the bad and the ugly. And, yes, it does get ugly.

1

The Early Days

'Every child is an artist. The problem is how to remain an artist once he grows up.' Pablo Picasso

That feeling you first exhibit as a child, after a few years roaming around the vicinity of your humble dwelling, learning the language, skills, habits and general ways of life that will hopefully stand you in good stead going into your crucial development years.

Before the hard work and stress of school exams, before girlfriends (or lack of) and the inevitable morphing we all go through into some kind of strange-looking and -sounding individual in our adolescent years.

Before that, before all the heartbreak and ball ache of becoming a teenager, there were the golden years of boyhood, between infancy and puberty, in which you could do whatever you bloody well pleased. It was a great time, the world was yours to explore and enjoy.

Once the stabilisers came off and you were brave enough

to venture out on the shiny, new bike that your parents had saved up all year to get you for Christmas, then a whole new world opened up. A parallel universe, one which was ten times bigger and better, thanks to the newly acquired superpower of being able to leave your cul-de-sac for the first time without needing to retrace your steps or fearing the backlash of not being back before the streetlights came on.

It is a great time for most kids. Knocking around with your friends, kicking a football around the park, and generally finding out what the world, or at least your own neighbourhood, was really like. DJ Jazzy Jeff and the Fresh Prince provided the soundtrack to those endless 90s summers of fun when the world was so much less complicated and the only thing getting in the way of adventure and mischief were the late August nights drawing in.

Your only worry was how late you could stay out playing before one of your parents emerged, aggressively shouting orders for the fifth and final time to tell you had to get back in the house, to be fed and put to bed, before you passed out asleep outside and the Candyman came to pick you up for not listening to your parents.

You were free, happy, content, creative and full of wanderlust, with endless ideas for what to do with all that magical free time just waiting to be filled with whatever your boundless imagination conjured up; consumed with how to squeeze the most out of every long sunny day in the endless carefree summer holiday.

As the child's world expanded, new frontiers opened up. You could finally make it all the way to the shops to buy a can of something fizzy and quench your thirst before the long journey back. You could explore places of interest you had previously only viewed from the car window, passing by on the way back from a shopping trip to the city. There were so many opportunities closed off to young people until they got hold of a bike, arguably the best bit of kit they were ever likely to own. It was this most simple of machines that would get you to other friends' houses, estates, towns, villages, beaches, shops, parks or any other place of interest that would previously have been impossible to reach under your own steam.

There it was, standing awkwardly on the sofa one Christmas, inside fluorescent red and green wrapping paper that didn't even begin to disguise what it was. You were already elated at the prospect even before you started ripping it off. And if you think I am overplaying the significance of a bike to kids of any era before the internet exploded, then you are obviously a kid who can't remember a time before the internet. This was *the* tool for accessing the rest of your world – the bits that really mattered – in the pre-tech age.

I am referring to the early 1990s, which for people of a certain age is not so long ago but for a younger generation is a kind of prehistory. Crucially, it's an analogue time, before the digital realm exploded and the world as we had known it became superseded by the World Wide Web. Of course, nowadays it's more widely called the internet, but either way this profound, disruptive invention would go on to change everything in our simple, everyday lives.

As a slightly odd-looking thirteen-year-old boy undergoing the physical disruptions of puberty – someone who had only just discovered Napster and was still watching Britney Spears videos on MTV (don't tell anyone I told you) – I found something liberating about being able to dial up this internet malarkey. Find any song in the world and wait for it to download within the next half hour, fingers crossed. (For anyone under thirty, that is not a typo – it really did take that long.) Only 20 years ago, given how long it took, downloading (not streaming) a song would be seen as an evening or weekend privilege when you were using a pay-as-you-go internet service provider to access the web, and when your siblings were just as eager to have their daily fix of early internet usage on the family home computer.

On a mobile phone in these prehistoric days you could call your mates, or text them with just enough characters to tell them you were alive or grounded, and you could even have a talk-of-the-town novelty ringtone based on the theme from *Titanic*, the Leonardo DiCaprio and Kate Winslet blockbuster from that era. These were much simpler times, like I say. Everyone wanted a desktop computer for the internet, and a mobile phone to let their mates know in under 130 characters that they wanted in on the 35cl bottle of vodka for Friday night. Still, these two very separate and expensive bits of technology were not yet at the stage of usability that would see them become accessible to almost anyone anywhere on the planet.

Fast-forward two decades, and changes in the use of mobile phones and the internet have been absolutely mind-blowing, and are now completely taken for granted. These tools have comprehensively changed the way we live our lives, interact with others, and access goods and services in a way that was utterly inconceivable only twenty years ago – a time when you waited until 6pm (when calls were cheaper) to call friends and family on the landline or order takeaways from your local Indian, Chinese or chippie.

These fast-food joints had cornered the market in takeaway business among hungry punters in towns or cities across the country until very recently, when technology delivery platforms emerged on people's mobile phones as simple-to-use digital-payment apps. In those days (both the bad-old days and the good-old days), landline phones would be dialled, orders would be placed (and always lost in translation) and, with any luck, in the next hour or so your food would turn up and you would pay the delivery driver, emerging from his beaten-up old car, with some cold hard cash.

Some of this cash would be ready to hand straight over to the driver. The remainder would have to be rescued from the bowels of the sofa, like a rare diamond dug out from a pitch-black mine, every cushion, wooden slat and fibre of fabric removed, the empty frame scoured for anything remotely metallic or shiny until eventually, if you were lucky, you found the 56p by which you were short of the right money, and the takeaway driver finally agreed to hand over the food. Then restoring the sofa to its original solid state so that it was fit to sit on could take just as much time and severely delay the enjoyment of your meal. It was all such a drag, but we didn't know anything else, so no one ever thought to complain.

If the sofa search was unsuccessful, it was time to raid every cupboard, jar, bedroom drawer, wallet, purse or siblings' piggy bank that you could lay your hands on or break open in time. This required lightning-fast initiative and barbarian-style hunting skills before the delivery driver eventually grew tired of waiting and decided whether or not to accept whatever you could rustle up as payment for your now-lukewarm takeaway meal.

There were emergency procedures, such as going next

door to borrow some money (always the youngest and most naive member of the household would be sent into battle for this most undignified task) or simply admitting defeat to the delivery driver and sulking, begging for a 'stupid prick' discount. This was the nuclear option in every sense. Not only was he not going to receive full payment for the food you had rung up and ordered three hours earlier, he wasn't even going to be recompensed for the time he had spent listening to everyone in your household deconstruct and reconstruct every movable piece of furniture in the house.

Looking at the routine humiliations the job involved, as a kid I never harboured ambitions to pursue that line of work. After all, I willingly took part in the mental destruction of delivery drivers on a regular basis, by which I mean every last Friday of the month, at a time when having a takeaway was still seen as something of a treat. This was normally when parents had just been paid or, very occasionally, when someone in the household had come home with a good school report. So the last Friday of the month was the most likely time for such a banquet.

Simpler times indeed. Maybe it wasn't so much fun at the time, given the process I've described of ordering takeaways back in the 1990s, but there was always some comfort to be taken in knowing that every delivery driver hated their job and hated waiting while you looked for the money, only to be paid slightly less than the amount that was owed. An amount which the restaurant staff had clearly stated at the end of the call, and you had verbally agreed, when you'd called up excitedly not really paying attention to such tedious specifics to place the order.

Not for the first time, you had naively reassured the person on the end of the line that payment would be swift, in full and not covered in the accumulated gubbins that lurked in the bowels of your sofa. Finally, after excavating the foundations beneath your feet in search of the extra money needed to meet payment, you admitted defeat to the now-impenetrable statue-like figure standing in your doorway with his bum bag full of pennies and twopence pieces as payment. Well, they shouldn't let kids ring up for takeaways, should they? This was before the days of risk assessments and health and safety (probably).

Food delivery is just one small and insignificant sector that the internet transformed once reliable online payment systems had developed to make such transactions simple and instantaneous. Before they did, I would never even have considered the prehistoric world of hanging around in sweaty chip shops, waiting to pick up a pizza and kebab to be dropped off to the family from hell (again), who never had enough change. Working every weekend. Never having a social life. No wonder these delivery drivers became robots in disguise. Blank expressions met you every time you tried to prise your food from their grasp.

As a child, I could quite never understand why they were so unenthusiastic. So it's hardly surprising that I had never considered going down that road in adult life. In any case, I was probably still blacklisted from every fast-food place in town by the time I was old enough to start applying for jobs. I did eventually pass my driving test and was ready to stand on my own two feet, but by then I was much more interested in new sportswear and trainers than rubber kebabs or greasy pizzas.

There were certain skills that I acquired as a ten-year-old which needed to be unlearned, as I found they didn't cut it in the world of work. Crying for attention, kicking and beating siblings for attention, leaving home for good, again for attention. Basically, competing for the love and attention of your parents and friends, brothers and sisters. There were also habits that would prove more difficult to shake off as you grew into an adult version of yourself needing to handle the big, bad scary world.

Picking your nose, farting, kicking and beating siblings (now more for stress relief and enjoyment than for your parents' attention), and still competing for some kind of love and attention from the people around you to shore up your sanity. Sanity which is now being further eroded with each passing year as each new strand of grey messes up your once-pristine and easily tended head of hair.

Generally, I had successfully managed to integrate myself into adulthood without too many dramas. This had come at some cost to the many dreams and aspirations I had once had as a child growing up. Playing football, becoming a pilot or simply building Lego for a living (is that a thing?). Living at my parents' house and playing computer games for the rest of my life (which is most definitely a thing and is currently trending around the world bigtime). Or simply just finding some hidden treasure somewhere and living it up in a mansion for the rest of my days.

Not one of these scenarios ever played out in the real world. You can point a finger at parents for never finding that treasure you had told them about, rather than acknowledge that they chose to work hard and put food on the table instead. Or that they never won the lottery despite having as good a chance as anyone else in the country, with them teasing you with what you would be entitled to if they ever did win.

But this is the real world, and I've never been much of a finger pointer anyways. You make your own damn luck in this world, and I was damned if I was ever to become one of those horrid, bitter, demented neighbours that everyone had growing up, the ones who never return your ball once it enters their back garden. Or worse still, one of those even more bitter fast-food delivery drivers.

Yet there was one key skill that I had successfully managed to fully integrate into my long and arduous journey to becoming a semi-functioning semi-adult, semi still wanting to hold onto a childhood version of myself. The need to escape from reality. If only for an hour a day or a weekend break. A week in Benidorm if you're on a budget. Or a few weeks in the Algarve for those who can afford it. A gap year in Southeast Asia if your parents are loaded. Or a private island somewhere secluded if you're in the top 0.01 percent.

For the rest of us, the time you have to escape from reality generally becomes more constrained as adulthood consumes us all and forces us into more selfless choices such as having children, mortgages, cars or insurance policies – and thus having to earn the money to fund all those choices. The list of routine obligations is long and for the average person seems to get longer with every year that goes by.

It therefore becomes vital that this small window of time you allow yourself to escape and unwind is treated as sacred amid the many changes that beset the life of an average Joe (or Jo) like you or me. It can be found in reading a book, going for a walk in the park, a day out at the beach, or diving into the pub beer garden for a few swift pints after work or on a weekend. Any activity that basically helps you switch off for a few hours and shed the many burdens of adult life.

I was at such a critical juncture myself, as I had just left behind a job I had done for the past decade or so, had sold my house and car, and had used some of the money to go travelling around California while I decided what I was going to do with the rest of my life. Well, not so much the rest of my life, but the next year of my life, while I was back at university doing a postgraduate degree in something that would hopefully stand me in better stead for something I really hoped I would want to do in the future.

As the Cali hipsters cruised past me along Venice Beach Boardwalk on their chopper bikes, all tanned and smiling, basking in the warm sunshine, I sat leaning back into semiphilosophical daze on the edges of a skate park thinking back to being a paperboy. Being out on your bike, battling the elements, doing an underpaid yet still meaningful job. There is something primal about riding a bike that satisfies your inner child, wherever that child may lurk.

There are fewer and fewer examples in modern life where such basic excitement can be had. We prioritise careers, money, other people, sedentary lifestyles and social media or Netflix binges to fill our ever-decreasing amount of free time in the complex and tech-controlled world we have given permission to flourish all around us.

Most cyclists cherish the sense of freedom and childlike passion you feel when out riding a bike. Whether it is going for a spin around your local woods, for a day out in the mountains, or simply for an hour before or after work to de-stress or rehumanise yourself before pretending to become an adult again. I've always used cycling as my main outlet for unwinding, relaxing, thinking clearly, focusing, or simply shaking off any sense of anxiety at times when things aren't going quite so smoothly.

All the health benefits you accrue are also helpful, but just as importantly is being able to eat the food that otherwise I would have to think twice about is a huge bonus too. The reward for a hard day out on the bike is always the consumption of a hearty meal to replenish energy levels and leaving you feeling all the better for it.

It's strange, but these feelings never quite leave you when you mount your bike and head for adventure, wherever that may be. That feeling of leaving it all behind: your life, your wife (or significant other), your troubles – all the anxious thoughts and feelings that sometimes seem to bubble up all at once. It may be work, bills, exams or even Donald Trump for that matter (though not so much since the Twitter ban and the Orange One leaving office). Anything that keeps you awake at night, those stresses so annoyingly hard to shake off when you find yourself caught up in the very real rat race of contemporary adult life.

As I got older, the escape route the bike offered me became more important as I travelled that unforgiving road, with its many complexities, hardships and lessons to be learned – the ones you have still to learn as well as those you will never seemingly learn – when it dawned on me that being an adult may be something I will never quite get the hang of. It was my bicycle that enabled me to reconfigure and readjust to these emerging realities of not being ten years old and out with my mates any longer. OK, so there were a lot of people in my life that also kept me together, too, the stability and eccentricities of each one helping me adjust in much the same way we were all adjusting to this crazy world playing out around us all.

As I processed these life-changing thoughts and feelings

that I was slowly becoming overwhelmed by, catching some early evening rays of sunshine on Venice Beach promenade as I sat watching the world go by, I knew it was time to get myself a cool-looking Cali bike for a few days to help me make sense of all the jumbled-up clutter that was starting to cloud my supposedly carefree trip of a lifetime before I headed back to the far less sunny climate of the British Isles. Looking back, it was the first thing I thought of doing when I had finally started to properly relax and unwind. It must have been my brain's way of telling me that this was what I needed in order to defragment all these life-altering possibilities swirling around my subconscious like a potent flaming cocktail.

A few days passed and I had made my way up to San Francisco. Much like a sex-starved individual's first time in the red-light district of Amsterdam, I found myself ogling the sleek attractions I could see in the many windows of bike-hire shops around the city when I had first arrived. Determined to find the perfect companion to offer me similar stimulation for half the price of a female escort (I assume), I came across a beautiful old racer with all the charm and character that typified the place I was now looking to explore over the following week.

Besides which, Bruna and Andrea, a couple of Brazilian girls who me and Liam, the friend I was travelling with, had met on a bar crawl on the first night in San Fran, had wanted to join us for the excursion we had haphazardly planned after doing one too many shots. We had drunkenly shared our initial enthusiasm for wanting to see the whole city by bicycle, and with rather sore heads and hangover stories to share, that fresh overcast summer morning after a strong coffee and bagel we were ready to mount the bikes we had hired and take in the many sights of this amazing place.

In my head, selfishly, I already knew deep down I didn't want to be dictated to by a couple of Samba girls looking to get a few tourist photographs and selfies along the route, already stopping after ten minutes to adjust their make-up and hair, and continue the small talk from the night before. I craved the open road, a large chunk of being alone and a dash of speed to get me going (from the bike, of course).

This had always been a problem for me in the past as I introduced girlfriends, family members or anyone else in my ambit to days out cycling. I do thoroughly enjoy the social aspect of cycling, more so with mountain biking, when you meet up at the end of a hard run or section of trail and trade war stories, looking for missing bits of skin that were torn away when you fell off on that particularly challenging rocky section. However, I have always found road cycling is best enjoyed alone, just you against you.

Anyone I've been out with in the past would verify this tendency I have, as single-minded dogged determination comes to the fore and flicks a switch inside me that makes me tune out of the real world and into the other side of me that demands special introspective attention. It can be annoying for anyone I'm riding with, hoping for a 'nice day out' on our bikes.

I was finally ready and primed to put some soul-searching, spirit-raising, properly introverted hard miles on the body clock after the past few weeks in Southern California spent lying on a beach reading books and getting better acquainted with strangers from around the world. Once along the harbour, and after another quick sports drink, I was screaming to be let loose from company. Like a German tourist armed with a barrage of towels desperate to be the first to nab a poolside lounger, I was single-mindedly driven in my mission and needed no assistance from anyone else.

As the girls yet again stopped along the harbour, reached for the cameras and handed them over to Liam to create a summer collection to be proud of, I politely stated I would be setting off alone for a few hours; already fifty yards ahead of the others and growing more impatient by the second, I said I would see them all later for some food somewhere on the other side of the Golden Gate Bridge.

My despondent looking roommate glanced over, a camera in each hand, with the faint contours on his face as I selfishly pulled away suggesting pure unmistakable horror. The hire bike beneath me was quickly coming to life, responding with grace to every subtle movement I made as I shifted my hips to the front of the bike to push off and leave. He eventually realised I was in fact being deadly serious, and was assigning him the role of team photographer for the rest of the day, without any male companionship for the scenic route ahead.

Presuming I would stay with the party and take my fair share of photographs, he now realised he would have twice the amount of work to carry out, and would likely have to cycle at a snail's pace for the rest of the day to satisfy the leisurely expectations the girls had of a 'nice day out' on the bikes. Once again, Liam, I apologise for what transpired.

I glanced back grinning and turned back to the front of the bike contentedly, feeling as if I had just finished work super early on a sunny Friday afternoon, with the promise of potential options unfolding before me and the overwhelming emotion of having bought myself some time, and freedom, in the process. I quickly settled into the rhythm of the ride much like a jockey does after sprinting out of the starting gate on a prized thoroughbred. He was welcome to any rewards from a day spent recording cherishable memories for two lovely *senhoritas* from São Paulo; I had more pressing priorities.

There's a symbiotic relationship between man and machine when you ease into the feeling of riding a racing bike at high speed. Subtle, almost invisible movements and moments that make you fully appreciate the bicycle you are simultaneously both using and an integral part of, and also what you need to do to ride the tiger when you let it go. Some days you simply don't feel it, but on some you do, and today was such a day.

I settled into the quickening rhythm of the ride as I zipped along the traffic-free coastal bridleway towards the Golden Gate Bridge, whose epic span was slowly emerging in the distance. Surrounded by such majestic scenery, in conditions that were cool and cloudy, my thoughts and feelings starting to reorder themselves into pieces I could analyse later on.

I could feel in my bones that this would be a memorable ride. Rounding the last bend of the coastal route, just before crossing onto the Golden Gate Bridge towards Sausalito to the north, I took in the vast expanse ahead of me, searching for the sense of adventure having arrived, the point of release for all the energy and anxiety which had been building up since Venice Beach, but had really been bubbling away since I had quit my job and sold my house.

Digging deep on particularly tough rides has always been a way for me to process whatever is happening in my life, good or bad, big or small. Setting my face against the often painful challenge of a tough ride is something I have used to help bring a clearer and more concise perspective to my life. Any problem, no matter how big or seemingly insurmountable, has far less significance and meaning after a day of blood, sweat and gears.

It's as if the brain fully awakens only under this kind of controlled duress in a way that simply isn't possible when we're procrastinating or sitting around doing nothing. This may be down to norepinephrine, a powerful neurotransmitter (the same chemical compounds that are targeted by anti-anxiety and anti-depression medications) that our body pumps out. This allows us to process information on a subconscious level and gives us that blissful feeling of suspended time. Serotonin (the happy hormone) rises and remains elevated during the day, and helps sustain that post-ride afterglow many cyclists (and runners) seek. We also experience a spike in dopamine, which also makes us feel good, hones our focus and speeds up muscle reaction times.

So science seems to back up the wonderful restorative functions I have always felt that cycling has on the brain, both structurally and functionally. Cycling acts as a kind of neural fertilizer, pumping oxygen and nutrients into this metabolically rapacious organ, creating rich capillary beds in our brain's grey matter and increasing the brain's capacity to grow, function and repair itself. Not only this, but as we pedal, we increase healthy blood flow to the entire body and brain, which actually builds a bigger, more connected brain. Cycling fires up extra nerve cells, intensifying the creation of a protein called BDNF (brain-derived neurotrophic factor) that stimulates the formation of new brain cells. This can double or even triple the production of neurons, which helps stimulate regions of the brain such as the hippocampus – which plays a critical role in memory formation and spatial navigation. [1]

A recent study has shown that the hippocampus of participants grew by two percent and their problem-solving skills improved by 15 to 20 percent after six months of cycling daily, while their ability to focus and their attention span were also greatly enhanced. Better still, all of these perks counteract the loss of brain function usually associated with aging, with cyclists' brains appearing two years younger on average than their non-exercising peers. [2]

Another recent study found that a group of older amateur cyclists' thymuses (the organ that produces disease-combating immune cells called T-cells) were found to be generating as many of these T-cells as the other, much younger adults, who didn't exercise on a regular basis.[3] So cycling seems to be a natural elixir, a key to the fountain of youth, if you still need convincing. If cycling were available in pill form, the whole world would be addicted to its verifiable effects.

Not only grey matter, but cycling also helps the white matter, boosting our motor skills. White matter acts like the brain's subway system – a conduit transmitting information between different parts of the body and the cerebral cortex – keeping our system running smoothly and boosting our brain functions in the process. [4] A lot of research now suggests that the brain is far more malleable than originally thought, and the evidence is growing that pedalling on a regular basis increases the integrity of white matter in the brain. The more white matter you have, the faster you can make important decisions, as your brain is better connected. [5] So cycling is clearly the complete package, with something for the mind, the body and the soul.

That's certainly how it felt as I traversed the final few metres of this iconic bridge, scouring the area for signs of a challenge to help awaken my senses and flip my current mood from that of an idle tourist - who couldn't work out where he was going - to that of a turbocharged sage ready to find a neat way around any and every obstacle life might throw in my path. Not only is cycling the only activity I've found that effectively deals with such issues so head-on, it also makes you realise, after a long day of punishing climbs and the pain that comes with that kind of effort, that these issues really aren't all that significant and can always be overcome without having to move any mountains or part any oceans. Distractions, busy thoughts and nagging worries simply evaporated when I immersed myself in this kind of adventure.

Cycling quite simply breaks life down into manageable, bitesize chunks, like the contours of a rugged mountain or a steep incline that needs to be dealt with on a turn-by-turn basis. Reach that next landmark and push through to the one after that. Reach that fork in the road, catch your breath and go again. Only stop if you really need to. Otherwise put your head down and grind it out, brick by brick, mile after mile, just like the journey of life. Out on a tough ride you are asked all the same questions that you are from life. How you answer those questions depends on what comes from deep inside.

The wind was howling from every direction as I approached the end of this elegant bridge, taking in the panoramic view of a glistening Pacific Ocean, with the occasional milky-white glint of boat or bird as I searched the horizon. To the Northwest I could see an imposing and fairly derelict series of rugged coastal peaks and knew right then that I had found my challenge for the day. I stopped and smiled wryly to myself before looking for subtle clues as to how I should approach the rather ominous initial climb.

An older American couple were approaching, out for a stroll

with their antique-style walking sticks. 'You're headed up Hawk Hill there. You'll need plenty of water, but there are points that you can stop at along the way,' they told me, their instructions delivered with boundless enthusiasm.

'I'll not be stopping today!' I burst out, feeding off their energy, feeling just about ready to tackle this rather daunting but inspiring challenge.

They spent a further five minutes trying to decipher my Geordie accent, and being completely overcome that I was indeed from the same part of the planet as the Queen and James Bond. Then they marched onwards, suitably refreshed but still rather unconvinced of my English heritage. For a brief moment before setting off up the spiralled climb towards Hawk Hill, I wondered whether I should try to smooth out and elongate my regional dialect to communicate more effectively with Americans, who in the main were having a very hard time understanding what I was trying to say, and why I was speaking at such a frantic pace (cycling also has this ability to somewhat quicken our sentences). But I decided to leave that for another day. I was a Geordie on a bicycle in the US of A. People would have to take me as they found me.

Their frowning expressions were a mark of their utter confusion at what I was saying and where I was from, and they treated the exchange like a game of verbal tennis, until they had exhausted every possible country I might have hailed from until it dawned on them with an incessant disbelief that was visible on their faces that I really did come from England. Admittedly, my part of the world is much closer in most ways to Scotland than it is to London, but it was still merry old England, though, alas, I didn't know the Queen or James Bond personally, whichever James Bond they meant.

This was simply unfathomable to most Americans I met.

I started climbing with a purpose, a steely determination I had not felt since arriving in California more than six weeks earlier. Out of the saddle, head down, with sweat droplets running down the inside of the handlebars, allowing me to tune in to the natural environment around me while letting my body do all the hard work. I looked up intermittently only to confirm the presence of other road users going past me, mainly cars and motorhomes, but a few other keen cyclists out too.

Reaching each individual vantage point on the short but steep inclines, as I rounded a near-blind corner and was met with yet another undulating section of uphill coastal tarmac trail, I was starting to see the wisdom of the older couple's advice to stop and take in a view and a drink of water. But my determination to keep going wasn't because I wanted to show off any kind of bravado. I had simply set myself a goal and wanted to get it done. It was purely for the personal satisfaction of setting out to achieve something and achieving it. And I instinctively knew I would get it done this day.

I passed many keen cyclists on the way up those beautifully sculpted peaks around the Golden Gate and looking east, down to the glittering ocean. I have always found solace in the mutual respect cyclists have for one another as we pass each other by, a feeling that lasts only for those few fleeting seconds but is always significant and worthy nonetheless. Complete strangers otherwise in life but united in those transient moments by a combined admiration for the labour of the other. You feel the eyes of others at the side of the road and along the walking trails as you struggle with your own personal journey up the mountain, lifted by a communal sense of everyone pulling together in the same direction. Cycling often personifies that struggle through life, embodies it and embraces it all at once.

I reached for the last few mouthfuls of water left in my bottle, which was tucked away on the bicycle frame. My battle had been hard-fought and was very nearly won. I could see the summit ahead and a mass of people who had gathered there after completing their own personal journey, however small or large it may have been. My legs were weary, my breathing was very laboured, and I was more than a little dehydrated but felt exhilarated all the same. I could have stayed at that same spot all day in a state of utter peace and contentment.

The panoramic viewpoint over the whole of the San Francisco Bay area was the most beautiful I had ever seen. I couldn't call it breathtaking, as the steep ascent up had near-emptied my lungs by then, but it was still a humbling and magnificent prospect. I lay down motionless on a grassy spot a little way over from the main cluster of tourists, propped up only by my elbows, slowing my body and breathing down to the level required after a short, sharp trip up an elevation of several hundred metres. Another cyclist completing the same journey pulled up nearby to do the same as me.

'Hey, man, good job you did going past me back there. You looked in the zone!' he said with the uninhibited enthusiasm that seemingly every American can muster.

I felt a twang of British modesty was needed to cool the overpraise. Americans use positive metaphors to start a conversation, and not at all sarcastically. The British thrive on being insulted and get to know others more intimately through the language of sarcasm and insults of the crudest nature. In most US states, as a typically stiff-upper-lipped

British subject, I can often feel a clash of social codes when adjusting to the more open and inviting American way of conversing.

From a summer working abroad as a lifeguard in South Carolina at the age of 22, having shared a large living complex with most nationalities from around the world, I found the Russian way of conversing and initiating social contact to be most in sync with what I had experienced growing up in the Northeast of England. Copious amounts of vodka, well-intentioned insults and slurs of one another's country, deep-rooted sarcasm and straight-faced heated debates added to the rich vein of Anglo-Russian relations I tapped into that memorable summer of 2008. Crumbling empires, mental scarring from world wars, and poor weather are possibly all to blame for this shared siege mentality, I figure.

'Sorry I didn't stop to talk, I just didn't want to lose my momentum coming up,' I said very slowly, trying my best to catch my breath but also to speak the Queen's English so that I didn't have to repeat myself and have yet another interlocutor ask themselves, 'Where's this nomadic idiot from?'

The cyclist told me that it was his day off from working in the city, that he came up this way for the challenge and the less-polluted air. I searched for the signs of any liquids he might be carrying, either on his bike or in various jacket pockets, but he appeared to be as ignorant as I was when it came to knowing the level of hydration and carbs needed for a punishing day out on the bike, though maybe not so punishing without the hangover.

'You have the perfect balance of city, country and beaches out here,' I offered, scanning the area for potential ice-cream vans or coffee cabins, but with little success. He proceeded to tell me how he went everywhere by bike, and worked as a cycle courier in the city for one of the large delivery firms. Well, when he said that, my jaw nearly dropped to the floor and smashed.

'Someone pays you to ride your bike around here all day and pays you at the end of it?' I said, half in awe, half in bewildered jealousy.

'Yeah, man, been doing it eighteen months now, it's pretty cool.'

There was a momentary air of silence as I tried to comprehend how magical his life must be. I looked towards him, eyes wide, mouth wider, suddenly as desperate as a gold prospector with a manically beeping metal detector to find out exactly how he could get away with having this kind of job.

'What's the catch, there must be a catch,' I pleaded.

He let out a calm and slightly self-satisfied laugh. 'Hills and pollution,' was the answer he gave.

It seemed like a very fair trade-off to me. You've got to die of something, after all.

"Are there any places to eat around here?" I asked. I was totally famished and starting to cramp up, holding onto my legs and pulling on my hamstrings, as I lay down on a nice lookout spot as the hangover finally started to take effect. My muscles were screaming out for any kind of liquid that would help to delay the inevitable reaction to a Jack Daniels-inspired drinking session from the pub crawl the night before.

"Nah, dude, try heading down to Sausalito, you'll get something there."

I tried releasing the pain shooting through my hamstrings, desperately searching for signs of somewhere to replenish my depleted stores of energy and a throbbing liver. He turned to leave, telling me he had a buddy in Scotland, and that we should cycle together whenever he happened to be going past my place, up in the Highlands.

'But I'm from England, mate?' I countered, but he was undeterred.

'You Brits crack me up. And remember this, if you can't do what you love, love what you do!'

He scuttled off, unwrapping the contents of a delightful-looking homemade flapjack and stuffing it into his mouth. Then he began the descent, the flapjack looking like a lion with a juicy rump steak in his gob. Lucky bastard, I thought to myself, completely exhausted and dehydrated as my stomach started to rumble aggressively as the effects from the past hour of near-constant climbing in 25-degree heat started to make themselves felt.

In fairness, it was already obvious as I sat alone at the summit how profound the experience of this bike ride would become. A true lighthouse moment, a beacon of light shining across the bay but bigger than the place or the moment in which I had felt it. Looking down along the coastline and the pearly blue sea below me, I saw a vision of the future, as the pieces of an elaborate jigsaw, previously unseen, had slowly fallen into place that cool and breezy San Francisco summer afternoon. It was the bicycle that had brought me here, to this special place, this fateful moment; it was the bicycle which now showed me where the last and most vital piece of the jigsaw would fit.

Later that day I met up for lunch with Liam and the São Paulo girls at a lovely small-town seafood restaurant in Downtown Sausalito, about an hour by bike from the Golden Gate Bridge. It took us all around two hours to get there, as I slowed my pace to stay alongside the others and enjoyed the scenic route that took us through some small and beautifully quirky waterfront towns along the way. I didn't mind in the slightest, my head had cleared after a hard slog up Hawk Hill. I was ready to enjoy the rest of my afternoon as my anxieties and worries had now been washed away. The wine flowed freely as the sun began to set, and the conversation turned to my apparently unchivalrous conduct, leaving my companions behind without any real explanation.

'You missed some really good photo opportunities today next to the bridge,' said Bruna, sat with me, wondering if she had upset me in some way back at the harbour, and clearly disappointed that I had not wanted to spend the whole day taking photos of her for the photo collage she would eventually make of the trip.

'It's OK, I got what I was looking for today.' I smiled contentedly, thinking that what I had got today was something that would stay with me for the rest of my life. I leaned back in the comfortable padded seat, sunglasses hiding my weary and dehydrated eyes as the cool white wine started to take effect and the sun gave off the last warm rays of the day. I could finally start to properly relax and unwind. I was completely at ease with myself. I had the answer I'd been looking for. The clouds had cleared at last.

The American dream came to an end, and we met with Bruna and Andrea at the airport to say our goodbyes and bid them well with the rest of their lives, with a promise that one day we would reminisce about some unforgettable nights, planning for future get-togethers once everyone had finished their studies. The true magic of travelling. Nights you'll never remember, with people you'll never forget, and will probably never see again.

Later when me and Liam were leaving to board our flight, Bruna asked me, 'What is it you had to go and get that day when you left me on our bike ride in San Francisco?' I gave her one final hug, grab her by the shoulders and kissed the top of her head.

'My future.'

She smiled and lifts her final bottle of Budweiser for the trip, to show how much she appreciated my response, and maybe understanding a little more of how I functioned as a human being.

'And you're completely shit on a bike, too!' I threw in for good measure, like a great British verbal grenade, instantly changing the atmosphere. She turned back to Andrea, her smile slowly turning into a slight frown that informed me that I had yet again spoilt another one of those moments. I walked off gallantly, passport in hand, ready to board my flight back home, eager to reunite with my two-wheeled companions.

Never leave them wanting more. Honesty is always the best policy. They never came to visit us, those girls.

* * *

Now before you have visions of me being some super-slim, Lycra-sporting nutter who spends more time on Strava at night than Pornhub, that simply isn't the case. I love cycling, for all those aforementioned reasons and many, many more. But I'm not in it for the marginal gains on hills or to be the best cyclist this side of the Atlantic. I have always seen cycling as a purely amateur, sometimes social hobby, that keeps me fit and happy as life carries on around me.

A very simple form of freedom that comes from a craving to be out in the natural world, experiencing new frontiers and meeting fellow like-minded enthusiasts, and as such a definite contrast to the banal and much safer, smaller world to which modern life so often condemns us and which can be so difficult to escape. This was the case even before coronavirus confined us all to our homes for a year.

Before starting the gig, I would have described myself as a fairly fit amateur cyclist, able to climb most mountains or bypasses thrown at me, barring a few impossible, near-vertical ones I've come up against in the time I've spent out and about. Here I'm thinking of the 25–30-percent-incline climbs in or around the Lake District, such as Hardknott Pass and Wrynose Pass, which are difficult enough for the best of cyclists and among the hardest in the UK. But just for the record, I was certainly no 8-percent-body-fat whippet with an appetite for hundred-mile races and endurance events in my free time.

I ran a few half and full marathons in my early twenties, but running – at 6 foot 3 and 15 or 16 stone – was never going to be my *thing*. Sore nipples, creaking hips, knees and ankles were partly to blame too. Also, having women half my height and twice my age, strapped up like the Terminator with multiple gels and sports drinks, striding past me with little perceived effort at a marathon in Kielder Forest a decade ago convinced me to return my attention back to cycling. Once I'd made enough money working at the leisure centre to buy as many bikes as I could physically store in my house, and a car to take them away in, the rest soon followed.

During this time, I'd always been a steady and stubborn 15–20 percent body fat. I used a gym occasionally, took part in a few fitness classes most weeks and was usually able to finish them without being sick or tapping out early. I worked alternate shifts at the same leisure centre where I also worked out, and was always fighting to sleep more than I did; changing shift patterns affect your body clock, effectively switching you between different time zones so that you are always out of kilter with your surroundings.

Exercise had to be squeezed in around this tight schedule, whether before the late shifts or after the morning shifts, to enable me to do my job with some degree of enthusiasm and effort. I could normally get around fifteen hours of decent exercise a week while still being able to function as a young adult and perform my initial lifeguard job without falling asleep (in the pool highchair) or falling in as I marched sheepishly around the same four slippery corners of the pool, trying to stay awake on the early mornings or the late nights.

Once promoted to duty manager, this level of exercise dropped off as I took on more responsibility and struggled to find the enthusiasm to look after myself to the same level as before.

So starting a master's degree back at university full time, while also taking full advantage of my ability to cycle to make a living, was clearly going to upend this rather conservative, traditional life I'd fallen into. But I would make it work, as this was a golden opportunity to do something that would make me healthier, happier and, with a little bit of luck (if I made it through the next academic year of my life), slightly more educated – and provide me with enough money to make it through to graduation.

It was on this most remarkable yet simple human invention, the bicycle, that I was hoping to make a living for the next twelve months of my life. I was about to embark on an ambitious project to flip the script and delve into the murky world of fast-food delivery. Something I had categorically written off as a child as being neither a viable source of income nor a credible profession. Surely, as long as I was on my bicycle, I would be able to avoid falling into the same trap as many of the middle-aged, morbidly rotund delivery drivers I remembered so vividly from childhood.

I reasoned that there was no possible way I would turn into one of those ancient relics if I was plying the same trade on a bicycle. The cycling would keep me happy. Keep me fit. Keep me sane. All those qualities that eluded delivery drivers in the age before the internet because of children just like me. There was a lot at stake.

2

The Rehearsal

'Every time I see an adult on a bicycle, I no longer despair for the future of the human race.' H. G. Wells

It all started after a cold crisp morning in October 2017, as I stood outside an abandoned railway station car park in the middle of Newcastle city centre. I was hoping to start my first new job in over a decade. I had packed in a secure career as a recently promoted duty manager at a leisure centre, having worked my way up from a lifeguard after my undergraduate days at university. Now I was going back go uni, so I needed to find work that I could fit around my studies as well as being something new and exciting.

I'd decided to a one-year master's course where I planned to ask why (or why on Earth) the UK was leaving the EU. How many debates could you could possibly have in the field of international politics without mentioning the name Trump at least a thousand times? I was about to find out. It seemed obvious that I would need a release from the brain strain as I delved into the issues facing the world during the Brexit and Trump era. In the past, that release had always come in the form of cycling.

Having arrived back in Newcastle after a carefree summer in California, it was time to get back to reality and find a suitable job that would get me one step closer to my dream of being paid to ride my bicycle. I had heard that courier jobs were rife in places like London, but had seldom seen any in my home town of Newcastle. Or maybe I had just mistaken such couriers for commuters or casual cyclists, having had no idea that there were such jobs available, or never really having the need to look or enquire in the past. Once settled into my new house share in Jesmond – a nice leafy suburb close to the university and city centre – with my first cup of tea in front of the computer screen in my bedroom, I excitedly typed *courier in Newcastle* into Google. Bingo!

The first job I laid eyes on was exactly what I was looking for. A new company called Deliveroo were hiring. I didn't even need to read the description. This was the one for me, thank you very much. I spent as much time reorganising my CV to hopefully impress the person reading it as I had done for in writing my application to study for a postgraduate degree. I littered my CV with examples of why I needed this job more than anything else on the planet, with a solid account of my glittering career riding a bicycle, from the tender age of three through to 30.

Well, not so much a glittering career, but a long love affair, with little sign of the relationship coming to an end. I needn't have gone to so much trouble. They must have figured I could ride a bike with some degree of confidence when I pulled up for the Deliveroo 'interview' with a large grin slapped across my Chevy Chase to the gig. And that was all I really needed to do this type of work. Perfect.

It was a dreary, misty morning as I pulled up on my cheap but reliable steel-frame road bike to sign up for the new *gig economy*. Something I had never even heard of before applying for the job. It was the sort of day Newcastle is famous for throughout the nation, the kind of day which southerners have always meant when they speak of life being 'grim up north'. For three hundred days of the year, they were generally accurate with such stereotypes, and today would be no different. If you narrowed your eyes just enough, you could see roughly a hundred yards in front of you. It mattered little to me.

As I approached the abandoned car park, that familiar feeling of new-job nerves which stays with most people all their lives and, if anything, gets progressively worse as the years go on, paled into insignificance compared to the overriding feelings of excitement and anticipation I felt as I got closer with every pedal stroke. Maybe because the environment seemed more closing-down pawnshop than the more formal dog-eat-dog, suited-and-booted, law-of-the-jungle hostility of the customary office interview, my mind was altogether more at ease knowing that the most challenging thing I was likely to be asked was whether I can cycle without stabilisers and not 'Give ten reasons why you are the best person in the world for this job' or 'Why does the company need to hire you here and now?'

I never felt quite right in a suit anyhow, with the first drop of sweat in warmer weather turning the experience of being around other people in a hot office into a case of nerve-shredding damage limitation. At least on a bike you have an excuse for being a little too sweaty, and in most circumstances this can be more easily managed by wearing the appropriate clothing.

Armed with nothing but a £300 bike, a helmet and a mobile phone, I was categorically not there as a budding contestant on *The Apprentice* but rather to promote why I was more than capable of riding a bike and to swear blind that I would try my damnedest to deliver a customer's food to them with as little drama as possible, (Note the use of 'try'; you'll understand why later.) As I was the first there, I waited and watched as another couple of keen amateur cyclists like myself pulled up.

As is always the case in such situations, bikes are compared, cycling war stories swapped and bodily scars pulled out to show who is the most dedicated to their hallowed sport. Enthusiastic growls echoed through the thick foggy autumn air. We were all genuinely surprised and excited that we would soon be riding our bikes whilst also getting paid at the same time. The feeling was tangible and magnetic as we huddled round to receive some guidance and training about the job. Today was a good day.

The whole process took less than twenty minutes. Fill out your details on a shiny new iPad. Download the app onto your phone. Receive your shiny new kit to show the world that you are delivering food for them, and sign a digital document promising you will try your utmost to be the very best version of yourself when representing the company out on your beloved two-wheeled steed. Armed with enough kit to slide into the background of a *Teenage Mutant Ninja Turtles* photoshoot, I cycled off dreaming of the day when I would finally be paid to ride my bike. I could hardly believe my luck.

A wise and contented gym instructor I had previously

worked with at the leisure centre once told me, 'Do a job you love and you'll never work a single day in your entire life.' He was right on both counts. He did love his job, and it showed when you spoke to him, asked him for any kind of advice, such as how to get rid of that annoyingly stubborn beer belly – the one that never really leaves a man after the age of about 26. His enthusiasm was infectious. He wanted only the satisfaction of getting you to change your wicked ways, all the while demonstrating his own repertoire of gruelling exercises to show you how insignificant and inferior you really were.

He had also never worked a single day of his life, as he spent the majority of his time lifting weights rather than cleaning them, which I suppose is what he really meant behind the cover of holistic wisdom. As duty manager I had often had to plead with him to try to introduce some cleaning into his taxing schedule of being content with life and lifting weights. But I was now finally beginning to understand how he had arrived at the mantra he was always passing down to me and many others all those years ago – in fact, to all of us in the leisure centre who actually *worked* for a living!

That once you find a job you love, you'll know it, and it will show in everything else you do in life. Not that I don't believe in a proper day's work, but you do reach a point in life where you can go from simply *doing* a job to *living and breathing* that job – where the job fully encompasses everything you are and everything you believe in.

Many use a job as simply a means to an end, a way to keep a roof over your head every month. But some see a job as something that they wake up for every single morning, a challenge they look forward to with a sense of excitement that comes from helping people or providing a great service.

There is a journey that many of us travel in finding our way to the kind of work that both interests and motivates us, from the student jobs we take during sixth form, college and university, to the first 'career' job or apprenticeship we manage (hopefully) to secure when we leave formal learning behind after school or further education.

Had I misunderstood the underutilised gym instructor all these years? I was beginning to feel this might be the time to find out. My own social experiment would be carried out while undertaking a full calendar year of postgraduate study, at the end of which I would hopefully receive a very expensive piece of paper saying I was sufficiently improved to be able to re-enter the *real* workplace in the not-so-distant future. But before all that happened, I was determined to get paid doing something I loved. Leaving behind a responsible, safe, well-paid job with all the benefits that a local government job entails. Plunging myself into the brand-new, little-known world of the gig economy.

Was I excited? Hugely. Was I nervous? Not one bit. I had rolled the dice. It was up to me to carve out a living from my beloved hobby. Hell or highwater. Did I have any idea how it would all play out? None at all. But there was no going back now and I was damned if I wasn't going to try to do it my way (as Frank Sinatra sang). This was my chance to live the dream, though who knew how long for?

I had given myself ten full months (the length of my master's course) to take full advantage of this temporary arrangement. Each day a new adventure, but in the background I was supposed to be counting down the days until life returned to normal sometime in the near future. The same four walls of an office to weaken the human spirit, the outdoor wanderlust we have somewhat lost on the way to becoming fully functioning capitalist beings. The same structured routine dictated to you by someone else, day in, day out.

But out in the wild, in the ever-changing life of a city as its heart pumps and you pass along its arteries like a blood cell in the stream – well, I had been waiting for something like this my whole life without ever having realised it until now. I had a short window of opportunity to immerse myself in this new challenge. A year off from the real world, and the chance of not having to work ever again, or at least not a single day for the foreseeable future. The time had finally arrived. It was time to go to work.

* * *

The first day of a new job can be excruciating on almost every level. The introductions. The tours around the building. The formalities. The names you will never remember of each and every new person you encounter – until you either find them on Facebook, or they find you, or you even become real-life actual human friends with them. You start out in your first real job trying to be a decent human being, interacting with your fellow colleagues, hoping to tick off most of the boxes they expect of you on the first day in your bewildering new working environment.

Teamwork, collaborating, sharing ideas, strong communication, critical thinking. All the ingredients needed to negotiate the sterility of 21st-century office life. It is not until a little later that you figure out that only pure chance put you together with this particular set of walking, talking human beings, who don't always agree with what you say or do exactly what you want them to do. Welcome to the real world, my friends.

All the things you never understood as a child growing up, which, if you had, would have helped explain why your mother and father weren't as happy and as carefree as you once had been. Why you never once saw them running around, laughing and screaming and having as good a time like you were, despite having way more money and a car to go wherever they very well pleased. Now, in the early, disorienting days in your new place of work, it all starts to make sense.

Compromise, taking responsibility, adapting to other people's needs. All vital parts of the social machinery you need to help deal with these additional strangers with whom you now share one third of your time with on the planet, hopefully to do some good with and to help each other in the process. It seems so easy when written down like that, in theory rather than practice. But people are complex beings, with evolving wants, needs, desires, agendas and a whole host of Freudian bullshit that, without getting too heavy on the subject, can be pretty unbearable a lot of the time. To be taken out of that rather intense arena of multiple competing personalities and office politics after such a long time is fairly liberating to say the least.

Think of having a time machine warping you back to being younger and having that first paper round. Rather than having to get up early and brave extremities of weather for a mere pittance, you can work whenever you want. Unless you're the sort of maniac who enjoys throwing themselves out of bed at 5 a.m., and can actually make it through the whole day without three naps or falling asleep during a meeting, in the lift or on the drive in to work, then the life of a cycling courier could well be better suited to your body clock.

No more early starts. No drawn-out pointless meetings while trying to stay awake. No more clock watching, hoping for the last hour to pass by quickly, so you can finally get home and onto your bike for that longed-for slice of daily freedom. No lying to big fat Sandra that she has lost weight while handing her the biscuit tin as a consolation when Mr Sandra has left her yet again. No one around to tell you to do your job better. No one to pick you up when you're having a bad day. Just you, your bike, the road, the restaurant, the customer. It's all about you.

It's fantastically simple if you are not a people person. If you are, as I usually was (or had to be) most days in my previous career, you'll quickly adapt to the other extreme of very little human contact and conversation after a few months on the job. No more being able to converse with others to solve problems that may arise during your normal working day. It's a huge adjustment from working with a team of over fifty people most days to being out on your own with only your mobile phone to look to for help or problem solving of any kind. All these thoughts were racing through my head as I left the house to do my first ever shift for Deliveroo. I would start off by doing a few hours. Dip my toe in. Slow and steady and all that.

How it all worked in the early days was like this. In theory you could work in any of the designated 'zones' that Deliveroo accepts orders within. Some of these zones are very large and densely populated with many hungry people. These are the main zones – central locations crammed with lots of office workers, city visitors and students. These areas are your bread and butter, so to speak. Some zones are smaller, on the periphery of larger ones, and likely to be either inner city or suburbia. These areas are generally quieter, with less of the people I have just described. More families, couples and the once-a-week orders, rather than the daily orders received from more regular customers inside the main zones.

Every Monday available hours were released through the app, and all you had to do was book the times of day you wanted to work, if they had not already been taken by other riders looking for the same hours, snapping them up as soon as they appeared online. As long as you could make your way to one of these zones, having booked the allotted hours through the system, the work was yours.

I sailed excitedly into the centre of the city. That's what you do. You find a busy area full of restaurants, or you try and find somewhere to sit while you nervously anticipate that all-important ping sound pulsating from your mobile – a sound that gives your whole body an upright jolt of excitement that makes you alert like a meerkat after a line of cocaine. The buzz that confirms to you that yes, you have been chosen at random to pick up this order, and should you be kind enough to click *Confirm* on your device, you will be the lucky rider who will make their way to the selected restaurant to take part in this new and exciting, real-life game of *Mario Kart*, getting this lovely-looking food to the happy and appreciative customer who ordered it by the shortest possible route in the shortest possible time. Oh, and trying not to get knocked off along the way.

Like a soldier about to be sent to the front line for their first taste of action, I sprang into life and marched proudly to the first job I'd been assigned. Show the restaurant staff your order number, wait for the food to be prepared, click on the app that you are ready to take it to the customer, up pops the address and off you go. I've done the whole bargain bin of crappy student jobs in the past. Office work, factory lines, retail and door-to-door sales. Basically, enough of them to know how lucky I was to be doing something that actually made me happy, healthy and for which I was also getting paid.

Despite having started my course and thoroughly enjoying the challenge of postgraduate life – reading academic books and articles day and night until my eyes became darkened in the process – I was beginning to think this job with Deliveroo was a little bit of me. My fifteen-year journey of work had led to this destination. And given the circumstances, it seemed a perfect fit.

My first day was a beautiful autumn evening. For many cyclists it's the best season for riding, their favourite time of year. Not too cold, not too warm, with the light reflecting and bouncing onto you from a low inviting sun and wonderful, glowing colours as the trees blush red and gold before fully undressing for the winter season. It's unquestionably my own favourite time of year to be on a bike, much cooler than summer but just before the dreary cold of winter hits, and you forget what it's like to see and feel the sun after three o'clock in the afternoon. Setting out that first day in October, I felt instantly liberated and a sense of complete freedom I had not felt in years.

Not only was I working for a living, I was doing my favourite pastime in the process. Gone were the days of having to race home in the car after work to quickly change uniforms and squeeze in the last two hours of daylight on the bike. I was combining both to deadly effect. I could barely contain myself. Weaving in and out of the rush-hour traffic as miserable commuters passed me by, some sitting in their cars, racing to get home to escape their conformist lives; some waiting for buses to take them to a world far away from the eight hours of drudgery they had just carried out as part of their contractual obligation.

I had once been part of that very real, yet now parallel universe. Times passes slowly. You want it to pass. You need it to pass. No longer was this the case. Every minute counted now. Yet every minute flew by regardless. Leaving behind one world to enter a very different one, a different existence altogether. It was simple, yet rewardingly physical hard work, pedalling around to deliver customers their food.

You drop off the piping-hot bundle of goodness to the very happy-looking customer stood waiting to receive it. You've just completed your first job. You've done your gig. One very small and insignificant gig. But it's a start. And you've just been paid £4.25, the same rate every time. Some deliveries take just ten minutes, some a little longer. You don't care either way, you've just been paid to cycle somewhere, anywhere. Nowhere is ever the same as anywhere else. You're always heading to someone or somewhere new.

The scenery is constantly changing. A new block of glass-fronted contemporary student flats, a row of delightfully elegant Victorian terraced houses, a beautifully converted Georgian building, an office block overlooking the glistening Tyne. Follow the map on your phone, and arrive at your customer's address. Ring them, let them know you've arrived. See happy and welcoming faces emerge for their weekly treat. Smile and greet them, it makes a small but important difference to the overall experience.

You often catch people in their happiest state: tired workers at the start of a long weekend off; a group of friends sat in the park on a long summer evening who collectively scream and shout at the arrival of the 'Deliveroo man' – that's you in your outlandish green reflective outfit; revellers during a house party (morning or night); couples after the birth of their newborn outside A&E; hotel guests staying in the city for the first ever time; or, most recently, people forced into isolation due to quarantine rules and in need of a little socially distanced human interaction.

You meet and greet people from all over the world, some keen to know the best bars and touristy things to do while staying in the city, others the different food they can order from on the app or the restaurants they can eat in while staying in the city. For a few brief minutes, you can sometimes become a mini tour guide, giving people ideas for places to visit or sights to see nearby. You can feed off their energy, and you never mind sparing a few minutes to find out what their plans are for the next few hours or days, it is as wholesome and uplifting for you as it is for the customer. When you spend your days alongside taxis or behind heavy, polluting double-decker buses, this brief friendly interaction is a very welcome distraction, much-needed boost to the ego.

However, you also witness the other side of the spectrum: overworked and dedicated hospital staff during the pandemic; folk after serious accidents at A&E; exhausted night workers in the morning after long night shifts, needing a meal to fix them up before trying to get some much needed rest; alcoholics trying to get booze delivered to them at home.

One time, I even had a seriously sick, mentally unstable

gentleman in a wheelchair attack me for a pack of cigarettes outside hospital. He didn't have any ID with him – Deliveroo insist that a form of identification must be shown to delivery riders by every customer, regardless of age – as he'd been brought to the hospital by an ambulance after one of his serious episodes, and went berserk that he wasn't going to be able to have a smoke after what he had been through. He grabbed hold of me by the neck, with me still holding onto my bike. I managed to wriggle free, but then thought it best to give him the cigarettes, given the state he had built himself up to.

He rang Deliveroo later to apologise for what had happened, but there's always an element of risk attached to certain parts of the job when dealing with orders that require identification or from difficult customers. Such instances are few and far between, but you are always out on your own, and you learn to deal with hostile customers with some degree of control and sensitivity.

Things can deteriorate quickly, but you can minimise the chances of such situations by simply rejecting orders that require identification. Deliveroo requires identification for any age restricted items regardless of age, which can come as a shock to older customers, despite being informed when placing the order that physical identification is required. A lot of riders see these orders as too much of a risk for such little reward. And too much time spent trying to justify the policy to customers.

The majority of your customers are always happy to see you, as you're always more enthusiastic than the average postman. You're riding a bike, for Christ's sake! Quite simply telling your brain to release happy drugs in order to do the job. How could you not be enthusiastic? Back into the middle of the city you go, with something new to look at and focus your attention on while you head back. I've cycled these roads a hundred times before, but there's always a new feature to occupy your thoughts, or a friendly cyclist to nod at as you pass them by, acknowledging the fact that you are both equally content with the current state of play. You're always on the move, with no time to stop and take it all in.

It really was liberating. You're part of a complex, ever-changing landscape – one tiny moving part of the whole ecosystem of the city. You wait impatiently for that next noise from your phone as you cycle back the way you just came, or sometimes take a different route altogether, maybe down by the quayside for the last rays of autumn sunshine glistening along the banks of the Tyne. You are about to do it all over again. You sometimes wait five minutes. You sometimes wait twenty minutes. But you are always alert: hoping, waiting, wishing for that next order.

It's very exciting in the beginning, to be involved in something from the ground up, when something is first taking root. You feel unsure and wary of the potential challenges, because you've simply not come up against any of them yet. It's all down to you now. You've been left to your own devices, with your own device, left to figure it all out. Time passes and you slowly figure out all the different locations you have to pick up from and drop off to. These are gradual steps on the way to learning how to get quicker in picking up and dropping off orders.

Some restaurants are very quick in preparing food, while some are very high-end and take more time to prepare what are often expensive dishes. All this means time spent learning the places to avoid, the places that are generally rather quick, the times of day that are better for collecting and the times that are worse, when places tend to be at full capacity and have a backlog of delivery orders to process. You can ask restaurants how long your order will take to be made, but generally you are an inconvenience to most of them, as they also have over-the-counter, fully-paying, eat-in customers they have to try to please in person.

Bide your time and be patient with staff. If it's taking longer than five or ten minutes, then ask about your order. If you're unsatisfied with the response, feel free to reject the order and move on. It can be a very tedious experience, but time is now very much money, as you are paid per delivery and not per hour. Don't be afraid to reject orders. You're your own boss, remember? You make the rules now. Like a highly efficient salesperson, you have to prioritise leads, and if something isn't quite going to plan you have to cut your losses and move on to the next one.

My first shift passed without any real drama. I enjoyed it as much as I thought I would, and knew right then and there that I had found the dream student job for the next year or so and could therefore afford to live within my means for the foreseeable future. But I soon discovered that the problem with finding your seemingly ideal job while studying is that you still have all the responsibilities of being a student, albeit I was back as a mature student doing something for which I really had a passion. Could I still balance all my new responsibilities for work and study with the extracurricular drinks and procrastinating that had also been a part of my lifestyle? The answer quickly became apparent.

Having too many activities intertwined, like a very aggressive Venn diagram, means you have to sacrifice a few to make way for the others, if these are to be done to any kind of standard! Could I continue to increase my hours in my new dream job while also being able to put away six pints of Guinness, make it into lectures semi compos mentis, and give a semi-articulate answer to something I'd read the night before? The answer to that would be a no, as I soon found out when, fairly quickly, things began to unravel.

So I soon began to prioritise university and work. By prioritise, I mean do nothing else. Apart from sleep, of course. Lots of sleep. Oh, and food. Lots of food. Which weren't sacrifices by any stretch of the imagination, as I've always been a huge fan of sleeping and eating. This meant my main sacrifices would be drinking and socialising.

I enjoyed both immensely, but there would be another time in which I could continue my amateur pursuit of these favourite British pastimes. And I was getting progressively less able to finish a whole bottle of vodka anyways, so who knows? I figured it might even be beneficial to my overall health, this newfound schedule of mine.

Students are well known for their consistent habit of sleeping when they ought to be doing voluminous amounts of reading (or perhaps due to that reading). For me this meant copious amounts of high-strength coffee and honey to keep brain and body in peak condition. It's a solution that may not be as rock'n'roll as what Pete Doherty once practised, but once you find something that works for you – and keeps you at peak performance – it's always a good idea to stick with it.

So coffee became my drug of choice, my kryptonite, my one and only. Gone were the days of living it up in Ibiza on other less scrupulous stimulants I took throughout my twenties.

Now it was to be the good old legal brown bean that turns weary sloths into fiery tigers. It gave me the wings I needed to get through long shifts without succumbing to the dreaded cyclist's bonk. In fact, my love of strong coffee enabled me to rapidly increase the hours I could work during that first winter, while trying to be a half-decent student at the same time.

Not that I was ever a slouch on the bike, but all this extra riding was quite a step up from cycling in the forest for a few hours on a weekend alongside once or twice during the week, with the odd spinning class at the leisure centre thrown in if I needed to lose five pints of bodily fluids or felt the urge to be surrounded by middle-aged women discussing the wines in which they would drown their sorrows later that night. Suffice to say that cycling was the best option every time. Just me on my bike. No small talk, no excuses. Fresh air to fill your lungs with and nobody screaming at you to go faster or turn your resistance up beyond the point where you can safely avoid having a near-fatal heart attack. Simplicity.

I know plenty of people who work in offices or call centres and hate the monotony and the dreary, uninspiring environment typical of such places. I've been in enough of them to know that such environments not only lead to complacency and bitterness among many who work there, they are definitely not where we were put on this wonderful planet to spend the majority of our lives. But such is the need to earn a living and pay our bills while keeping a roof over our heads that some kind of job is essential to carry on progressing up the ladder – or at the very least to earn your keep and keep the mortgage company, or landlord, happy.

Some people asked me when I sold my house, left my job,

went back to study and started renting again if I was either crazy or didn't really appreciate what you needed to do in order to get on in life. It's a very valid proposition, that makes the path I have chosen difficult for many to understand, given how our parents grew up and lived, and given a general fear of the future that we were always urged to plan for. In some ways the fundamentals haven't changed much: job, house, car, partner, kids, happily ever after and retire to the country – all that Disney propaganda we firmly believed and were drip-fed as kids growing up.

Once I had stripped away the house, the car, the mortgage, and paying the bills every month on time, there's only really you left to focus your energy and time on. All the external distractions and responsibilities I had built up and maybe used as an excuse for not pursuing other things in life had simply dissolved. I was left with a much clearer and broader perspective on what was important to me and how I could go about taking advantage of the new opportunities that came my way.

But the times we are living through are very different to those that existed even 20 years ago, and someone was offering to pay me to ride my bicycle at a time when suddenly all my adult responsibilities had disappeared. Yes, the dice had been rolled, and rolled well.

3

The Main Event

'I don't ride a bike to add days to my life. I ride a bike to add life to my days.' Unknown

It was all I had hoped for and more, with all the positive connotations that could come with cycling and earning a living at the same time. It was a lot like being a paperboy, but on steroids and earning decent money, too. Better still, there were no early starts, as who orders nice takeaway food at eight in the morning, right? Working when you wanted to suit *your* schedule.

While the rest of my university companions strolled away from campus to stack shelves or pour pints, or even to party and enjoy being a student while they still could, I was off to recapture a little segment of my youth - riding around on my bike, seeking out new adventures and seeing a side of the city which in the past I would have been far too preoccupied to fully appreciate. My only problem seemed to be leaving myself enough time away from cycling to make sure I could fulfil my academic goals. I guess nothing comes easy.

The beginning was a learning process. Every new restaurant. Every new drop-off location. Every student accommodation block. The most efficient routes to take, without ending up on dual carriageways or being stuck behind double-decker buses inhaling all those noxious gases. Waiting an age for students to finally emerge from their newly built skyscrapers, ultra-lavish places where every single need seemed to be catered for. It would take about three or four months to learn all the complexities of the various routes, but in the meantime you could always use your phone's GPS for directions.

Phone in jacket pocket, wired earphones to tell you to turn left or right, or turn around when you missed your street altogether. Swear. Stop every few minutes, check the street name again, swear again. Turn around again, start all over again. It takes time to learn the layout of a city, even one you think you know and have visited hundreds of times before.

I had a new respect for taxi drivers and what those London cabbies had to go through when they did the Knowledge, as their test of professional competence is known. Or the couriers who traversed London with only walkie-talkies and giant maps to guide them, long before the advent of GPS on mobile phones made the job of getting to places so much easier. Now I saw these people as mini oracles as it took me an age to navigate roads, side streets and dodgy back alleys – trying to get some food to a customer in the faint hope it was still lukewarm by the time I actually arrived. Not that the two examples are anywhere near comparable.

In the early days of Deliveroo, the zone that could be delivered within was fairly small – a 2.2 km zone in most places, designed to optimize early delivery distances and times

[6] ; at that time there was only a small number of riders who were signing up for the work, along with a few others who had been there since the very beginning, predominately on scooters. Those original riders had been on hourly rates of £7 per hour, plus £1 per delivery, rather than the fixed fee per delivery that was introduced later as demand grew.

But the low numbers of riders working in these zones in the early days meant there was a large supply of orders, though the original pay structure must have acted as something of a disincentive. With a new structure in place, the company could attract the riders it needed. As a result, it took off among the target demographic of students, professionals and office workers in highly concentrated metropolitan areas, offering a whole host of popular restaurants not available on other delivery platforms. Low delivery fees were offered to the customers, and, latterly, fair wages to the couriers delivering the food.

It would take time for word to get out about the opportunities available in this new kind of work, but anyone who did sign up found everything they needed to carry out their job in one simple-to-use app. There is no office to sign in at, no human resources department to plead with to get your wages. No superiors watching you, no one to tell you to perform better or to complain to if things weren't going so well.

You choose the hours you want to work, ride into the city, tap the 'go online' button, and off you go. Streamlined simplicity. I could get used to this. So naturally, as I was being paid to ride my bike, I booked as many hours as I possibly could. Days off from uni, nights after uni classes had finished and, of course, weekends when uni classes didn't take place.

Daytime shifts were harder to come by – as the demand was

far less than in the evenings, and was usually prioritised for scooter drivers in those early days. But I would take what I was given, and gladly so. Any spare hours that flashed up on my screen I would happily devour. Sat at my desk studying, I would see these hours appear out of nowhere, flashing at me seductively and tempting me to the chance of some spontaneous cycling. Faced with the only alternative of another couple of hours spent reading heavily condensed journals late at night, I would often choose the boon of a few hours racing around Newcastle in the early autumn moonlight. I could always catch up with my extensive reading in the morning over a coffee.

I finished my first month, high on the feeling I got from cycling. I was learning to adapt to this new reality of no early alarms being set, no more waiting around to go into work for the late shift, no more desperately looking forward to my next batch of days off, no work-related stresses or extracurricular hang-ups. Just riding my bike and studying, or studying and riding my bike, I kept reminding myself.

Working to my own schedule, day or night – studying during the day, cycling in the evenings. No days off, I didn't need them, as every single day I was doing something I loved to do. The difference was night and day. I was buzzing, and everyone knew it – my parents, friends, housemates; basically anyone I could bore to tears with my enthusiasm for the life I was now living.

In those early days of Deliveroo the money was pretty good too. At that time, the laws of supply and demand very much worked in my favour, as there was a lot of demand for this newly emerging city-centre fast-food delivery and relatively few riders to meet it. For riding a bike, with the sole responsibility of simply getting some piping-hot food to a hungry customer, it was very good. I had signed a digital contract paying £4.25 for every delivery carried out. That's how the gig economy functions. It's piecework: you are paid for what you do – every job, every task, every delivery. Nothing more, nothing less.

On the downside, there really was nothing else – no holiday pay, no time in lieu, no finishing early on the company's time (one of life's great perks for the masses). There was also no nice juicy pension to show for it all after fifty years' service, just accumulated earnings for what you have done during each and every shift. If you can't do the job, you don't get paid a dime. I even had to pay for my own rider kit at the time, which then came from my wages as I worked those initial few weeks in the company's debt. These days the kit is provided free of charge.

If your bike ceases to function, tough luck. If you get a puncture, best learn to fix it quickly – or better still, march with vigour, dragging your deflated,bulky and burdensome bike alongside you to your customer's location. If your bike is stolen, best have another bike handy or you're jumping on the first bus home to rue your loss, wondering in the meantime how you can continue to work (more on all of this in later chapters).

But none of that mattered too much for now. I was a student doing the gig part-time and only had to make enough to cover my rent, food and coffee. My rent stayed consistent, but my food and coffee bills would rise rapidly as the weeks flew by and my legs grew stronger.

The fitter you get, the faster you deliver. The better you learn the layout of the city, the less you have to look at your phone for turn-by-turn directions. The better kit you have to do the job, the easier it is to work in the torrential conditions the British Isles can throw your way on any given day – though only slightly. Like most jobs, experience is the key. If you're already a keen all-weather cyclist, this also stands you in good stead.

For being outdoors means being at the mercy of Mother Nature. With the right waterproof kit and warm layers, you will soon be able to cope with most things thrown at you, without looking to the heavens and wondering why the fuck you decided to wear shorts and a T-shirt when it looked so sunny and picturesque outside your bedroom window just a few deceivingly dry hours ago.

Being such a keen cyclist in all seasons, I already possessed most of the clothing that would help me cope with the winter that lay ahead. Waterproofing yourself is a must, even if rain is not expected. It's the best advice I can give anyone thinking of doing this job on a regular basis. Of course, I didn't always follow my own advice during my early days as a cycle courier, but it's out there, so you know anyway. Don't say I didn't warn you.

It certainly makes economic sense to invest in the right kit, as you can't properly function beyond a few hours in miserable conditions without the appropriate clothing and gear. It's an uncomfortable, unforgiving, wretched experience otherwise. There is only one courier I have ever met who flouted this rule on a regular basis, who on most days only wore short shorts (like a footballer from the 1980s) and a lightweight T-shirt, no matter what the forecast. I'm sure he wasn't all there, and neither would you be if you pedalled around the city eight hours a day in all weathers wearing such an outlandish getup.

He didn't last long, though – most likely got sectioned once the temperature dropped below five degrees. Wearing the wrong gear is mental as well as physical torture.

As the weeks passed, I learned how to best equip myself for doing the job smarter, quicker, more comfortably and therefore more easily. Little things made a big difference. Touch-screen waterproof gloves, wireless headphones with a built-in microphone so you can ring customers without reaching for your phone from your pocket every few minutes while cycling (very dangerous!). Waterproofing your whole body. Covering your face when cold. Anything that stops the heat escaping and the cold from coming in. A handlebar mount for your phone is essential so that you can actually see where you are going on the road while safely following the map at the same time.

A lot of pedestrians have little to no idea that cyclists use roads and cycle paths, so it also helps to strap some kind of sound-making device to your bike to let pedestrians glued to their phones know that you are coming their way. A small bell will probably suffice for this task and will do the job more politely with typically British understatement. All these small additions to my cycling arsenal meant I could take the hallowed step up from working three-hour evening shifts to long days 'roo-ing' from lunchtime to late at night.

I was on the way to becoming a fully fledged cycling fanatic. I already had the enthusiasm and the right kit to get me there. Solid enough foundations, yet there was still a stubborn bit of body fat left to burn through, even as I spent longer and longer in the saddle. I had even bought a brand-new coffee machine, instinctively knowing it would prove to be one of my better investments for the year ahead.

All I needed now was the energy and a lot of extra coffee beans in the cupboard. As my hours on the bike started increasing, so did my food intake, coffee intake, sleep intake and Tesco Clubcard points. A bike doesn't ride itself, after all – though some of the new electric bikes now do most of the work for you, and unsurprisingly are widely encouraged by the delivery companies as they generally make for faster delivery times. As for me, when I first started, I had to rely on what I had got from the parental gene pool to get me from one job to the next. That and a very reliable £300 road bike.

There is nothing quite like exercise in promoting the wellness and proper functioning of your body. You can try other ways and means of making yourself feel better or happier. But in my experience, they are all a substitute for the rush of happy drugs your brain releases during any period of intense physical exertion. In fact, this motivation to go out and ride your bike is an evolutionary leftover of our primitive instinct to explore and seek sustenance. This kind of exercise leads to a fall in levels of a fat hormone called leptin, which lets our brain know that the body has enough energy. When leptin levels are low, we experience an extra boost of motivation for physical activity as a means to 'pursue food'.

When we give in to this urge and go for a vigorous ride, our bodies are flooded with a cocktail of happy drugs including norepinephrine, dopamine, endorphins, anandamide and serotonin, which allow us to keep riding longer and harder, and which keep us coming back for more. We have literally evolved over the past two million years to respond to these increased activity levels that reward us for engaging in tasks such as cycling that combine mental engagement and aerobic exercise. [7]

Our brains act like an amazing pharmacy; through exercise we are able to create heroin and cannabis substitutes, happy drugs which are in the brain already. Dopamine is a reward-based drug. If you set yourself a goal and achieve it, you'll get a dopamine hit as you feel good about doing it. Endorphins are released by the brain when we do hard physical exercise; even half an hour is enough to get this release.

Endorphins are essentially morphine-based pain relievers, much like heroin. Compared to heroin, an endorphin molecule is probably a hundred times more powerful, meaning you would need a lot of heroin to get the same effect as a small amount of endorphin. This partly explains why people may get addicted to exercise, or use it as their means of release or escape most days.

When you've been cycling for a few hours, this also leads to increased blood levels of a natural cannabinoid called anandamide. These naturally occurring cannabinoids are the natural marijuanas of the brain, releasing different neurotransmitters and allowing us to exercise for long periods without pain. This anandamide is much more effective and specific to the brain than marijuana, and it affects our energy, appetite, mood and perception of time. [8]

Cannabinoids affect the same part of the brain acted upon by marijuana and opiate use, which is why people feel a 'cyclist's high' during a longer ride. This activation of the endocannabinoid system gives cyclists a boost of euphoria, anti-inflammatory effects, enhances creative thinking and helps us find novel solutions to problems. [9] The incredible, completely complimentary, miraculous magic of cycling. Perfect for a born-again student!

Drugs like cannabis and heroin can chemically enhance your

experience in a similar way. But as they say, what goes up must go down. Extreme activation of the dopamine/opioid system results in the drug taker having a crash. This is caused by depletion of the neurotransmitters that gave the drug taker the overwhelming feeling of happiness when the drug took effect. The brain has used them all up and is now in a deficit of these neurotransmitters.

As the drug taking increases, the person taking them builds up a tolerance to the drug of choice and requires even greater amounts of the drug to reach the same level as that first initial rush. Eventually, if the drug taker is dependent on the hit, it may not even produce the original feeling of pleasure, but the drug will still be craved.

With lots of high-intensity exercise, you need to build more sleep and recovery into your schedule. Because exercise is natural, you don't get the same spike surge as you would from drugs, meaning you won't get the same resulting comedown. Sleep seems to restore and normalise these levels through the night, meaning when you wake you feel more refreshed and don't suffer the same peak and trough you get from taking drugs. [10] Still, during long bouts of intense cycling you have to listen to your body, and later in the book you'll find examples of what happened when I didn't follow this simple rule of thumb.

Now, I admire anyone who can live their lives by the well-worn mantra of wake early, work hard, strike oil. The ability to wake at 5 a.m., before the rest of the population, and go to work is a sign of dedication in any profession. But it's not something that will work for everyone, and certainly not those who value their sleep. For AM-ers, or larks, this task will feel more natural than those who go to sleep later and wake up later – the PM-ers or owls – and this is largely due to regulation of melatonin and serotonin production to get us going for the day ahead. Each of us conforms to one or other chronotype, controlled by our genes, with these habits being something we usually develop after we pass the peak of the late-running clock typical of most adolescents, a natural daily schedule which from around the age of twenty starts to get earlier the older we get.

Sleep is the most essential function for allowing your body to properly repair, recover and rehabilitate after a long day of work or cycling. Our brains effectively wash away waste toxins during sleep, potentially highlighting one of the key reasons why we do it. Failure to get enough sleep and clear out these toxins is linked to a host of neurological disorders, including Alzheimer's. Put simply, in the modern world we aren't getting enough of it. In fact, on average we are losing between one and two more hours' sleep a night than we were used to getting in the 1950s.

It had always been a huge struggle for me doing the early shifts at 5 or 6 a.m. at the leisure centre, and I never felt quite right or sufficiently human during those early morning slogs when coffee would be used as a substitute for lack of sleep the previous night rather than to give me the extra energy needed for the rest of the day. Professor Russell Foster, Director of Sleep and Circadian Neuroscience Institute at the University of Oxford, says: "Disrupted sleep, such as in shift workers, can lead to a multitude of problems ranging across suppressed immunity, greater risks of cancer, an increased risk of coronary heart disease and even metabolic disorders such as type 2 diabetes."[11]

In light of this, those who are woken up before nature

intended or still awake long after they should be asleep, simply because they are contractually obliged to do so, are putting themselves at risk. It seems to me completely nonsensical when you think of how we used to live before the dawn of artificial light and the Industrial Revolution. Eight hours' sleep, that's what most people need. Work, rest, play. Eight multiplied by three. It's a simple formula that points the way to how we ought to be living. Of course, such simplicity is hard to achieve, but as the template for a balanced life, it's hard to gainsay.

Yet here I was, stretching that formula out of sheer necessity. They had it harder during the Industrial Revolution, during any war, or during any other time in history, to be quite frank. And I was my own boss now, wasn't I? So it was totally down to me to cut down the 'play' angle of that equilateral template when I needed more of the 'rest'.

After all, sleep is the best way to reset mind and body. Bad day? Toss and turn, eventually getting to sleep, wake up, hopefully feeling slightly better. Good day? Great, well done, you! Go to sleep happy, wake up refreshed and strike oil whenever you're ready to go again.

We all need sleep – but sleep is a slightly different beast when you are trying to push your mind and body to the upper limits. It serves a vital physiological function and is arguably the single most important factor in exercise recovery. Both increased quantity and quality of sleep helps athletes improve performance in many areas related to the demands placed on them. Elite athletes are encouraged to get at least nine hours of sleep a night, and treat sleep with the same importance as athletic training and diet.[12] Cycling has a positive healing effect on the brain which helps calm anxiety, a key cause of insomnia.

Sleep debt, however, reduces your body's ability to build muscle and leads to a higher chance of injury. This also leads to the amygdala, the area of the brain that controls emotions, being up to 60 percent more active than normal when sleep-deprived. This in turn makes you more prone to emotionally charged reactions to negative situations, affecting your performance and making you far more irritable. And a ranting and raging courier is a potential danger to both themselves and others.

So getting enough sleep is vital, as there is so much to focus on while you're out on the road that you need to be mentally as sharp as possible. Performing at your best tactically and physically requires a lot of brain power which a lack of sleep can inhibit. [13] I found that even an hour or two of missed sleep could be hugely detrimental to my cognitive functioning when out working all day – as I'll explain in more detail later in the book.

Not that I'm comparing myself to a Royal Marine in describing what I was doing. It was nothing out of the ordinary – cycling twenty to forty hours a week, reading and writing the rest of the time in between bouts of coma-quality sleep. Plenty of keen cyclists and fitness enthusiasts will have similar schedules built around their job and favourite hobby. It's just that I wasn't fulfilling the role of a small-town librarian either. I was trying to cram the most out of every day in my new circumstances, so that I could not only survive, but thrive.

If you've ever been a student in any kind in a post-school environment, you'll know that very large amounts of academic reading can leave you feeling very tired in a fairly short amount of time. If you study from home like I do, this can be exacerbated by the fact that your desk is never more than a couple of feet away from your bed. I've always been fine with going to a gym to put me in the right type of environment to be screamed at while working out around others. But when it comes to studying all day in a busy library, I have a serious case of inferiority complex.

Having enough food and drink (coffee) to keep me going for long study periods proved impossible in such a building. Also having enough natural light to keep me switched on, as the fluorescent lighting that you commonly find pouring out in these gloomy communal spaces has an unenthusiastic glow and slight buzzing sound that makes me instantly want to place my head in my hands and have an hour's kip. Again, thank the drop in serotonin from a lack of natural light for this, switching your body clock into rest/siesta mode.

It's something that is very easy to do in a library, where it's always so quiet and peaceful. So peaceful, in fact, that I always felt inhibited walking into such a space, worried that having an elongated stretch of my limbs and muscles, or merely breathing out loud, would elicit the groans of other library users with far greater discipline and powers of thought – those who supposedly never feel the need to exercise these perfectly natural physical functions during the course of an arduous day of study in a sterile, cold, antisocial and energy-sapping environment.

Add to the mix the constant cycling I was now putting my body through, and I began feeling pretty tired in brain and body most of the time anyway, no matter what the stimulants I reached for. So sleep is the cure for everything. As I worked and studied more, I slept more. I needed to. An early start at uni meant sleep afterwards – followed by more study upon waking and then perhaps another nap.

Then I would go to work in the evenings, grab some supper when I got back home, and sleep until my next scheduled class the following day. This polyphasic sleep is completely natural, and hugely beneficial in helping us digest chunks of our day and also in improving memory retention. It was very much the norm before we started adapting en masse to eight-hour shifts and lightbulbs.

Elite sports sleep coach Nick Littlehales, who works with Team Sky, Olympic athletes and many top football clubs, looks at sleep more holistically and suggests we treat it incrementally over the course of a week. An ideal week is 35 sleep cycles, with each sleep cycle being ninety minutes, which we can aggregate into our daily lives beyond the usual pattern of sleeping only when we go to bed at night.[14] Anyone who has the luxury of taking regular naps and recovery periods during the day can relate to this, both athletes and desk jockeys alike.

Trying to get people back to the office, post-Covid, after so many of us during lockdown developed natural habits of proper rest and recovery, and have felt the benefits, will be extremely difficult and possibly even counterproductive for many businesses going forward. In a recent survey, 65 percent of workers said they would be more productive in a home office, 75 percent of workers said they will be more productive due to reduced distractions, and 83 percent of employees felt they did not need an office to be productive. Two-thirds of employers report increased productivity for remote workers compared to in-office workers.[15]

The structured routine of a 9-to-5 never appealed to me on any level throughout my early life. School was a constant battle to stay awake most mornings until I could make it to the canteen. I routinely slept through my early alarm, had to skip breakfast and sprint through the estate to get the bus yet again. A constant state of teenage 'social jetlag' – fighting our internal sleep regulators, our age-related chronotypes [16] so as to get up early for school – is a big impediment to optimum learning, due solely to the need to make teenagers conform with the work schedule of adult life.

At least as an undergraduate away at university I was finally able to draw up my own rather unproductive schedule, to enable me to make the most of the available hours in a way that suited me. By then I had realised that I as just not very good in the mornings, and if I got up too early it could leave me feeling groggy and unproductive for the rest of the day, no matter what I tried to do or drink to overcome it. Gradually, it had dawned on me that I was a PM-er – more productive later on in the day and someone who needs that extra bit of sleep in the morning to function properly when I'm awake.

Seven to nine hours is said to be optimal for most human beings. Slightly more if you're approaching the fitness levels of an athlete, which was what I flippantly told my friends and family I'd now become. College athletes are among those who need the most hours of sleep to be mentally and physically at their peak; it's a high peak and needs a lot of maintaining. [17] Some captains of industry can allegedly get by on as little as four or five hours a night, but if I was ever to try rebooting my operating system in such a small timeframe, I'm pretty sure the lack of sleep would leave me unable to pedal a bicycle with any kind of genuine fluency, precision or enthusiasm.

While I'm now in my mid-thirties, I still cling to the vague notion that I am someone who needs a lot of sleep and is therefore entitled to it. Despite being a bang-average student and an amateur cyclist at best, the upper end of the sleeping scale is where I aimed to be, and as a rule when I set myself to achieve something, I do tend to follow through. Research shows sleep is essential for overall health and well-being.

The physical benefits of a good night's sleep allow your heart to rest and the cells and tissue to repair themselves, which helps your body to recover properly. As you progress through different stages of sleep (there are five stages in total), the changes in your heart rate and breathing throughout the night promote cardiovascular health.

The deep sleep of stages three and four is when your body releases human growth hormone (HGH) to repair muscles and bones – perhaps familiar as a banned performance-enhancing drug which our bodies produce naturally and whose effect is powerful. While asleep, you also produce cytokines, which are hormones that help your immune system fight off infections – helping to prevent illness or recover from illness. [18]

But it was not only my body that needed to get used to the new schedule of intense physical activity; my brain was also adapting to the new regime, as I discovered when I woke from prolonged periods of deep sleep. Some dreams now consisted of me cycling through seemingly abandoned and fairly featureless urban environments – most likely tracing the many assorted routes I had taken through the city centre the previous day.

Sometimes they were fairly vivid images, and I could remember certain landmarks as I navigated the cityscape in the dream; most of the time however, turn by turn, they were journeys through unremarkable terrain as the brain made sense of, i.e. cognitively processed, what my body had gone through during eight long hours in the saddle. This processing helps us to form memories, and contributes to improved performance in the future, helping me subconsciously to memorise my daily routes as I learned every inch of the city whose streets were now my daily working environment.

Luckily, during this stage of your sleep your muscles are paralysed, probably to stop you acting out your dreams as they occur. This condition is known as atonia. During rapid eye movement (REM) sleep – the sleep where most recalled dreams occur during the second half of the night – respiratory and eye muscles stay active but your body's muscles are stopped, to help prevent you acting out your dreams and injuring yourself (and potentially others!)[19] About 20 percent of your sleep is spent in this state.

That's not to say as you transition to different stages of sleep that your body is completely immobile throughout the night. Muscles gradually relax during each stage of non-REM sleep as you transition to deeper sleep throughout the night. On the whole, brain activity slows, but there are still short bursts of activity.[20] I've received numerous complaints in the past of being an unintentional nocturnal abuser, on account of various kicks, knees, elbows, legs thrown over and even uncontrollable spasms during episodes in which my brain must be replaying a day spent out on the bike.

'It's like being in bed with Alan Shearer,' an ex-girlfriend once remarked. Granted, she was a Sunderland fan, but it must have been hell on earth after I'd spent a long weekend mountain biking in Scotland or the Lake District. Far worse than the consistent cigar-induced snoring that drove my mother into a separate bedroom from my old man, as at least with snoring it becomes a near-constant white noise that can be filtered out like traffic, becoming part of the background aural environment.

Waking up throughout the night with bumps and bruises can't be much fun, unless you're into that sort of thing, and unfortunately I'm yet to meet anyone who's a fan of late-night cycling sadomasochism. Still, they say there's someone for everyone. Nowadays, I place some memory-foam pillows strategically between abuser and abused. Early morning accusations of physical assault have all but disappeared since, though for a while I was watching anxiously as the #MeToo movement gathered pace worldwide.

* * *

So, anyway, I was sleeping more, which was brilliant. I was also cycling a hell of a lot more after a few months. Another tick. This also meant the amount of food I required to keep body and brain fuelled was considerably increased to combat any possibility of fatigue or lethargy, which quite simply I couldn't afford to be afflicted by over the coming ten months of intense workload. I already had half an idea from going out mountain biking all day that a big breakfast, followed up with any simple sugars during the ride, would suffice to keep my legs turning most of time without risking any kind of serious side effects.

Whilst diet is important to a certain extent, I have always enjoyed indulging myself after exercise, and for a decade or so had tended to eat almost anything I wanted after a long day's cycling. Now, faced with the reality of becoming a full-time cyclist, the world of food had blown wide open – so much so that I imagined myself eating six meals a day of whatever I fancied without ever having to worry about staying in shape.

In reality, this would never work. If I had a full English breakfast every morning, followed by a mouth-watering curry before I turned in most nights, my heart would be less filled with joy and happiness, more with excess saturated fat and cholesterol. I would have to find a middle ground, a pragmatic way to fuel the engine without flooding it. A way to combine my love of food with the need to take on loads of extra calories to keep me going each day. It was a genuinely mouth-watering prospect, though one I would have to budget for from my earnings.

It's very easy to add extra snacks and calories into your day. A few extra Weetabix for breakfast in the morning, a few spoons of sugar, full-fat milk. Honey does a great job too. You never have to worry about these extra calories when you are exercising so often, so sweets are also fine when you're out on the bike. I tend to think of them as lumps of sugary coal for keeping the fire burning brightly. Simple carbs will always do the job: bananas, apples, Haribo, jelly babies and cake. Calorie-dense foods such as nuts, flapjacks and dark chocolate do the job just as well. The list is endless. Carbs sometimes get a bad press, but for cycling couriers they are essential in your quest to keep your legs turning for prolonged periods.

Slow-release, low-to-moderate-GI (Glycaemic Index) foods two to three hours before cycling, then high-GI, rapidly delivered carbs during riding hours, then back to low-to-moderate-GI foods again after cycling. The GI is a rating system for foods containing carbs, which shows how quickly each food affects your blood sugar (glucose) levels when consumed. That's the advice for the pro cyclists (and the dedicated stoics) anyways. The pros have nutritionists telling them exactly what to eat and when to eat it. They don't have unfettered access to a Greggs every five hundred yards when they are out training in the Alps.

Top yourself up little and often. It can all go wrong without adequate energy to keep you going all day. As my university life settled into a routine and I got to grips with further education again, I was throwing everything, including the kitchen sink, at doing more hours at work on the bike. In October I had started by doing occasional evening shifts, three or four hours at a time. Nothing too strenuous considering my cycling past. This quickly morphed into six-to-eight-hour evenings and longer weekend shifts after the first month, and the busy influx of orders rolled in as the cold of November begins to bite.

I was also starting to notice some profound changes in how my body was responding to all this extra exercise. I didn't have a solid stool for a month (I know, too much information, but stay with me), while I dramatically increased the hours I was working, although I was also experimenting with pretty strong Turkish espresso coffee at the time too. This is fairly common in people who work out for long periods or participate in intense forms of exercise such as cycling.

Usually, diarrhoea relating to working out is caused by intestinal blood flow that slows down and is directed away from your intestines – instead being redirected to other parts of your body with more need of the blood and oxygen, such as the muscles in your legs when cycling. [21] This is also what leads to a bloated stomach, something I suffered with for majority of the time as a cycle courier, and something I will go into detail about later in the book.

I was also waking up every morning to a pillow covered in hair from my head which had fallen out during the previous night's sleep. I had first noticed this fairly dramatic increase in hair loss when showering after longer days working for Deliveroo, thinking of it as loose hairs which had been dislodged due to the helmet or cap I'd been wearing, or maybe from when I had wiped my brow and head to remove the excess sweat and trapped heat during and after a shift.

It's normal for most people to shed between 50 and 100 hairs a day. Anything significantly greater than that is considered excessive hair shedding and is known as telogen effluvium. There are many triggers for this, but the main one seems to be experiencing a lot of stress or after a particularly stressful event in life. [22] I couldn't confess that I had been under a lot of mental stress in the previous few months, but I was certainly starting to put my body through a lot of new physical stress, which may have accounted for the various symptoms I'd noticed regarding hair or stool.

In the winter you need more energy to sustain yourself, as the cold weather burns more calories when your body is working harder to maintain its core temperature. In that regard, as early as the third week on the job, I discovered one of the undeniable perks of working for Deliveroo: what the customer does not pick up is yours to consume as you see fit. Oh boy, was this music to my ears! I was already stockpiling foods from my weekly shop that just a few months ago I would have considered rare treats.

Now this unexpected benefit would give me the chance to randomly sample some of the city's finest food while not paying a penny for the privilege – in fact, being paid to do so while burning off the calories in a process of guilt-free consumption. Two birds, one stone. A lovely fresh meal for all my hard work, ready to be devoured as soon as I got home and needed to refuel, and all without having to go anywhere near a saucepan or kettle.

Now, in the good old days of paying cash on delivery, it was a loss to the business if their seemingly loyal customer didn't have the necessary funds or, for whatever reason, was not answering the door when the food arrived. The customer got nothing, but the shop had made the food that they now wouldn't be paid for. The delivery man took it back to the shop to be thrown out or more than likely to enjoy as a freebie if they had the guile to suggest it to the takeaway owner.

Looking back now, all the takeaway delivery men who came to our house seemed to be long-serving members of the big boys' club, whose entry requirements were set at twenty stone plus. No wonder they refused insufficient payment when they had been waiting at the door for more than ten minutes while my household tried frantically to gather up the correct amount of loose change from every bit of furniture in sight. The undelivered meal was likely to be a bonus for having their time wasted.

Technology helped change the basic ground rules on how to run a takeaway delivery business. No longer did the customer have to provide the cash to pay for their favourite Friday night nosh. The customer now prepaid Deliveroo directly through an app before they got their meal, so that the delivery driver, or now rider, could just concentrate on delivering that meal.

Of course, this is time-saving on all fronts, but what if the customer doesn't come to the door to collect their food? They've paid for it, after all. It belongs to them. But they also know that, so it's their decision whether to take delivery of what they've paid for; the rider is still paid for the delivery, whether the customer comes to collect the order or not.

To take one example shortly after I started the job, I was standing outside on a freezing-cold early November night, waiting for a student to collect their paid-for goods, and several minutes had ticked by since I had first called the customer and been put through to voicemail. Nothing too unusual there, I thought. No phone signal is common in a lot of apartment blocks. You aren't allowed into the student accommodation blocks, and many concierges at the time wouldn't accept food orders being left at reception areas. The students also don't put their room numbers on the order, as they know that deliveries have to be accepted from the main entrance.

No big deal anyways, they'd be doing cartwheels down the stairs or pressing buttons furiously on the lift to get to their food soon enough. I looked down at my app, I'd already been waiting five minutes. *Five minutes*, I thought. How rude! But maybe the lifts had broken? Maybe they had just fallen asleep? More than likely they'd been drunk when they ordered and had since passed out, or maybe even better, they'd got lucky with the fairer sex. All scenarios were possible, and frankly I didn't really care what had happened as long as they came and collected their food quickly. I wanted to get off to my next job - and earn enough money so I could afford the food I needed myself to give me the energy to keep doing the job.

I was perplexed as the minutes passed. It was time to use my initiative to figure out what should happen next. Nothing to do with the restaurant, I thought - they simply make the food, get paid for it, and hand it over to an intermediary like myself to deliver it. Since I had not encountered this problem up to then, I started clicking random buttons on the app. No one had told me at my very informal interview (no more than a gathering, really) in October what to do should the customer not arrive for their food.

I was too busy comparing bikes and trying on my shiny, new reflective clothing – thinking that bragging about my ability to do more than a hundred miles in a day was a better way to introduce myself than enquiring about what the job really entailed. It was too late for all that now. I would just have to wing it. It was a block of flats, with no flat number and no contact from the customer yet. I decided to ring Deliveroo and see what was going on.

"You're through to rider support. How can I help?"

"A customer hasn't turned up for their food, they haven't even called me back, and they live in a student block of flats which I can't even get into. I don't know what to do. Can you tell me?"

"Certainly, can I have your rider ID?"

"No idea, sorry, I've just started." I gave my name.

"I need your rider ID, please."

"Can you tell me where it is, please?"

"You should have been told it when you started."

I eventually found it and was able to give full vent to my frustration. "What do I do now, please. I've been stood outside in the freezing cold for about ten minutes?"

"OK, I will now try and contact the customer. Please stay on the line."

Great, I thought, she's going to ring this customer and will also go straight through to voicemail, and we'll be back at the start. This was tedious. Can I not just leave and go home already?

"OK, I've just rang the customer and I cannot get through to them, sir."

"I've already told you this!

"OK. Yes, I understand sir. I will now send them an email saying that you are here and to pick up the food as soon as possible."

"OK. So how long do I wait for them?" Perhaps until he wakes up and decides breakfast has never looked so good, I thought?

"Please wait ten minutes, sir. If the customer has not arrived you are free to continue to your next job."

"And the food?" I was still none the wiser as to whether I should return the food to the restaurant or not.

"You are free to do as you wish with it, sir. Dispose of it, give to the homeless, it is up to you."

Interesting, I thought, and said, "OK, no problem pet." The Geordie dialect always comes out a little in me when I'm giddy or excited or otherwise anticipating getting something for free.

"Thank you, sir, ride safe."

"Thank you!" I said gleefully as I hung up the phone, wondering if the lovely polite East Asian girl I had just spoken to, working in some call centre thousands of miles away, would have any idea of the meaning of the word 'pet', or if she would see it as an attempt to undermine her professionalism. No doubt, wherever in the world she was based, she had to help a whole range of Deliveroo drivers from many places on the planet, deciphering their deeply challenging accents and dialects of English.

Dealing with Geordie – half Scottish, half Viking – had to

be a hell of a tricky task. It was hard enough to understand or decipher for the average southerner, who no doubt assumes that all Geordies still go to work down the pit and drink fifteen pints before going to bed of a night. They are perhaps more accurate on the latter of the two stereotypes.

Still, I had ten minutes to wait until the first potential free meal of my short riding career. Just ten minutes, hoping, waiting, praying that the student doesn't wake up and check their phone or walk down the street towards you and realise what you are there for. After a seven-hour shift in the dark, vacant, stale, moody streets of Newcastle, all I was thinking about now was food.

Maybe a nice warm shower too. But above all food. Lovely, warm and much-needed food. Seconds went by. The sun seemed to set and rise in those ten minutes. Even the fog was clearing over the Tyne – such was the length of time since I had first arrived at the customer's address.

Nine minutes pass. Nine minutes thirty seconds. I pick up my backpack, I zip it up, I walk away and reach for my bike. Nine minutes fifty seconds. I look graciously up at the block of high-rising rooms, safe in the knowledge that this poor student's loss would most certainly be my gain. I pedal away, with a huge grin slapped across my frostbitten face. Supper, all cooked and all mine, free of charge. A large thin-crust pizza with a side of dough balls, and a bottle of coke to wash it all down with. Thank you, kind sir, you have paid my wage and helped feed me for the night, too.

In the euphoria of getting my free meal, I cycled home in triumph and conveniently forgot about the last hour that I was scheduled to work. It had been a long day, and I had not found the time to make my usual bowl full of pasta and cheese to devour before coming out that particular evening, meaning that for the last few hours my stomach had been growling relentlessly to put something wholesome into it. I set about articulating to my housemates upon arriving home how lucky I was to be riding my bike while also being fed at the same time. I might even have shared a few of the dough balls in the delirium that followed. After a decade of being chained to the one employer in the same building, it felt like a just reward.

I mentioned that the money was good – £4.25 a delivery. But when you picked up a double delivery (two orders from the same restaurant), this was multiplied by two. And as the work kept increasing, such double orders became more frequent. This was the cause of some envy and admiration among other riders. You informed the sixteen-year-old at the counter that you were here to pick up two orders. Your fellow rider, waiting there for his single order, would blurt out excitedly, "You've got a double order?"

"Yeah. £8.50! and it's only down the road, both right next to each other."

"Jammy twat, take you fifteen minutes max, ten if you're really quick."

"Not bad for ten minutes work, eh?"

The spotty sixteen-year-old looked on flustered and bewildered, wondering where he went wrong in his job-application process. For my part, I was baffled as to why every person in the country who owned a bicycle wasn't applying to do this job.

"Well, mate, hopefully you'll get a double later, eh?"

"I'm not complaining, already made £70 tonight in less than three hours."

Alright, mate, no need to brag. We're British here, so keep

it together. Don't let other people in on our little goldmine. I watched as the sixteen-year-old started throwing chicken slightly more aggressively into a bucket for the next lucky rider, who'll get a similarly handsome reward for his toil.

"Nice one, have a good night!"

I eagerly exhaled as I bolted out of the shop, knowing that I would have to push my body to the upper limits of what can be achieved on my bike, just to make it within the ten-minute timeframe that I've allotted myself. Anyone working as a cycle courier will know this same mentality. Time is money. Keep pushing. The more you do it, the quicker you get. Repeat, repeat, repeat. Much like a well-practised and well-rehearsed salesman. Close the sale then on to the next punter, as fast as you can manage. Much like every delivery I was now carrying out in the shortest possible timeframe.

I was driven to squeeze the most out of every shift I worked on those busy winter nights. It was exhausting work, but I had a naïve appreciation of this new type of work I was now doing. The pay was better than a typical student job, but the money was almost secondary to the feeling from cycling for so many hours, week after week. I was now getting fitter, not fatter, doing a job based around my life. Not fitting my life around the demands of my previous job. I could barely contain myself. And I was only getting started.

To begin with, the whole process is time-consuming. You need to accustom yourself to the intricacies of the city or town that you're working in. Not that I'm any kind of anarchist, but on a bicycle you can take advantage of certain obscure, undesignated routes within a metropolitan area that you simply can't get away with by car or scooter. One-way streets, wide pathways, pedestrian bridges, riverside routes, high streets, graveyards. Okay, use your common sense a bit, too, as you always run a risk if you pass a policeman in a fully pedestrianised zone.

You are a road user, after all, and you pose more of a threat to unassuming pedestrians if you don't follow the laws of the road. Delivery riders in general get a bad reputation from the few that quite blatantly abuse the rules regularly, so don't be one of those renegades who ruin it for the rest of us. If you wouldn't do it on a scooter, you shouldn't do it on an electric bike. A red light means stop. Not stop only if you have a petrol tank. Of course, you do have a slight advantage in some ways over those pesky scooters and cars – if you play your cards right and use the infrastructure around you to trim a few minutes off your overall delivery time.

I would use my own grandmother as a ramp if it meant bypassing a few shards of glass on a road – though I doubt that's what she meant when she said she would always be there when I needed her most. There are many and various obstacles to be avoided – broken glass, oil, tramlines, black ice, expanding and multiplying potholes or hard-to-spot but not-so-subtle speed bumps – which can either slow you down or stop you in your tracks entirely. You need to have a laser focus at all times to stop your bike from throwing you off at any given point during the day – and remember that sleep is vital for this strenuous task.

But the more you fall from a bike, the more you learn how to fall safely in future episodes. Mountain biking prepares you well for a career as a cycle courier – as would figure skating or any kind of activity for that matter where throwing yourself gracefully (or not) onto a hard surface at speed is a fairly routine activity. Worse still are those road users (think taxi drivers, bus drivers or anyone else with an engine and a steering wheel) hell-bent on knocking you off your perch, as they consider you to be the lowest form of traffic commuter there is. The battle is endless, so respect the road and the various people and vehicles that use it. Or you will end up on your arse more times than the poor contestants on *Takeshi's Castle*.

Swipe *Delivered* on your app and accept your next job, hoping the next order is close by and therefore easy to get to. If it isn't, you start rejecting these jobs, as by now you will be learning that you can't afford to stray too far from your own patch. It is a very busy Friday night. There are lots of orders and lots of hungry weekend warriors needing the well-deserved takeaway that they have slaved away for all week. And that's just fine. You are learning all the rules of the game and getting better, faster, fitter and richer in the process.

You are self-employed. So you are not contractually obliged to accept every single order. Just log in to the app once you're inside the delivery zone, stay logged in, and complete the delivery jobs as you see fit. Tired? Log off. Need a break? Ditto. Craving more sleep? Simply cycle home, leaving the app running in the background; if you live quite far outside the zone, you tend not to be offered any more jobs as you are too far away from the bulk of the restaurants to be considered.

If you actually live inside the zone, well done you. You are way ahead of the game. You have a base that you can quickly return to when things go wrong, if you need a cuppa, have a puncture, or if the weather turns bad and you need a change of clothes or a cattle prod up the arse to get you moving again. Otherwise, you are stuck in your zone for the duration of your shift, making good use of every public toilet and park bench you can find, every corner shop and Greggs bakery, to keep you going in the role of pawn in what is an algorithm-optimised game of fast-moving human chess.

And in the early days of Deliveroo, when it was making its mark in cities across the UK, your earnings were what first united you with your fellow riders. Discussing them on a nightly basis, comparing how many doubles you had picked up on any given day or how many orders you had managed to complete in a busy single hour. It was all there on the app, a living, breathing real-time analysis of how efficient you were, how much money you were now making and how much better you were than your fellow comrades in squeezing every minute out of every hour as a way to be the very best of the best. Computerised workloads, data-driven performance.

It was the Strava equivalent of being king (or queen) of the road (or roo- Deliveroo). In the beginning, it was not uncommon that you could squeeze in five or six deliveries an hour in the course of a busy night's work – something that's very uncommon these days as the overall rider supply is far greater than customer demand. Fast food, fast riders. Choose the right places, choose the shortest distances, ring ahead to your customer so that they're ready to collect their food when you arrive. Deliver, accept your next job, get there, hope the food is ready to collect when you arrive back at the restaurant. Repeat the same steps again and again.

Simply brilliant when it all fell into place, though this was only ever the case during really busy periods – if the weather was terrible and the many fair-weather riders disappeared to escape a torrential downpour, or simply if you knew exactly what you were doing. Not that you couldn't afford to spend a minute or two in the restaurant with your new colleagues, discussing your accumulated daily total or, better still, your daily target before you sprinted off to deliver the food then sped back to the city centre to do it all over again.

The pay packets generally tended to increase as the weeks rolled by from autumn to winter and you learned the quickest ways to get from A to B, from C to D or E to F. And as you got fitter, you also got faster, which meant quicker deliveries. Demand also seemed to grow as the winter went on and the weather turned colder. November was, and still is, the best month to work as a courier for Deliveroo, with my earnings in this month being consistently higher compared with other months in any given year.

After the sharp drop in temperature from the autumn, all the students are still in the city at this time, with the fun and frolicking at the start of term now somewhat behind them, and still time before the present-buying pressures of December come to the fore, meaning any disposable income would be spent less on pub crawls or meaningless gifts for ungrateful relatives and more on the weekly indulgence of a takeaway meal.

But it was far from one-way traffic on the road to consistent pay packets to help me cover my rent and other expenses. Students keep you busy in this line of work, and when they disappear, your earnings can take a big hit. Still, some of these students stay all year round, and these are ones you count on to pay your rent on time.

The key demographic served by Deliveroo tends to have plenty of disposable income, more free time, city-centre locations, and they're happy paying for the convenience of having their food and drinks delivered to their newly built ultra-modern skyscrapers. Many of the high-rise cranes that have plagued the skyline in major city centres across the UK over the past decade have been helping to meet a chronic undersupply in the amount of student accommodation, as the growth of successful universities and the rising number of non-UK students has driven demand for decent accommodation. Only the US (with 28 percent) attracts more of these 3.3 million students who leave their home country to study in OECD countries than the UK (with 13 percent). [23] And the international students are your lifeblood, your most loyal subjects, and the ones who will ensure that work is constant all day, every day.

International students stand on the highest rung of your professional gratitude – above the likes of domestic students, office workers, city visitors, young professionals and suburban/inner-city households. They are minted. They order breakfast, brunch, lunch, tea, supper, cigarettes, alcohol and anything in between for that matter. It's these customers who keep most full-time city-centre delivery drivers on the road all day – who keep the cogs in the machinery properly greased, so to speak. They're the real VIPs in this line of work. Non-EU international students are the most frequent faces you see – Chinese and Middle Eastern (but also Indian) students tend to be the customers you deliver to most often.

This may be because they don't spend so much of their budget on nights out drinking like domestic students, but in any case research suggests they do have more spending power than EU students and domestic students. The latest assessment of the economic impact of international students in the North-east shows off-campus expenditure of £256 million, supporting 2,032 jobs. They are worth more than £25 billion to the UK economy as a whole,[24] supporting 206,600 jobs in university towns and cities across the UK and spending £5.4 billion off campus on goods and services in 2014/2015 alone.

A recent report from the Higher Education Policy Institute highlights that students from outside the EU, who pay higher fees, are worth £102,000 each to the UK economy. Nick Hillman, the think-tank's director, recognises that their spending has become a major factor in supporting local economies, bringing "economic benefits to the UK that are worth ten times the costs of hosting them... fewer international students would mean fewer jobs in all areas... literally the sandwich shops, bike shops, taxi drivers, nightclubs... [and] some of the local resident population would lose their jobs." Newcastle came second only to Sheffield on the list of urban centres with the biggest economic dependency on international students.[25]

They certainly help in paying my wages most of the time. How they chose to spend their money before the advent of app-based delivery firms I have no idea. But you soon learn that this young, apparently wealthy urban elite will keep you in employment for the foreseeable future. Some you deliver to most days, some even a few times a day, and with some you'll soon be able to guess who it is when the order first flashes up on the screen.

I remember fondly in my own undergraduate student days at Leeds, when I would manufacture some half-hearted excuses to my lecturers by email for missing morning (pre-noon) lectures when I all I was doing was waking up late and anxiously waiting for *Deal or No Deal* in the afternoons, while dining exclusively on Sainsbury's finest nine-pence packets of noodles. Sure, I ordered the odd takeaway, but this meant using the temperamental cashpoint machine, speaking to another human being on the phone, collecting cash from other students (akin to pulling hen's teeth), then waiting an hour or two after eventually phoning in your order, having made sure you could club together enough cash to pay for it when it had finally arrived.

The entry of the app-based delivery firms has technologically gentrified the sector to appeal to the new generation of young, savvy mobile-phone shoppers, making the old way of doing things irrelevant almost overnight. A tech intermediary had entered the game, and found its ideal user group in this ever-growing and very well-heeled cohort among the student body of large parts of the British university sector. I ask myself, would I really ever have been able to justify paying upwards of twenty quid in my undergraduate days for a single, albeit delicious meal? The answer was absolutely not.

That was a good week's shopping for me. Noodles, hot dogs, crumpets, pasta, cheese, milk and tea – that was my standard diet in those days. Cheap and mostly cheerful. Being thrifty was a necessary skill to learn, so I could afford the finer things that university life had to offer – by which I mean pub lunches, pub crawls, clubbing, house parties, books (yeah, right!) and rent. These were the days just before Netflix, Facebook, Instagram and Twitter consigned us to staring at our mobile phone screens for most of the day.

I guess it all comes down to priorities, with today's students being more likely to pursue fitness and a healthy lifestyle than those of previous generations. I would happily have spent the equivalent of a Deliveroo meal on a night out when I was a student, whereas many students now prioritise convenience and health over those six treble vodkas and lemonades I would get through of an evening.

Fifteen years seems like a lifetime ago when you consider the changes in how young people are now growing up and accessing goods, services, information and their own individual lifestyle choices. It's less treble vodka and mixer these days, more skinny chai latte with almond milk. The Starbucks is probably, on balance, slightly better for you!

Newcastle has 27 fast-food outlets per 100,000 people in the UK, which is second only to Cardiff with 30. Students now spend £925 a year on takeaways – an average of £102.77 a month, which is more than the £67 a month they spend on food shopping.[26] The UK saw a 34 percent increase in fast-food outlets between 2010 and 2018 due to this insatiable demand. Students, despite having tighter budgets, spend four times as much on takeaways as the average Brit every month. Figures show that smartphone-based delivery companies have caused a 73 percent surge in the money spent on home delivery of takeaways in the past ten years.

Deliveroo, UberEats and Just Eat now have a combined total of over 600,000 daily users.[27] The total food-service delivery market in 2019 was worth around £8.5 billion, thanks largely to the rise of online delivery – meaning there are now over 24 million users of such apps in the UK. That's big business for those looking to extract a larger market share in the sector, with estimated revenues of around £4.26 billion in 2020 projected to grow to approximately £6.78 billion in 2025, helped of course by the pandemic which has accelerated an existing trend towards ordering more frequently online.[28]

International students nowadays are an essential feature of any modern multi-cultural city, not just for what they contribute to its vibrancy but for the part they play in the way it functions. They spend lots of money, going out shopping and socialising and doing all the things that you're supposed to at that age. As the vast majority of them live in the heart of the city and can access the menu of any given restaurant in any given language, this makes ordering food in the unfamiliar place (and its language) where they have come to study a simple and streamlined process.

As Deliveroo tend to offer the cheapest delivery fees amongst the various delivery companies operating in the city centre, most folk who live there find Deliveroo the cheapest to use for the food they want. Deliveroo Plus, the paid monthly subscription service, also helps keep these customers ordering from the company time and time again, much like the Amazon Prime model has done for Amazon. Today's undergraduates have also grown up with the internet from a very young age. Being early-years adopters, they have taken for granted everything it has to offer for more or less as long as they can remember.

These students have become the lovely folks I deliver to day in, day out. No hassle. No fuss. Young people from all corners of the planet – from China and from Asia more broadly, from Russia, from Europe and from South America. All of them are happy to be here and excited to receive some food to brighten up their days. Some speak fluent English, some are still learning how to get by and communicate with others from the other parts of the world. We exchange a few pleasantries, and I ask them about the countries they have come from, eliciting thoughts and impressions of how they find being in Newcastle, with any luck leaving a good impression of my own in the process.

Sometimes I have wished that I was back in their shoes or more specifically back at their age. I bid them farewell and ride off into the sunset and await my next gig. And in the months after I had started doing this job, as the weeks rolled by and it was clear that this was indeed a viable way of earning a living, I began thinking to myself, what would the younger version of me think of the grown-up Ryan riding a bike for a living?

All of the freedoms and carefree thoughts I had enjoyed as a child riding a bike were now front and centre all over again. That same warm, fuzzy feeling of being out in the elements, not being constrained by cul-de-sac boundaries or housing estates, nor by office walls or dead-end jobs, not in the sense that there was no career progression – but that career progression was the life-limiting point of it all.

On a bike, you always get that warm, fuzzy feeling that anything is possible, that you may stumble across something new and exciting, even dangerous. No longer bound by the limits of being stuck in the same place with the same people for the same amount of time five days a week - you find that every bike trip reveals a new landmark, a fresh face, a different location.

The sense of adventure is something fundamental to being alive, something we develop a taste for as young children and, if we're lucky, never lose. I had defiantly chosen to cut all ties with my previous life. Being a cycle courier was my new adventure, with a whole city to explore and new faces to greet along the way. It was all ahead of me, all around me, that sense of a bigger world I had felt and experienced as a ten-year-old child – going out of the cul-de-sac and into the periphery. I had unconsciously returned myself to that earlier, easier, freer time in my life, when everything that lay ahead of me would one day be discovered, all thanks to my bike.

* * *

At certain points in life, we are faced with choices that can seem as hard to make as solving a Rubik's cube. Life is finite and we have to balance expectations, ambitions, the need for safety, security, prosperity and a pleasant old age with the needs of the present. For many people, it isn't as simple as having a job that allows you to be content, with enough money coming in to put a roof over your head and food on the table, getting you from one week to the next.

And in that regard, I was putting myself through further training with a view to better things. I was back at university studying for a master's degree in something I thought would offer me better employment opportunities, open new doors that got me closer to what I thought it meant to be an adult. Most of my friends were in relatively secure forms of employment after all. Some of them did jobs they enjoyed with a passion, while others turned up every day simply to pick up a payslip at the end of the month. A further few had learned a trade after leaving school, while another lot were going it alone and setting up their own businesses.

All in all, it was a very broad spectrum. While I had put a lot of time and effort into working my way up the ladder of leisure in my previous role, I always craved a little something extra that will always be hard to get from a job that dictates your weekly schedule and leaves you little time to focus on other areas of your life. There's an undeniable element of freedom and entrepreneurial spirit that can be harnessed when you are unshackled from the constraints of a full-time job and the responsibility it entails.

In the end, the reasons why people work at the jobs they do are as varied as the individuals doing them. Some do it for the money, some for the advancement into more senior roles, some to inspire new minds, and some do it because family connections give them an in. Some are good with their hands, while others seek to play their part in society and to help improve the lot of others. Some grit their teeth and work simply to keep a roof over their heads, so that they don't end up back at their parents' house - having finally shown them after all these years that they have indeed grown up and can stand on their own two feet after all.

Once you get to a certain age and you can go it alone, there are certain hopes and expectations that are placed upon you. Take your parents as a starting point. The biggest investment they ever made is in you. They have brought you up, given you invaluable life lessons, tried with every fibre of their being to get you into a good school, to get you a good education, so that maybe you have good prospects for the future, meet some good friends and become a good person in the process.

Some of this also depends on how you adapt to the world around you, but these initial steps go a long way to determining the kind of person you eventually become. Why shouldn't they have certain hopes for you? They love you; they want the very best for you and hope you can get on in life and access opportunities that maybe they were denied due to a lack of these fundamentals when they were growing up themselves. With a bit of luck, they will recognise that you also want to be able to get some joy out of your life and from your work. They want you to have better chances than they did, so it is completely natural that they should want you to grasp whatever opportunities come your way in this highly globalised and interconnected world.

Anyway, you meet your friends for drinks once in a while, share experiences of what it is like growing up and becoming an adult, the complex games of negotiation, adaptation and sometimes humiliation that result from interacting with other adults. Long gone are the days of simply running off, kicking and screaming, when things go wrong. This is the big bad world you sensed all those years ago when your dad was having a rough time, choosing to console himself with a cigar rather than burden his carefree, if somewhat troublesome offspring with the huge pressures of adulthood.

Looking back, those pressures never seemed that bad from the child's point of view. After all, Dad seemed to have the money to buy whatever he wanted, and all I ever got was a couple of packs of football stickers every week and a pick'n'mix if I kept my nose clean and didn't come home with troubling notes from teachers on my lacklustre performance at school. When I did, they all said the same thing: how impossible it was for me to concentrate when I was surrounded by all my best mates, sniggering audaciously at the back of the class at the most inappropriate times, at the most inappropriate things.

So, anyway, your friends ask what you are doing with your life as you start on your first silky-smooth pint. You no longer snigger inappropriately every five minutes, as life in your twenties has toughened you up somewhat; now it would take some seriously strong weed to induce that kind of infantile reaction. Those hedonistic episodes of Amsterdam aside, the young adult you have grown into is, with any luck, a much more rounded and responsible citizen. You have watched *Newsnight*. You pretend to understand the intricacies of the

Middle East. You vote, you pay your bills on time, put your bins out once in a while and do all those things you never would have dreamt of doing when the world was a much simpler and happier place all those years ago.

I tell my friends I bike around town delivering the finest food the city has to offer. Some laugh, some ask questions, some wonder if I have lost my mind altogether, and some try to tell me you only ride a bike as a child, or as an emergency backup when your car has broken down or public transport ceases to function. But I'm an adult now, able to form my own opinions. I can argue the case, debate, confront; if I ever got the chance, I could even stand up in parliament and put forward the case, as I'm doing in this book, for why this constituent should not be denied their basic human right to be happy in their work.

4

The Good

'Cyclists see considerably more of this beautiful world than any other class of citizens.' Dr K.K. Doty

Doing what I do goes against many preconceived adult ideas of how to earn an honest living. Unless you play football, sell out concerts, push drugs, inherit a fortune or keep company with Warren Buffett, money never does come easy. Never has, never will and never should. What it can and does do is determine the conditions under which you live, your place in society, what you can afford to eat or drive, how long you may live for, and how you can best spend whatever free time you have remaining when you are not busy earning money.

By stepping off the unabating career treadmill onto a familiar feel-good pedal, I had somehow disturbed this delicate ecosystem of work, rest and play. I was looking to work and play within the same parameter of earning a living. *Was I crazy?* said the niggling voice in my head. Get back to the office and slog it out like the rest of us so you can appreciate your free time more, you enemy of the state, my subconscious howled to me while I slept.

When awake, I had endless internal disputes, tossed around the arguments for and against and, in the end, put them right back in the box they'd come from. I was committed, cooking on gas and stubbornly against even thinking of my previous existence. My friends understood I could make a living from this disruptive new technology platform, but some were very concerned about my inability to sink more than three pints now that I'd exponentially increased the number of hours I spent on the bike.

It couldn't be helped. This kind of moderation goes with being any kind of round-the-clock athlete. Of course, I knew I wasn't really an athlete, but this now became my excuse for avoiding any more than three pints or a few mixers before I needed to call it a day. Drinking copiously was never my strong suit at the best of times, but now my tolerance and reluctance to drink was becoming embarrassing.

In Newcastle, if you don't drink alcohol, chances are you are a religious zealot or a recovering alcoholic. What I mean is that a normal social life can be pretty hard to carve out and maintain if you don't participate in this very northern habit of seeing acquaintances for a few drinks (and then a few more) every so often.

It became clear that some friends were less than impressed by this pursuit of happiness and a healthier lifestyle. When I suggested alternative venues in which we could meet and catch up – coffee shops, gyms, places that prioritised food and non-alcoholic drinks – well, this was more than some could take. Instead of trying to understand the choices I was trying to make, perhaps meeting up with me in some of the places I suggested, they withdrew their comradeship quicker than the once-loyal Geordie depositors who had queued outside the branches of Northern Rock to get their money out when the bank went bust.

Also, as a lot of friends were taking on more responsibility in their careers and buying their first houses and settling down, it became much easier to be less distracted by what was going on in your social circle. This is a natural by-product of your thirties, as your hard-earned money goes into more sensible investments, rather than the footloose and fancy-free pastimes you enjoyed in your twenties. But while everyone around me was settling down, I was speeding up, going against the grain in ways that seemed completely incomprehensible to many.

I've always quite enjoyed being outside the natural comfort zone, the norm. A job for life made me feel claustrophobic and tied down. A job with no security and living week to week produced the opposite effect. Rather than counting down the days, you simply make the most of every single one. This job insecurity ignited a burning desire deep inside to do more, to learn more, cycle more, live more.

This short-term, insecure mentality made me think long-term of what I wanted most from life. The long-term, secure job and career had the opposite effect, making me think from week to week – my escapes, weekend breaks, the next night out and so on, always counting down the hours to my next days off. Of course, some of this will come with age anyways, but dropping out of the rat race profoundly changed my outlook from taking everything in life for granted to taking nothing at all for granted. Each and every week in my old career I had the same feelings of needing to reset my faux professionalism and enthusiasm in order to re-enter the workplace.

From this new reality of insecurity and uncertainty, I had found contentment and an inner peace I had never really experienced before. It's strange how we can adjust to these situations when flipping the script and accepting life on our own terms. My work and leisure time now merged effortlessly into one another, which allowed me to move away from my old habits of feeling the need to go out most weekends – to let off some steam and release the pressure – after another hard week of contracted labour had come to an end. Now I was releasing the pressure by going *to* work, a complete contrast to my previous existence.

So, not being able to drink as regularly and be as sociably up for it as I once would have been after a hard week at work, I found solace in increasing the hours that I spent at work on the bike. And of course, the time when most folk want to go out and have a drink after a hard week at work happens to coincide with the period when most other folk want a comforting takeaway meal to cheer them up after slogging it out all after the same kinds of hard week – like I once had. It meant working most weekends – Friday, Saturday and Sunday nights – the busiest times of the week for takeaway food delivery.

Weekend shifts were the ones I had normally loathed in my previous job, as they took away the time I spent with friends drinking myself to oblivion chasing bright lights and big-city life (or on other occasions spent mountain biking somewhere new and exciting). In a way that would have been inconceivable to me just a few short months before, I was now turning away from such drunken escapism. My sole focus now was attending classes, cycling and delivering enough meals to make an honest living.

* * *

Now I couldn't tell you a great deal from what I learned academically during my time as an undergraduate all those years ago, just before the financial crisis turned Cool Britannia into Poor Britannia. As the great cultural philosopher Jez from *Peep Show* once declared, 'Who cares about that shit? I didn't go to university to get a degree.' But I do remember in my undergraduate studies being vaguely interested by one very profound lecture topic, which related to psychology but was widely applicable to the real world of experience and personal fulfilment.

The psychologist's name is Csikszentmihalyi, pronounced Cheek-sent-me-high. It's not the easiest name to remember or to spell if you're not Hungarian (he's Hungarian-American), but give the man credit where credit is due. He established the field of positive psychology, but despite the vague interest I had shown at the time, I hadn't thought of him or his ideas in the decade since then.

Now I found that for some strange reason something I had studied over a decade earlier, when I was young and carefree, was finally starting to sink in, resonating deeply with what I was doing and feeling as I started working longer shifts over that first fresh, cold enchanted autumn and winter on my bike. I'm sure most people would have felt something similar at some point in their own lives.

Allow me to paint the picture. It's a chilly, sense-tingling winter night in the city – your breath almost leaving an invisible trail behind as you streak effortlessly past many familiar landmarks en route to your next destination. The

Christmas lights are glowing seemingly with the same excitement that emanates from frantic shoppers as they pass you by, dashing between the seasonally decorated buildings, creating a tangible feeling of energy surging through every one of these similarly engrossed human beings as they take in the scenes all around them. Young people out finding gifts for their first loves, old ones dashing to find the same Lynx Africa gift set that hasn't failed them for the previous twenty years. Parents out likewise, hunting for the season's must-have gifts for their children.

Every building is lavishly decorated to seduce you into being similarly lavish with your hard-earned money. Markets buzz with gatherings of people eager to consume the latest fashionable food item or sugar-laced drink, refreshing both body and the Instagram account they so carefully curate to show that they are keeping up with the Kardashians (who cares about the Joneses these days?). The energy is magnetic and palpable. The buzz is all around you, much like the phones flashing away, capturing millions of cherished moments.

Of course, you can only ever notice this energy if you stop and take it all in. But life moves fast, people don't stop, for we are all too consumed in our next conversation, selfie, Snapchat video, or the next stall along selling blocks of fudge for the same extortionate price as our next inevitable dentist's bill. You are part of that same flow of endless activity, at once a moving part but never stopping long enough to take it all in. A flash in the night, much like the flash from a photograph, only coming and going in a brief moment of time as you focus on your next subject, your next point of attraction, your next assignment, your next gig.

Think for a moment of the large office block where you

work. You know every nook, cranny, shop, one-way street and traffic light in the surrounding area. Now imagine that all your office furniture is outside, moving sporadically through the streets as the city fills with people looking for a place to eat, drink and be merry. No longer confined within four immovable walls answering emails from your colleagues about milk missing from the fridge or broken toilet seats or supplier problems, angry customers, angrier staff. You are now completely unshackled from that parallel world of office politics and crushing monotony. It feels good. You know what it was once like, and are conscious and cognizant of the life you traded in to experience such moments of joy as you often feel amid the tumult of the city.

I had been cycling all day, which had settled into one of those perfect early December evenings – cold and crisp with an underlying tranquillity, as if there really was a divine benediction just around the corner. There were people all around me as I navigated the streets I'd chosen as my own dedicated workspace. It was getting late.

The coursing energy acts like a subliminal support team, willing you on as you navigate the happy shoppers, the busy restaurants, the festive displays of hastily-erected wooden chalets and flashing lights – swarms of Santa hats industriously filing out into the city, buzzing with purpose to the next bustling, vibrantly glowing public house through the oncoming darkness.

Coffee shops were closing all around, with the smell of cinnamon and pretzels perfuming the air, while the tiny clinks of the glasses of workers and shoppers alike - quaffing between bouts of splashing all the cash they had - sounded like the festive tinkling of bells.

As the last of them finished their pricey cocktails and picked up their Christmas extravagances, I had the melodic sounds of ambient house music playing in my headphones, and a feeling I had never quite experienced so profoundly in all my adult life. I had stopped to take in the scenes playing out around me. At once I knew what it was I was feeling.

I was contented and alive with heightened perception, as the multiple sensations of the city resonated through my body and brain. It was like finally discovering the precise wavelength on that analogue radio you used to have – the one that took constant adjusting and readjusting to reach the optimum transmission frequency for what you were trying to listen to.

Back to Csikszentmihalyi. He introduced to me an idea which is beautiful in its simplicity, as the best ideas mostly are, a term from positive psychology which he called *flow*. It's an idea that describes those moments when we are completely absorbed in a challenging task. The best moments in life, Csikszentmihalyi says, occur not during passive, relaxing times but when a body or mind is stretched to its limits under voluntary guidance to accomplish something difficult or worthwhile.

It came to me, like a sign of the wisdom of my life-changing decision, as I was riding home after my first ten-hour shift on the bike, as the city I had left behind turned into a faint blur and only the peace and darkness of the empty snaking road lay ahead. It had been non-stop, with no breaks, but with a nice little kitty built up from a hard day's work to show for it all.

It wasn't like I had never experienced this feeling of flow before, on longer rides on the bike up around the Lakes, during high-intensity fitness classes, boxing, or after handing in a particularly hard assignment or a final dissertation. These were special occasions, however – points of relief in what was otherwise a life of tedium and toil. I was now experiencing these moments of flow on a daily basis. I was so entirely immersed in the challenge ahead of me that nothing else mattered in the world.

My senses were heightened, perceptions increased, as my levels of adrenaline surged. I kept telling myself this feeling could only be temporary, like most good things in life. Enjoy these rare moments as they don't last forever, I repeated over and over in my head. And I did, never taking them for granted. Like a lottery win in later life, it's better to have it late than never to have it at all. And in this case, it may have been better to have it now than at a younger age, when perhaps I wouldn't have fully appreciated the opportunity. I had the flow and I wasn't going to let it go.

I was now doing 60-mile days on a regular basis in the leadup to Christmas, and the world seemed completely at ease, as all other insignificant problems seemed trivial by comparison. Nothing else really mattered that much, as in the context of such a heavy workload every day, everything else seemed easy to solve. In a flow state there is no boredom, anxiety or depression, only the feeling of joy or even rapture in the activity you are doing. This carries nicely into other aspects of life, too.

I was looking forward to the little break from my first semester of uni, and the prospect of a Christmas dinner and unlimited chocolate would be appreciated this year more than any other. I had a week off from Deliveroo as I eagerly arrived at my parents' place to eat, drink, be merry and willingly gain a few pounds in the process.

My increased energy levels were a great counterbalance to the uni work. I could concentrate solely on the essays I needed to write and the large volumes of academic reading I needed to get through. I had happily received my huge dose of cycling throughout the autumn and early winter season. Come a cold, crisp Christmas Day morning in the previous few years, I had always been excited at the prospect of cycling the 25-mile coastal route to my parents' house in Northumberland, to help set me up for a decadent few days of festive overindulgence. But I had given myself the day off this year - on account of the amount of cycling I'd been doing in my new life as a courier.

My body was starting to send strong signals that a few too many drinks were becoming harder and harder to stomach, and I found myself moving towards the biscuit tin more often than the drinks cabinet. As it had been my first full week off from cycling and the uni boxing club in three months, I prioritised recovery over decadence, and let my body repair itself from the regime of intense activity I had recently put it through.

Then, after the festivities were over, I received an email from Deliveroo just as I had started writing one of my essays at my parents' house, saying how New Year's Day is one of the busiest days of the year, and that was enough for me to prioritise a few extra days on the bike rather than on the lash. I developed a rather efficient reward-based system for days spent reading and writing essays over the festive period, much like my first term at uni. Most of the day I would work on my assignments, then as a reward I would go out in the evenings and do three or four hours as a courier.

The mental benefits from doing this were simply incredible.

I was able to concentrate for long spells without distraction, information was more easily absorbed, and in terms of writing creatively cycling was proving to be a huge help not a hindrance – I had fully expected the opposite when first starting the job. The activation of the endocannabinoid system in the brain is largely to thank for this. Even as I have done re-edit after re-edit of this book, cycling has provided me with the necessary creative-thinking and novel problem-solving skills to defragment ideas, thoughts and segments of the book, and helps provide fresh ideas and a different perspective, though only when I'm not overdoing it.

It's almost like the brain pieces together fragments of information and is able to more efficiently join them all together. Which of course is precisely what it is doing behind the scenes. The cocktail of neurotransmitters and happy drugs in our brains gives us a boost of euphoria and, crucially, makes us feel more relaxed, more focused. Creativity peaks when flooded with these feelings of flow.[29] No wonder I never wanted these feelings to subside.

Considering I had only been back in higher education a few months, I was delighted when my winter uni results came back, scoring low to mid 60s in most assignments. Once again, I allowed myself a few long shifts cycling as a reward, and settled back into a busy schedule of study, sleep and work, respectively. I had enjoyed the many challenges that winter had thrown my way, upending my work–life balance for the better. There had been some cold and wet evenings out on the bike, but they were nearly always an enjoyable counterbalance after long days debating in class, as well as reading and writing.

I felt physically and mentally more attuned than I ever had, and this new lease of life meant I could focus all my energy on doing well in class and pushing harder and getting faster on the bike at the same time. The two activities were entirely complementary, both mentally and physically, pushing me to become a more wholesome human being, more interested in what I could achieve in this regard than any by external distractions or temptations.

Winter was slowly turning into spring, and the long dark evenings spent dressed head to toe in waterproofed warm clothing would soon translate into fewer layers and lighter nights, along with a healthy dose of sunlight and Vitamin D for good measure. Deliveroo turned five years old, with 15,000 riders now working up and down the country. Before spring had sprung, however, a rather extreme storm that brought the country to its knees catapulted me out onto my bike.

The Beast from the East, the Arctic weather front that stretched from Siberia to Western Europe in late February and early March 2018 came with the dreaded Met Office red weather warning, meaning a potential risk to life. As I sat in the library - after picking up a few books before heading home, watching the first lashings of snow descend upon the city - somewhat excitedly I saw this as a chance to *really* challenge myself, rather than the very real source of danger that perhaps it was.

But a bout of bitterly cold weather wasn't going to stop me from earning a living. OK, so I had to slide into work, much like a footballer sliding into a Love Island finalist's DMs. But the extra financial incentive to work was good, the distances from pickup to delivery were very short, and if you weren't put on this Earth to challenge yourself once in a while then why even bother being part of it all anyway?

Rather than being sat at home studying, all cosy and

comfortably wrapped up with a cup of coffee beside me, looking out intermittently from the bedroom window onto an icy landscape with an overwhelming sense of wanderlust, I could be out there in the Arctic tundra, trying my very best to break my first-ever bone in a stiff and tensed body (luckily, I was unable to, despite my best efforts).

I managed three full days in those Arctic conditions, a completely nebulous memory, and even now I couldn't tell you how it felt or how I got through them. Good old-fashioned, character-building days, let's call them. Not something that can be transferred onto the closing statement of a CV, covering letter or LinkedIn profile, but you can self-efficaciously stick them into your idiosyncratic bank of life – and pocket the experience with compound interest – as another tale to bore the grandkids with one day.

There was only one other rider I saw working as consistently as me in the Arctic blast the Beast from the East brought with it. As senseless as I was perhaps, he was always out in the worst of conditions, and usually always smiling too. We still talk about those days whenever we cross paths now. The thick, battle-hardening Russian winter snow. Long unrelenting late nights and no one else around for miles. He worked his arse off that first year, taking on as many hours as he could possibly stay awake for.

I never got to know his name until a few years later, but you never really have to with other riders you meet while out navigating the city. A mutual respect is usually enough to get you through the days, as you are only brought together in brief momentary encounters when waiting for orders in restaurants or pulling up alongside each other at traffic lights – with just enough time to swap war stories and mishaps you've suffered along the way. I simply referred to him as the Guroo (see what I did there?).

His real name is Abdul, and there are only a handful of riders in the country who have completed more deliveries than he has. He rarely has a day off and knows the city and the job better than most others. There is probably at least one Guroo in every city, someone who everyone seems to know and admire in equal measure. A few YouTube clips show riders down in London who have done 24-hour-plus shifts continuously during busy periods (albeit on a scooter). While I certainly wouldn't recommend this extreme form of couriering in the slightest (it poses a real danger to yourself and others), it goes to show that you probably need a few loose wires to be even considered for such a hallowed title.

Then again, after that first winter spent working day and night on a bicycle, Abdul eventually upgraded to a motorbike himself, as soon as he had saved enough money to do so, so maybe he was the sane one after all. He's never gone back to riding a bicycle in all the time since, preferring the motorised speed of a scooter or even the warmth and safety of a car to complete his deliveries. I can hardly blame him. He must find it hard to comprehend why I have not done the same in the past few years, all else considered. But I argue my case each and every time I bump into him!

After the Beast from the East had subsided, the lighter and brighter days finally started to appear once again, after what seemed an eternity of dark, damp, dull days. Checking your app in case extra shifts had appeared was now as ingrained in the psyche as checking Twitter or Facebook, as the job became an intrinsic part of who you are and how you function. Straight after lectures, classes, boxing sessions, during the night when you woke up, even during sex, too – only joking; as if I had any time at all for that kind of thing!

Dressing appropriately had been a constant challenge of two extremes during the first winter. A cyclist's clothing offers flimsy protection in sub-zero temperatures - but bear in mind that when pedalling as fast as you can between destinations, you feel like you're going to burst into flames - so exactly how much and what cycling paraphernalia you should wear to accommodate those extremities of heat and cold is always a delicate balancing act.

One minute you'll be standing waiting for fresh pizzas to come out the red-hot wood-fired oven inside a fancy Italian restaurant, then ten minutes later you'll be outside a big block of student accommodation doing mini star jumps to stave off the cold. It's something of a game that you can never truly win, but you do learn to fine-tune your apparel over time by prioritising areas where heat is lost the quickest: keeping your head, feet and hands warm will go some way to conquering the chill of a long drawn-out winter.

The Beast from the East was a late blast of real winter, but when it had gone, spring began in earnest. The snow from the Beast gradually melted. Longer days and longer shifts were now the reward from the past six months of toil in near round-the-clock darkness and study with artificial lighting in my bedroom/bike room. I was leaner, faster, smarter and sharper from it all, and wholeheartedly ready to increase my weekly dose of prescribed cycling to coincide with the longer, brighter days that lay ahead.

I had found the sweet spot in my work–life balance, managing to cycle around 25 hours a week most weeks. My sleep quality was better as a result, I was sleeping slightly longer, and also having the occasional nap during more intense bouts of reading and uni work. This equilibrium had helped me to concentrate better, de-stress from classes and process information much more effectively than if I had not had cycling as my main outlet.

Besides which, there was a whole new world of work-related perks that were opening up, though I didn't know about them yet. Like most things in life, you adapt to your new surroundings, hopefully making the most of every chance that comes your way. Getting to know every restaurant in your neighbourhood can be seen as both a blessing and a curse, depending on your appetite and your ability to converse with the staff.

I was being let in behind the beaded curtain, so to speak. Like most people, I love my food. When you cycle all the time and need supplementary calories to sustain you, at times you develop a powerful and ravenous hunger that grows stronger by the day, and the pasta and cheese you have in the cupboard and fridge can only be combined in so many ways before becoming bland and boring.

Be a good person, I was always told, and you will be rewarded. So you become friendly with the chefs and the waiting staff in the places you start picking up from on a regular basis. In a world where you can be anything, be nice, and they will usually be nice back. Ask them how they are, and they will ask you the same. Sometimes you are good, sometimes tired. Sometimes you are in a rush to make your next job, sometimes it is fairly quiet and you have time to drool over whatever culinary delight is being made which, with a heavy heart, you then have to give away to the paying customer.

But you try your luck sometimes; shy bairns get nowt, as they say. When they ask you how you are, let them know you are hungry. Well, it's more than likely you always are. You've been cycling all day or all night, and the labour is relentless, insatiable. You have your emergency jelly beans, dark chocolate or snack bar to help keep the coals alight, but they only last for so long. What you really crave is hot, hearty, greasy, artery-clogging, smile-inducing food. You can pick up the occasional bit of free food that the restaurant has no use for.

It's not often enough, but it may be an irregular, or slightly burned pizza that can't be sold; fresh but wonky bread; any uncollected order from a few hours ago; or food otherwise going to waste at the end of the night that might as well go in your mouth as in the bin. And when it does come your way, it's a metaphorical pat on the back, your just reward for sticking in there, never giving up hope that after all those draining hours on the bike, there would be free food to enjoy at the end of it.

As you gradually increase the number of consecutive hours, the length of shift you are physically capable of doing, you rely less on the big meals that sustained you at the beginning of your cycling career before heading out to work all day or all night; less, too, on the snacks you usually had stuffed into your backpack or the sugary drinks you once needed to stave off the worst of your problems if out on the road and your energy drops below the levels you need to keep you moving forward.

This is the dreaded cyclist's bonk, a physical phenomenon where the rider experiences a sudden drop in energy levels when they haven't taken in enough carbohydrates to fuel the body. As a result, glycogen stores in the liver and muscles become depleted, leading to fatigue due to abnormally low levels of glucose in the blood. Luckily, I've only ever suffered from this a few times during all my time as a cycle courier. Mostly, I can hold it together, with regularly released carbs of any kind refuelling and replenishing the legs sufficiently to keep me moving well enough in the saddle most days.

Regular water is also needed to replenish the fluid you lose in perspiration from your body. Some of the places you pick up orders up from will be kind enough to the riders to ply you with enough coffee, so you can make your next delivery without falling asleep at the handlebars. You should never fail to make the most of these places if you are in need of a caffeine pick-me-up to see you through the rest of the evening.

Caffeine highs aside, another marvellous perk of cycling for a living is that you become a leaner, happier, healthier version of yourself. Never is this more obvious than when you finally start speaking to those other riders, after spending most of the first few months on the job flying past them in between orders. There's no doubt they're enjoying themselves as much as you are: they often smile as you go past them, and you smile back conspiratorially, acknowledging the common feeling that exists among many riders of contentment, elation and freedom.

All other 'riders' – be they on a scooter, motorcycle, car or even chopper (limited service) – have much sterner faces, expressions and demeanours that are immediately recognisable in any restaurant you pick up from. It could be the extra burden of having to pay insurance, petrol and road tax, or for shelling out for fancy leather leggings and jackets.

I've never quite been able to put my finger on it, but the

cyclist is generally a much happier breed of courier than those in what we could call the motorised wing of the sector. It could be down to the lack of physical exertion that floods the cyclist's brain with endorphins, maybe? Of course, they have the added luxury of comfortable seats, engines, water-repellent kit, roofs over their heads, and anything else that helps protect them from the elements.

However, you can trump all that and more by simply being able to ride your bicycle. Sure, there's a bit of maintenance to make sure it runs smoothly, and the odd puncture to add a degree of occasional stress and agony to your daily schedule. But generally it's plain sailing. Look after it, service it, tuck it in at night and keep it away from the very worst elements and it'll be good to you, too. It'll help you pay your bills, help you de-stress, help keep you fit and also burn off most of the calories you consume as quickly as you can shovel them into your super-efficient, fat-blasting engine room.

I started to tweak my tried-and-tested sweet spot of hours at work as the nights became much lighter, students came back from their Easter breaks, and I had finished my next lot of assignments and essays, which once again had gone remarkably well. I had started doing the lunchtime deliveries some days, going back home to study or start work on my dissertation thesis, then back into town in the evenings to blow off some steam. Weekend evenings were spent doing the same, but I had started to notice I was incapable of reading or writing for any longer than a few hours at a time without needing hour-long power naps.

With my desk being a few short feet away from my bed, and choosing to work from home due to added luxuries like the coffee machine and mini desk fan, this was starting to capsize my overall balance of study,sleep and work. Sleep had increased, work had increased, study had slightly dropped, and my social life was by now non-existent. I classed my social life as being out as a cycle courier, able to converse with a few fellow students in the same boat as me, going through the same experiences – with each one seemingly delighted at being able to use this newly-established line of work as a means of escaping the humdrum brain drain of long bouts of academic study.

As Deliveroo continued to grow, so did the zones it encompassed and the distance you could travel to complete deliveries. What had started as city-centre delivery covering a 2.2km radius, quickly branched out to inner city, suburbia and beyond. To encourage riders to carry out deliveries over longer distances, Deliveroo changed its business model to distance-based fees. From the original hourly rates, they had already changed to the paid-per-delivery fees a few years earlier; now that £4.25-per-delivery contract changed to a new distance-based fee system, based now on overall distance travelled.

Deliveroo stated these were 'fairer, distance-based fees: paying you more for longer distances', a calculation based on the entire journey from 'accepting the order and travelling to the restaurant and delivering to the customer'. They stated in the rider newsletter, 'We believe you should make as much, if not more, from this new, fairer fee structure. If you don't, we'll pay you the difference in July and August.'[30] Minimum fees were now £3.90 (in Newcastle), 35p lower than each delivery I had carried out before the changes, or an 8.24 percent decrease.

Cyclists would now have to travel further to make the same

amount of money as before. Many riders could envisage the sweeping changes would be permanent, and that this was only the beginning of greater distances they would need to travel and lower overall fees to come. Their gut feelings would prove to be right.

As the delivery distances increased, I was also beginning to feel the effects of overdoing it on the bike, along with the overall increase in hours I had been working of late. Warmer weather brings with it a different set of challenges for the courier. Staying properly hydrated and suitably cool is the name of the game during the summer months. Again, it can be easy to dismiss such formalities when work is busy and the wind against you feels sufficiently breezy to keep you cool and your body temperature as close to a homeostatic 37 degrees as possible.

But you still need to drink little and often to stay properly hydrated, to help replace lost fluids and salts. I had a few days during that first summer where I dismissed such formalities, where I was just about able to fight through the pain barrier and dismiss the heat as par for the course. I always arrived home exhausted, visually thinner, having shed a few kilos, and much more defined, even gaunt, than before, with headaches and terrible cravings for sugary substitutes for the next 24 hours or so.

I somehow let myself believe this was good for my appearance (probably to rationalise the extreme decisions I was making when working in such conditions), but I would always end up like a basking shark the next day, drinking litre after litre of water to properly hydrate myself once again. If you disregard the need for water, you are merely delaying the inevitable after effects and the familiar crash feelings.

Dehydration is the main reason for the majority of problems faced by riders in the peak of summer. The core body temperature rises to around the 39 degree mark when you're cycling in the heat, and this can lead to heat exhaustion or, worse still, heat stroke if it creeps over the 40 degree mark. Your blood thickens, so the heart has to work harder; your ability to process glucose and turn it into energy drops as energy production requires water; the blood and oxygen supplied to your legs fall as blood is being redirected to the surface, your skin, to cool the body (the process of sweating helps to maintain this temperature sweet spot).

While in the winter you have a natural heating mechanism – your exercising metabolism – in the summer it is much harder for your body to cool down than it is to warm up.[31] There are a few things you can do to help, however. Wearing light clothing, covering your head with a helmet, cap or hat, wearing sunglasses and covering yourself in factor 50 (regardless of skin type!) will all help on the longer days you spend working in the heat.

Avoiding working at the hottest peak times of summer days – mainly lunchtime and early afternoons – is a good idea for the full-time cycle courier. The motorised fleet pick up much of this work, as do some students and those doing shorter days. Early mornings and late nights are better for your overall health, and help you avoid the worst of the damage the heat can inflict upon you unknowingly day after day.

Just like a nice cup of tea and a warm shower in the winter can help restore some of your lost body heat and help you feel more human, you can find similar respite and solace from the opposites in the warm summer months. I started freezing bottles of water in the summer months to help my body cool down during and after long days in the saddle. I would take a few frozen bottles into work in my backpack – allowing them time to thaw and become drinkable during the day.

All of my water supplies were kept in the freezer rather than the fridge (much to the annoyance of all the housemates I have ever lived with), making it easier to cool down when my body felt like it was burning up. Random bottles were scattered sporadically throughout the house and kitchen, acting like mini fire extinguishers in the extremes of heat experienced throughout June and July when I would pop back for quick five-minute breaks between deliveries.

On many of these days, you can drink fluids all day long, and barely feel the urge for a pee, though you will certainly sweat, with liquids acting to rehydrate you and replace lost water as your body tries to cool itself. This is in stark contrast with the colder months, when your body feels like it's holding onto water, or you simply block out the urge to pee when you are too busy to be listening to your body (when really you should).

Around this time, I had started experimenting with cold showers - initially as a way to cool down after long hot days when sticky, salty deposits you have sweated out seep not only into your clothing but also every conceivable pore in the body, too. Warm showers had started to leave my skin feeling very dehydrated, making it very uncomfortable to sleep at night due to the raised core temperature that comes from cycling all day, then blasting myself with a long warm shower at the end of it all.

There is substantial research to back up the traditional wisdom that cold showers and ice baths after cycling are very beneficial as part of any post-ride recovery. While it may seem ludicrous and fairly extreme to consider doing this, shocking the body in such a way cools you down rapidly and evenly. This cooling effect directs blood flow rapidly to your vital organs and allows the muscles space to release any build-up of lactic acid and repair themselves. The cold water forces the blood vessels to narrow, known as vasoconstriction, and the damaged tissue becomes cold. This can help mitigate swelling and bruising from the build-ups of fluid and waste that are your natural output from a hard day on the bike.

Hot showers are great for stimulating the blood flow to muscles and skin (vasodilation), dispersing lactic acid and helping alleviate muscle aches – heat is also a natural pain reliever. But it is the cold-water effects that will actually speed up the healing process and help you to recover faster.[32] In the past few years, I have found alternating between hot and cold temperatures is also massively beneficial to recovery and well-being.

Starting with hot water, which opens the blood vessels and allows the blood to rush out and be pumped through to the muscles and organs, then switching to cold water, which constricts the blood vessels and allows all the blood to be redirected to the middle of the body. This triggers the circulatory system, causing blood in your deeper tissues to circulate faster to maintain core temperature, helping to reduce inflammation.[33]

I'm yet to experiment with ice baths as part of my recovery process – bath tubs in shared housing can be a grim experience – but if they are used habitually by athletes of all sports in their recovery programs, I'm sure they would be every bit as effective (if not more so) as cold showers for cycle couriers.

Before the worst effects of the summer heat and increased

hours cycling had struck, I had largely been able to study with a clear head, to fully concentrate while reading and then make it into class and be semi-articulate with no major issues. Now, as the crucial last few months approached, I was overcompensating with sleep and struggling with anything approaching a good outline of my dissertation thesis, on a topic which I had previously looked forward to, having chosen it even before I got accepted into uni. This was massively frustrating, but I knew it was simply a case of laying off the bike for a good few weeks to help clear my head and let my body recover a bit.

It can be very difficult to let go of something you enjoy so much, especially as your brain is drip-feeding you so many of the happy drugs while doing it. It wasn't like I really needed the extra money at the time, as I had built up a few quid over the winter and hardly went out socially anymore, bar the odd pint or wedding that had been pencilled in from six months beforehand. I just really, really enjoyed riding my bike and being out in the city as the seasons changed, while making the most of my time doing this dream job while I still had the chance to do so.

I had three weeks off from the bike, which allowed me to start feeling more human, or more refreshed, again. It was the first prolonged period I had taken off since I had started the job, and when I look back now I can see how much I needed a break. It also coincided with the time when most students leave the city en masse over the summer. My master's thesis was due to be handed in at the end of August, so I had a few months to get my house in order, so to speak. The time off in June helped me to recharge the batteries and gave me the ability to start chipping away at the final project of the academic year.

I eventually reverted back to the tried and tested approach of evening work, as well as the odd weekend shift when I was particularly sick of reading and writing and had run out of creative steam for the day. Much as it has been during the process of writing this book, this approach worked very well for me, but reading and writing is very difficult to do with any kind of consistency or enthusiasm when trying to cycle more than twenty or thirty hours each and every week. It's difficult to do most things with any kind of enthusiasm when going over this threshold, I found, and as you further increase the hours spent cycling, this only becomes worse still.

So I finally started to properly prioritise my dissertation thesis, and my sleep gradually came back down to a much more acceptable level, around 8 hours rather than the 10 I had been having of late. Cycling was used as an outlet rather than the full-time job which I had subconsciously allowed it to become over the previous few months. The dissertation took shape, I watched England play in the World Cup (with even less enthusiasm than usual), my rewards being the free meals not picked up by customers when working, along with intermittent weapons-grade-strength espressos at my desk to give me the energy to bash away at the keyboard with some of the enthusiasm I hadn't used up during the England football team's performances that summer in 2018.

Caffeine and cycling addictions aside, the academic year had gone remarkably well for someone who had re-entered higher education after a decade in the leisure industry. All of my grades had consistently been in the 60s, and I was able to leave uni with a 2.1 classification overall. I just missed out on a first-class mark on my dissertation thesis, but I didn't blame cycling for that – quite the opposite. It had helped raise my ability to perform beyond what I had ever thought was possible just a year earlier. It's impossible to sum up just how much cycling had transformed my life over that year. I'd put 20,000 miles on the body clock, but felt ten years younger - and a few years wiser, too.

* * *

It is hard to overstate the overall physical and mental health benefits from cycling, so what follows are just the basic facts. Cycling greatly enhances your cardiovascular health, builds stronger lungs and legs, cuts heart disease and cancer risk; it's also a low-impact workout compared with the constant aches and pains of running. It strengthens your immune system, makes you sleep better (and sometimes much longer than necessary!), boosts brain power, helps fight depression, decreases your stress levels and increases your overall energy levels (when done in moderation, of course). There's also the increased libido – think Duracell bunny once you've built up a habit of cycling most days.

Basically, in terms of overall health, you'll soon become a 2.0 upgraded version of yourself, minus some of that stubborn fat and some of the other nasty excesses you've built up from years of overindulgence or neglect. This will lead to greater overall endurance, you will be able to enjoy your food more (all in moderation of course), and it can help grow your social circle through meeting other riders, joining cycling clubs and heading out on trips to ride with and meet fellow enthusiasts.

Cycling to extremes can have the opposite effect on your social life, as you'll discover later on in the book.

Most folk you meet while out mountain biking and road cycling are friendly, helpful, receptive individuals. Some are out doing fast laps and focused on racing, but most are simply enjoying their precious free time, and especially the social element to cycling. If you're thinking of taking it up, engaging with cyclists when out and about is one of the best things about cycling.

Cycling has even been dubbed the 'miracle pill', with near miraculous health dividends that could help save the NHS.[34] It could help save the planet in my humble opinion, if only we think more long term about our own health and that of the environment we inhabit. As the saying goes, prevention is better than cure. Better infrastructure is of course the key. Build it and they will come. Things are starting to finally take shape, thanks in no small part to the Covid-19 pandemic, but we need bold plans and they need to be executed *now* to encourage more folk onto their carbon-neutral, two-wheeled companions.

There is also what health experts call a pandemic of preventable illness connected to physical inactivity. Both physical activity and physical infrastructure need to be prioritised in equal measure in order to build back a better, happier, healthier, more wholesome society. This natural elixir for your brain, and also your body, is certainly the cheapest and most accessible miracle pill on the planet. Cycling regularly leads to a longer life. I'll go out on a limb and say that it leads a much happier life too. Maybe I am biased. Go out on your bike and see how it makes you feel.

In the years I spent sitting on that ancient, straight-backed office chair when I was managing the leisure centre, cycling was nearly always my tonic after a long day of stretching out intermittently to release some of the tension built up in the back and neck from a few hours sat hunched over, responding to the flurry of emails that clog up the inbox throughout the day. I rejoiced that that was all firmly behind me, and all that lay ahead was the open road between me and the next pick-up, the next delivery, the next adventure.

They were good days, those early days, when I was high on the thrill of something new and different, an escape from the monotony of a different life, a different era. University had finished, and I was about to embark on a new path, a new career – a new life perhaps. But nothing lasts forever. There must be a catch, I hear you all scream.

You learn that from a young age. The countless summer holidays spent chasing dreams – at the beach, in the pool, on the playing fields, in your back garden doing Punch and Judy for the neighbours. Behind the garden shed for your first-ever kiss. Running away and laughing uncontrollably, clinging to the football that you've just retrieved from *that* neighbour's garden, moments before he emerges, knife in hand, looking to deflate your footballing dreams for the rest of the holidays.

But without wanting to turn the rest of the book into a Morrissey album, or worse still his autobiography, there are certain truths discovered in adulthood which hold true in this case, too: that nothing is ever quite what it seems, that nothing good lasts forever and what goes up must indeed come down.

Yep, you've been taken on a gentle ride to the very top of the rollercoaster, and we are slowly rolling over that last brief crest of track before the big drop, the big reveal.

5

The Interlude

'Life is what happens to you while you're busy making other plans.' John Lennon

After the initial euphoria of finishing my degree had subsided, and I had picked up a rather expensive bit of paper, my certificate, confirming successful attainment of a master's qualification, it was time to head for pastures new. To prove that packing it all in and going back to study was the wisest of choices I had made on my journey through adulthood. I would head to a new place, for a new start, rather than try to hang on to fond memories of the past year, which I had spent riding my bike and getting a little more wise about the world in the process.

The only problem was that I was going to have to start the process of finding a job all over again. This brought the obvious difficulty of having to reimagine your whole professional life in a way that would appeal to prospective employers. An altogether more exacting task than when, as a naïve teenager looking to make his way in the world, I had handed in a CV to the sports shop that most suited my wardrobe choices – keen for the staff discount I'd be entitled to on the latest sportswear and trainers to hit the shelves.

Gone were the days of walking into shops and stores, handing in poorly constructed, light-on-experience and dubious-looking CVs and covering letters. The whole world had gone digital in the 15 years since then as everything had moved online. I would have to do the same.

I would have to update my whole corporate image if I was to slip seamlessly back into the world of full-time hours and the benefits that accrue from pledging sole allegiance to a single employer. The same employer who wants you to be a poster boy for them until your best days have gone up in smoke, keeping you in lockstep with the rest of society, that artificial construct we are told is the only thing holding anarchy at bay. So I followed my contemporaries onto the brave new world of LinkedIn, the social network of jobs. Good jobs. Jobs that I now wished to be considered for.

I created a profile, a shop window for why employers would be crazy not to have me in their workplace. It was time to sell myself to the world. Something I hoped that I would never have to do again, to be honest. The alternative, clearly preferable for most of us, would be for a family friend to slide you into a comfortable sixty-grand job for life. Yeah, right.

I wasn't from the Hamptons, and nobody I've heard of makes that kind of money as a graduate these days anyways. So there's an enthusiastic yet vastly oversupplied pool of graduates or even postgraduates like myself fighting over an ever-decreasing pool of suitable jobs. As higher education has opened up, there are huge disparities between the kinds of work new graduates manage to find compared to the nature of the degree subject that they have studied. The latest figures published by the Office for Students (OfS) show profound differences in outcomes depending on where students study and their subject between certain high-ranking Russell Group universities and those offering an array of low quality subjects.

Less than half of undergraduate degree holders with Sociology, Social Policy and Anthropology degrees go on to either a professional occupation or further study 15 months after graduation, followed closely by Psychology, Creative Arts and History - highlighting massive disparities between university courses and the jobs to match them. Some universities such as the University of Bedfordshire had just a third of graduates in relevant occupations after graduating, according to the OfS.

While 85 percent of Oxford's Philosophy and Religious Studies graduates met the job threshold after leaving, just 59 percent of students taking similar courses at the University of Southampton did so.[35] This pattern seems likely to be repeated not only across the country, but all over the world, as more students gain access to higher education, and supply in the job market continues to lag behind demand from recent graduates.

While it is admirable that any society should allow people the chance to study what they want, or something they may even want to make a career of one day, there is little sense or social good that comes from charging (taxing even) students a small fortune to better their chances in life when they graduate if they could just as easily have attained the same non-professional job they could no doubt end up in after graduating without the huge expense of an underutilised and unrelatable university degree.

This educational arms race will no doubt likely still prove beneficial for those who graduate from a top university with a relevant degree, with many others left to enter the job market with misaligned job prospects. You are setting young people up for a huge reality check when they emerge from years of hard work only to end up getting a job in a restaurant, call centre or supermarket. Not that these jobs aren't vital and necessary to any society; it's just that the setting up of the expectation in so many youngsters of career advancement and fulfilment as the rewards of the hard academic slog of a degree or higher degree is a recipe for mass disappointment in many who may never get close to those ideals.

It's a brave new world out there, but in most places outside of London and the other major cities, the only kinds of jobs you'll find are the same as existed in previous generations, aside from the new opportunities created in the service sector, which now makes up the majority of the UK economy. Graduate schemes, internships and pools of tech jobs are few and far between in places like Newcastle, and even less so in towns and rural communities left behind by successive governments, both red and blue.

I would be lucky to start on a salary I could live on, and I simply couldn't afford to go down the route that opens up to graduates whose parents have deep pockets: having to prostitute myself for a whole year as an unpaid intern for some global giant that could easily afford to pay me a salary, to prove that I have what it takes to be worthy of a paid position at a later date. Besides which, I had turned my hobby and passion into a viable source of income – allowing me to switch from being an unwilling institutionalised employee into a born-again free agent.

124

Instinctively, this is perhaps what I had craved most from leaving behind my old career – the freedom to choose when I wanted to work, according to a schedule that suited me. Playing it safe can and does lead to becoming institutionalised and complacent about the future, whereas the risks involved in being out on your own make you question yourself and hold yourself accountable far more often, forcing you to think about how best to use your time, skills and abilities.

I was heading for something of an epiphany. There was a multitude of paths that could take me anywhere or nowhere. Paths that could open the world for me or take me straight back to the start, to the same job I had been doing, while I searched for the right opportunity in the meantime. But those days were behind me, and if I've inherited one genetic trait from my father other than an early propensity for grey hair, it would be a quality of outright stubbornness. No going back, only forward.

The blissful summer of endless cycling, humid pressure-cooker libraries and England coming so close in the 2018 World Cup was now firmly behind me. With the daunting prospect of having to carve out a whole new existence, shit was getting real, so to speak. There was dread, excitement, apprehension, and a feeling of sheer elation from having actually finished it all. There was also a deep-seated feeling of emptiness from having enjoyed the previous twelve months so much that it had all passed by far too quickly for me to even consider what I wanted to do next.

The overwhelming emotion I was wrestling with after handing in my final dissertation was like being stuck a crossroads. One being a path of uncertainty and a life much like before, the other a sense of adventure and spontaneity much like the previous ten months had been, and one that I was nowhere near ready to leave behind. Academically, yes, I was happy to tap out and never read a cited journal again for as long as I drew breath.

However, the endless cycling, the unfettered freedom, the newfound sense of liberation, the free food and coffee, being your own boss, and the constant alluring buzz and dynamism of the city were going to be massive things to give up in turning my focus toward the new career that was supposedly the point of all that studying.

Not that cycling around town for a living was always living the dream. In fact, as we all know, when things are finally looking up, life has a funny way of bringing you back down to earth with a bump. It's what we mean when we talk about 'real' life. My old man's favourite motto was that "it's nice to be nice, but business is business." He happily retired from business many years ago and hasn't spoken of it since.

Businesses need to change, to adapt, to survive, to thrive and most importantly of all to try to make money in this brave new world of tech disruptors backed by venture capital, each of them seeking to emulate the success and scale of what are now household names throughout the world to become the next Amazon, Facebook, Google or Uber. These tech giants have successfully followed in their bid to eliminate the competition and achieve market domination, even monopoly – aided and abetted by some very patient venture capitalists.

The stakes are high, as are the rewards. With the right backing, growth can be prioritised over underlying profit – that is still the case with Deliveroo, for example – in the pursuit of ever-greater market share and customer retention, changing the habits of consumers and dislodging existing industries in the process. And customer convenience is what is paramount to these newly dominating tech companies. Shaking the very foundations of long-established business models and employment laws in each and every country where they have set up shop in (if not always registered to pay tax). Acting like political lobbyists, these companies have communications teams full of special advisers that would rival any corporation on the planet.

Customer convenience is being built off the back of inconvenience for riders, as pay has slowly deteriorated over time. Making companies like Deliveroo profitable will come at the expense of those preparing and delivering the food, not those ordering it. In that regard, as a publicly listed company, its responsibilities are now less to its riders and much more to its shareholders. These include Amazon, which in 2020 took a 16 percent stake in the company, and Will Shu, Deliveroo's CEO, has acknowledged Amazon as the "most consumer-obsessed company in the world."[36] With these investors looking for better returns on what they put into the company and extracting value in the process, cutting costs and increasing wages are not a likely route to profitability for a newly listed public company, if the model pursued by the established tech giants is anything to go by.

Even Uber, founded in 2009 as a ride-hailing company in 70 countries and now also in the food delivery game in 34 countries, continues to lose money, while promising investors in their latest prospectus to be profitable by the end of 2021. And even mighty Amazon failed to generate a profit for its first 14 years, instead focusing on growth at the expense of profit. Now that it certainly does turn a profit, other companies such as Deliveroo (in which Amazon still has an 11.5 percent stake) look to it as a reliable, replicable business model to justify long-term growth ahead of short-term profits.

Yes, I was riding my bike and making a living from it. But if it really was that good, wouldn't everybody else just pack their jobs in, dust off the bikes lying dormant in the garage, give the boss the longed-for V sign on the way out of the office and become a much happier, healthier version of themselves in the process? The money was fairly good in the beginning, relative to other kinds of short-term or zero-hours-type work, but Deliveroo continued to grow at a rapid pace, and was always looking to change the way it operated in order to sidestep any legal obligations it should have had to its 'riders', who it treated much like employees but audaciously classified as self-employed contractors for the purposes of employment law.

In fact, this kind of casualised arrangement has grown up so quickly, and is now such a significant aspect of economic activity in many countries, that governments have struggled to keep up with the pace of change. For a born-again student trying to make his way through twelve months of education, however, it enabled me to pay my bills and afford the daily trips to Tesco Express to fill my basket full of pasta, cheese, dark chocolate and nuts. It was still less money than I had earned in my previous career, however, with none of the benefits accrued from working my way up the hierarchy and into a job for life, if there even is such a thing these days.

There was no pension provision, no sick pay, no holiday entitlement, no clocking off on a Friday half an hour early, and certainly no prospect of being able to afford to buy a home ever again on the money I was earning from being a cycle courier. I was now truly pay-as-you-go, earn-while-you-try-to-learn. I just had to make sure not to get sick, to keep my bike working at all times, prevent hangovers at all costs, live like a Shaolin monk and put the right fuel into my body every single day. No pressure then.

Most importantly of all, I had to adapt to the environment around me. By which I mean the weather. The dreary and unpredictable British weather that descends upon us all – though in the North we definitely get more of it – is what tells you on any given day whether you are going to be really busy, really bored or really wishing you had gone to the pub rather than sitting on a rickety old park bench, scrolling through videos of friends boomeranging their drinks together like they were living in the last days of Rome.

This most British of obsessions is famously the starting point of many conversations in this country - whether out of politeness, social custom or a sheer lack of imagination. And don't get me wrong, I try my utmost to uphold this most British of traditions. After all, how would I be able to bond so easily with my gran over a pub lunch if I couldn't call on extensive knowledge of how indifferent, unpredictable and even infuriating the weather can be? It's a natural ice breaker, even when outside there's no ice to break and it's chucking it down.

And chucking it down is something that happens more than anywhere else in Britain in the place I decided to move to when I finished my master's. I had made up my mind. After all the hard work and countless days spent on the bike over the past twelve months in my hometown of Newcastle, it was time for a change. With the prospect of applying for graduate jobs embedded deep in my subconscious like an aggressively pecking hen, it was time that I took advantage of this new kind of employment (sorry, self-employment) that I could just as easily pursue there as well as here, thanks to the magic of an app that was always just a fingertip away.

Deliveroo was nationwide by now, having started in London before spreading the length and breadth of the country in less than five years. And I was part of it. I could go anywhere. Do anything. So that's precisely what I did. I moved away and took the job with me. A couple of good friends, Dean and Michael, who I had gone out clubbing with during my twenties, were relocating to Manchester for work. So I decided to go with them to start a new life in a new city, while trying to carry on cycling for a living for just a little bit longer.

It was to be the beginning of something new. I truly had no idea which of these two paths life would lead me down. On the one hand, it was time to apply for real jobs and become a real person again - or so I thought and even hoped at the time. I figured there would be more opportunity in Manchester anyways, as I never quite fancied working down the pit or at the shipyards back home. (That's a joke, perhaps a bad joke these days, as there's not much of either anymore.)

So perhaps I could reinvent myself in Manchester. Or better still, see a whole new city from the saddle of my trusty bike. Yes, that's what I would do. New life, new city, same job. The same familiar feeling of every new day being an unscripted, unrestrained adventure while I also applied for jobs that would lead me towards another new life. So this was just an interlude until that new life appeared on the horizon, and until it did I felt more than content doing something that made me happy.

Equipped with a bucketload of experience from my first year in the saddle, I was hopeful I could move to Manchester and make a go of it. A large, growing, vibrant cosmopolitan city, friendlier than London, bigger than Newcastle. The land of one-pound buses and pints, coupled with enough curry houses to keep my plumber busy for the duration of my stay in the city. Yes, this was quite a plan. A way to properly immerse myself in a city I had never had the pleasure of staying in for more than a few nights at a time.

A way to see all the sights, the sounds, the culture and the people who call it home. All the places to eat, drink and be merry. Record shops, bookstores, charity shops, marketplaces, libraries, museums, art galleries and much more besides. It's all there for you, in your very own personal office space to use as you see fit. A proper look at how a city really works from the inside. It very much appealed to my sense of adventure and spontaneity after being bound to the same place for such a long time. And it was all made possible through my mobile phone and bicycle, two bits of paraphernalia that would allow me to make the move to a new place and thus to make a new start.

It's all thanks to the app-based work system - which uses global positioning system (GPS) technology to track your every move, from logging into your zone when you start your shift to delivering your customer's hot food and every other movement in between. All of this in the palm of your hand, telling you where you need to go for your next order and how to get there, as well as the name of the restaurant, the quickest route, the fee you will receive, the customer's address and their contact details.

It spurs you on to make yourself, and the company in the process, as much money as possible. You can watch your earnings build up, compare your daily, weekly and monthly figures, like a giant flashing stopwatch. You brag to your fellow cycling colleagues that you have made over a hundred pounds today. You've earned it, every single penny, with every turn of those bike wheels. Every single concrete flight of stairs you've scaled or foul-smelling lift you've had to endure.

Here I was, making my way in a new city, one I was hardly familiar with. I wasn't too concerned, as I trusted that the app would tell me all I needed to know. Every new turn, every new street, every new restaurant, every new block of flats. Eventually memorising it all just like the city I had left behind. Every piece of the puzzle needed to fit together just like before to make me quick enough, and thus fit enough, to survive in this great northern city.

It does take time, however, to learn it all, the intricate complexities of a new city. Manchester took slightly longer than Newcastle, as I had no previous experience of traversing it at all by any kind of transportation, including a bike, and thus no idea how to access certain buildings or navigate the many streets, main roads and tramlines, the last of which left me on my arse many times in the very beginning! It took me about five months to truly grasp it all. Aside from anything else, Manchester is a much larger city with a much wider choice of restaurants and fast-food places to pick up from. Once you do, though, life and the work itself becomes far quicker and easier, and you start using your brain rather than the phone's GPS for guidance.

And I was soon finding my way around, earning my keep, enjoying all the benefits that come with moving to a new place. To anyone considering a city in which to work as a cycle courier, Manchester is a no-brainer. There are loads of students and a constant stream of jobs from the many offices and thousands of young professionals who work there. If you can cycle more than a few hours at a time, the place will treat you well and make you some money. The topography of Manchester city centre is also very kind to the cyclist, with very little elevation to slow you down on those longer days on the bike.

As far as I know, unlike Newcastle, there are no steep embankments or narrow cobbled Victorian lanes to force you to get off and push. The steepest section around Manchester I can ever remember cycling from my time there was Cheetham Hill Road, and even that wasn't half as bad as some of the more unforgiving gradients in and around Newcastle!

Newcastle has more beautiful architecture, however. There are more listed buildings, plus a cheaper cost of living and cheaper nights out. It's also closer to beautiful beaches, has less rainfall and is the home of cheesy chips. It's known as the 'friendliest city in the UK', according to a recent report [37] – though clearly, the fieldwork was not carried out on a Saturday afternoon when the football team inevitably gets beat again. Last but not least, it's also the home of Greggs, the staple diet for any true cyclist.

Manchester pulls in more students, however, ranked third among cities in the UK for student numbers (Newcastle is eighth). And as you will know by now, students, especially international students, are the most dedicated users of delivery apps, especially Deliveroo. Manchester is regularly voted the UK's most liveable city in global surveys [38], with better jobs and more opportunities than Newcastle, as well as fewer hills. My favourite bands of the past few decades – Oasis, The Courteeners, The Smiths, etc. – hail from this neck of the woods, whereas Newcastle has struggled to produce any real musical icons since the likes of Sting and Mark Knopfler.

Not that I was overly concerned with such things as I increased the number of hours I worked in this urban jungle. Up to now, I had mainly just been gigging on nights and weekends, with the occasional lunchtime or full weekday when time had allowed. Towards the end of my year back at uni, I had managed to do about a dozen weeks of full-time hours, but these had to be planned for and recovered from appropriately. They were taxing on the mind and body, and would mean an extra day or two off to recharge my batteries and get my energy levels back up to anything resembling those of a functioning human being again. But now I planned to make the step up from small-time to big league.

I arrived in Manchester with boundless enthusiasm, and to begin with I thrust myself into the digital world of internet jobsites and LinkedIn. I aggressively applied for any job with the word graduate in, hoping that my hot-off-the-press qualification would get me one step closer to a better job, a better life. I threw my hat in the ring for most of the big graduate employers – KPMG, EY, the odd Civil Service job, along with the likes of BP, Shell and Gazprom (who have offices in Manchester). No longer were jobs based around hastily scribbled CVs and covering letters (and adolescent interests or work perks).

Competency assessment tests were the norm with such employers. If your CV or covering letter stood out, or more likely met the data algorithm requirements when processed, then you made it through to these brutal online competency and aptitude tests, designed specifically to sort the best from the rest. I try not to shy away from most challenges, but these were an altogether more terrifying prospect.

I managed around half a dozen of these digital intelligence

investigations in my first few weeks in Manchester, propped up at my desk, wondering how I had ever managed to acquire a postgraduate degree given how cognitively subservient I now felt, not making it through to the late stages of any one of them. The boundless enthusiasm I had acquired of late was quickly reined in with every test I was now undertaking - and failing.

I wasn't too disappointed at the multiple rejections I received from these companies, which probably meant that I wasn't too emotionally invested in the jobs on offer in the first place. I could soldier on regardless; it wasn't like I didn't enjoy being a cycle courier on my new patch. Quite the opposite, in fact. Those competency and aptitude tests served as early litmus tests to inform me of the types of jobs that I might be more suitable for at some later date. Of course, I was gutted not to make it all the way through the selection process to interview, but more so for my ego and pride than because I had any grand plan for my career.

Your skin grows a little thicker, your confidence takes a hit. Then you lick your wounds and get on with it, much like everybody else who is trying to climb the ladder. *Welcome to the layer cake, son.* My last job rejection, at the tender age of 18, had been for Northern Rock when I had first left school and wasn't sure what route in life I wanted to take – my CV in those days even had DJing higher up the list of interests than cycling (the nerve!).

That job rejection led me to move away and to study at Leeds. Every door slammed shut in your face is a chance to find one that opens. Every rejection teaches you much more about yourself then any job offer or promotion ever could. "Whatever you do, don't congratulate yourself too much, or berate yourself either. Your choices are half chance. So are everybody else's."[39] You can use a rejection constructively to make you prioritise what you really want to do in life. So I did just that.

The moment had arrived to embrace the gig economy full-time. Despite being newly endowed with a master's degree, I was evolving into one of those people you read about in magazines, throwing in the corporate towel and going it alone. The first few weeks as a cycle courier in Manchester were much like the first few weeks I had spent doing the same work in Newcastle. It was exciting, fresh and invigorating, stimulating every sense I had. Slipping off every tram line I crossed, absorbing every new side street and canal route that took me off the beaten track on what promised to be a quirky little shortcut along the arteries flowing out from the heart of the city.

Every new tower block, every new office block, every new area in this great city unifying 19th-century industrial heritage and 21st-century glass-covered, sun-glistened, high-rise buildings. It promised so much, but I knew I was going to have to get serious if I was going to make the step up from part-time, student money-making scheme to doing the job on a full-time basis. Would I even be able to work the same long shifts I'd got used to if I had to do it five days in a row?

Sure, I'd been able to work part-time hours during my studies, but this had meant sacrifices in other parts of my life, as well as a lot of additional sleep to help my body recover from the gruelling longer shifts I became accustomed to. Now going full-time meant that I would spend an even larger proportion of my weekly wages trying to replenish energy levels while working so many extra hours. At the same time I would also keep up the job search on days off, searching for the next best thing in life.

It soon became a fragile ecosystem of work, sleep, and bashing away at a keyboard drinking high-strength coffee, trying not to fall asleep in the process. In that sense, it was a lot like the last year of my life, only now the number of hours spent cycling had increased quite dramatically, as had those I needed to spend recovering, mostly asleep in bed. Studying had been replaced by job hunting, but I gently reminded myself I had all the time in the world for that.

Think of other careers that large numbers of people would trade their spleen to work in. Being a DJ, for example. Something I'd had my own lofty dreams of becoming once upon a time, mixing vinyl in my bedroom instead of revising for my GCSEs. Hoping Northern Rock would somehow see potential in someone who can seamlessly mix together a few vinyl records of a certain, very particular taste with such panache.

You are up onstage having it large, in front of all those people, hundreds or maybe even thousands of them, off their heads, buzzing from the song you're spinning. A curator of people's lives for those very special moments of connectedness and self-transcendence, helped in many cases by a discreet use of ecstasy, but still a special, shared, communal moment of the kind that is hard to achieve in the modern world.

A sense of community we've been sold by numerous corporations from Coca-Cola to Facebook. In that sense, the connectedness of the internet is the continuation of a trend that's been present in western life since consumerism and the prosperity it reflected started turning us into individuals making choices independent of any group allegiances we may once have had. People recording the event on camera phones to showcase to friends rather than being present in the moment, enjoying it with others who are there. Don't get me started.

What a job, mixing some tracks you love, that you believe other people will love, too. You get paid for it, go home to bed, wake up, mix together some more music, go to a club the following night, get paid again and return once more to your humble abode at the end of it all. And all with the satisfaction of knowing that you are doing something you love and being paid for. It sounds like a dream job, but I've read enough tales of famous DJs and the demands of that non-stop nocturnal lifestyle to know better than to think anyone can cut it at the top.

Many DJs fight a near-constant battle of alcohol and drug dependency. The environment they work in, the need to be in the zone all the time, the pressure of being, quite literally, the life and soul of the party takes its toll. They are surrounded by alcohol, drugs and all that goes on at after parties. They can't simply go home to sleep after each gig, then wake up and walk the dog the next morning, suitably refreshed.

It's a very different lifestyle to the average Joe, who has a very structured routine and wakes up at the same time most mornings. I'm sure you can see where I'm going with this. For better or worse, there are different expectations and altogether different realities entailed in the different paths that each of us chooses to pursue – for better or worse.

Would I enjoy a night working as a DJ? Undoubtedly. I have done a few times in the past – for friends' birthdays, hosting nights, one-off events, at house parties. It's a huge buzz, and afterwards I would spend the rest of the night talking about it with friends until we all eventually fell asleep as the sun came up and spent the next week recovering from it all. Could I have made a career as a DJ? Not a chance. The parties, the drink and drugs, the travelling, horrendous sleeping habits, and then recovering from it all.

The huge highs but also the crushing lows, invisible to all except those who actually live and breathe it. The potential damage to your mental and physical health that many DJs are known to suffer for those few hours of work on weekends would mean the good times would not outweigh the potential damage this lifestyle could do to other aspects of my life. I wasn't built to have it at the Hacienda every weekend. I was built to ride a bike.

So ride a bike I did, up to 55 hours a week, this being the maximum amount you could work when booking shifts at the time. I was now entering the big league, throwing everything I had into making sure I could work as much as my body and mind would allow. Manchester was super busy all day, every day, and I was slowly figuring out how best to get around the vast city space and where the best places were to eat and drink, filling myself with just enough calories to get me through the long day ahead.

And the same lessons I had learned in Newcastle served me just as well in Manchester: the restaurants that are super-quick to pick up from, the ones to avoid, the nicer areas of the city to deliver to, and the not-so-nice places that are either difficult to get to on a bike or simply the kinds of places you don't want to end up in at ten o'clock on a pitch-black winter night.

And as the first few full-time weeks passed by, made all the better by students flocking back in droves come September, the world was alright with me. Late summer and autumn had been very good, allowing me to settle into a rhythmic existence, after the stresses of all the punishing competency tests had been washed away with every pedal stroke since then. All was new and seen from a tourist's perspective.

Enjoy it while it lasts, this isn't forever, I told myself once again during those picturesque autumn days and evenings that make it such a blessing to be a cyclist. Engross yourself in every aspect of this new life, for one day soon you will be back in the office, romantically reminiscing about your short, sweet career on the bike.

The autumn leaves blew away. My physique resembled that of a racing whippet by now, the direct consequence of solely and exclusively riding my bike and sleeping over and over, day in, day out. Clean living, deep sleeping, and what little fat I had remaining was being stripped away at an unprecedented rate.

The bathroom scales in my new house told me I was down to 14 stone. Bloody hell. I've never really put much store by bodyweight, but this was the lightest I had ever been since I was at school, and my abs were even starting to poke through as I looked down at the scales to weigh myself.

I had dropped about 2 stone over the last few years, despite being able to eat almost anything I wanted, although the energy my body would now accept as fuel was starting to become slightly more wholesome than what I had put in my body in the past. I was lean, my body was quickly starting to adapt to the daily stresses of riding the bike, and my brain was downloading the newly forming cityscape most nights after long days in the saddle.

* * *

Things were looking up. I was seeing a whole new city in a complete and absolute sense - living and breathing it all around me, part of the ebb and flow of its natural existence. A tiny organic component, like an antibody charged with doing my bit to maintain the health of the whole - the elaborate universe of concrete, brick and glass through which people flowed in and flowed out every minute of every day.

Just as day becomes night, so autumn becomes winter. Autumn is usually a good companion to the cyclist. Reliable, sometimes difficult and demanding, but with more good days than bad. Winter is a different proposition altogether. My first winter in Newcastle had taught me all the lessons I needed to survive the coming change of seasons.

The lessons were many indeed. Cover every inch of your body. Multiple layers are essential, not simply necessary. Wear thick gloves. Waterproof everything if possible, socks included. Keep your hands, feet and head warm- and you're ready for the battle ahead.

I've taken part in a few pretty gruelling events over the years. There were a few shifts over that first winter in Newcastle that could be thrown into the same category as those marathons and bike rides that require every last ounce of willpower to get you over the finish line, including the Beast from the East. It may rain heavily all day, with super-strong headwinds; it may be freezing to the point that your phone ceases to work, before stopping you in your tracks; or snowing so heavily that you can't see ten yards in front of you, cheeks hardening into immovable features on your face.

These are all challenging conditions – frustrating, too – as they limit your performance and change the basic job from simply riding a bike into what feels like pushing a giant brick strapped to both feet through quicksand while blindfolded. Approaching me now was a winter in Manchester, which sits at the foot of the Pennine Hills and in close proximity to the Irish Sea. The weather is famously wet, and much wetter than the place I had just left behind me. In fact, it never occurred to me that moving away from Newcastle would lead me to an even worse microclimate, but it did. I'm still learning, just like everybody else.

But nothing could stop me now in my quest for adventure. A winter in Manchester lay ahead of me, one that was going to push me to my absolute limits as a way simply to pay the bills and maybe have a bit of fun, too. The dark clouds were looming, and I was scrambling to find as many waterproof items of cycle clothing as possible, so that I could go on living the dream, or the wet dream, as I refer to it now, looking back. Well, minus the orgasm, the warm bedsheets and the cosy relaxing environment.

Maybe the wet nightmare is a better way to describe it, one that lasted for what seemed like forever.

6

The Bad

'The race is won by the rider who can suffer the most.' Eddy Merckx

Manchester. The only place on the planet where I have ever considered owning an umbrella. I say considered. My old man would turn in his grave if he knew I had actually bought and used an umbrella to go about my daily business. But some people do use them quite frequently over there. And rightly so, too. The weather is diabolical. And that's a word that I haven't used in conversation in years.

To illustrate the point, Manc weather is incomprehensible even to the locals. Even the weather app on your phone can't predict what's going to happen over the course of a day there. That's not something I've ever had to worry about even in places as wild and exposed as Scotland, the Lake District and North Wales, where conditions are predictable enough that they can be dressed for appropriately.

Never in a million years did I think I would be able to move away from Newcastle and actually brag about the fairer (if colder) weather in the Northeast. It's quite unbelievable really. Unless I was ever to sail solo around the world, or end up as a deckhand on a vessel somewhere in Alaska, I had always presumed anywhere I would move to after Newcastle would have a much better climate. How wrong I was.

Two weeks into the job, I got to experience first-hand the worst that Manchester had to offer. It had been a fairly busy Friday lunchtime, as they always are. It's one of the better days to work for Deliveroo in most places in the country. Offices start you off, as workers give in to the familiar Friday feel-good factor. Once the offices have had their lunchtime fix, custom usually tails off into the first student orders: those who have just woken up or have just got in from lectures or were too inconvenienced and unwilling to pop across the road to pick up their favourite meal or snack.

These student orders could be very lucrative in the grander scheme of working for Deliveroo, as I was still making the minimum distance-based fee of £3.90 a drop from when Deliveroo had changed the fee structure a few months ago. This would soon change again, but for now I had found a fairly easy way to make decent money throughout the day working in Manchester, doing deliveries over a very short distance on a section of Oxford Road that had a KFC and a Taiwanese bubble-tea shop called Chatime across the road from each other.

These two shops were a stone's throw away from a newly built ultra-exclusive student accommodation block housing mainly Chinese students. Sat around the corner from the KFC and Chatime, I received regular orders from both places throughout the day - with the many hundreds of students ordering regularly through the app from their accommodation - despite them being a short walk away, due mainly to the super-fast delivery times and very low delivery fees (99p) that Deliveroo was charging at the time.

Many Deliveroo riders wait outside certain restaurants or busy areas, since you are normally assigned orders based on the rider's proximity to the nearest possible restaurant. Both outlets were literally a thirty-second walk over to the high-rise block of predominantly Chinese students. International students are big money, in this case paying anywhere from £13,107 for a 'Lite Studio' up to £25,347 for an 'Ultimate Vita' 40sqm room during a typical 51-week stay in the city.[40]

Those are eye-watering amounts that various groups of international students are able to stump up in their pursuit of a western education and lifestyle, and in that context, what's a few quid here and there on a takeaway - and why not pay a little bit extra to have someone wait on you from across the road, as a two-wheeled waiter is effectively what I was for those students.

On such orders I simply locked my bike up outside the bus stop between the two outlets, then having already phoned ahead to the customer while picking up the order, marched over intently, with my backpack still strapped to my back, to drop off these regular orders. It was pretty easy and painless work: five to ten minutes waiting around for the items to be made and then a hundred yards walk over to the customer waiting outside the building for their daily treat. Ideal when you were tired of cycling longer distances and needed a bit of a break!

I was booked in to work my normal allocated hours, which on a Friday usually meant a twelve-hour shift, from ten in the morning until ten at night. It had taken a bit of time to get used to working such long days, but the terrain was flat and the overall distances I needed to cover were relatively short, made easier by the fact that I stayed around a certain section of Oxford Road when I was tired or needed a break from cycling around the city. When you are still high off the whole feeling of finishing uni and moving to a new city, then the extra bit of energy and enthusiasm you needed to get you through these longer shifts certainly helped.

By now I would wake up just in time to make it into town, log in to the zone within the first fifteen minutes of the shift (for attendance) and spend the first few hours of the shift gradually waking up and consuming enough food to sustain myself throughout the day - despite the likelihood I would end up with a bloated stomach from not being able to properly digest when cycling. It's similar to how you spend the last few hours of any long shift - putting any kind of sugar or simple carbs into you, trying your best to fend off the dreaded cyclist's bonk, to give you just enough energy to make it home so you can cook some pasta and cheese to replenish lost reserves of fuel.

Cyclist's bonk did happen on several occasions during my time in Manchester, during those initial twelve-hour shifts I had slowly started acclimatising to in the winter, when having foolishly gone without food for more than six or even eight hours at a time, it hit me like a juggernaut – more a head-on collision than a bonk. Usually, a hearty meal and some sugary drinks or sweets would be enough to pull me back to being a semi-functioning courier again.

However, on one occasion it hit me so hard that I had to lie down for an hour under a canal bridge along from Deansgate, with a terrible pulsing headache and uncontrollable shakes. I had a carrier bag full of sweets and disgusting convenience-shop sausage rolls, which I had purchased impulsively when I'd started to feel the bonk coming on. I had also foolishly downed a whole can of full-sugar Monster to put some instant energy into my system, but this sent my heart rate skyrocketing for the last few hours of work.

My advice is not to have energy drinks when cycling all day, as your heart rate is extremely elevated at most times of the day without adding to the punishment. I barely slept a wink that night, as my eyelids and stomach fluttered uncontrollably throughout the night, as I lay in bed sweating and cursing my inability to properly hydrate and fuel myself during the longer hours I was now spending in the saddle.

I vowed to myself from that day on that I would start to implement a more structured routine of regular food, drink and rest during quieter periods, to allow me to work more effectively during busier periods and never again end up like a hideous,delirious troll sat hunched under a dark, abandoned bridge feasting on stale leftovers.

The hours after lunch and before late evening are normally more relaxed. These are the moments when you actually have a few minutes spare to grab a coffee, replenish your rations, wash your face or empty your bladder. Some couriers spend these hours resting at home or stopping for food. I had never done that previously but was slowly starting to allow for short periods to refuel and relax.

Once I had completely stopped, that was nearly always the closing curtain for me. If I had cycled home for a mid-afternoon break and relaxed for just an hour, it would be nearly impossible for me to get back out again, as I would either quickly fall asleep on the couch, the poor weather would signal the end of my working day, or I would simply cook such a large meal that would seriously undermine and deteriorate my evening productivity.

Just stay upright, stay focused, and if work is busy the time flies by anyhow. If it stays dry, everything usually goes smoothly. No need for that extra waterproof layer or the change of gloves you have hidden away with your sweets and bananas. But when it rains, and it has a habit of doing so very quickly and very heavily in Manchester, then the minutes suddenly turn into hours.

It can take a matter of minutes for a dark cloud to eclipse the once prominent sun across the whole of the city. Sunshine at four-fifty, pissing down at five. Today was one of those days. The day I learned I would need to buy extra waterproof gloves, waterproof socks, waterproof shoes, waterproof undercrackers and also a waterproof cover to help protect my phone. Wet balls I could just about get away with, but if your phone isn't up to the job of staying switched on when the rain hits, then you really are in trouble.

Before the day in question, the job had seemed so simple, so inviting, so easy to dress for and so dry. How I was to miss being dry. My once-reliable weather app was now lying to me on a regular basis, telling me I could go out to work and would only encounter sunshine and cloud on my travels. It was not only lying but cheating on me big-time. Not even suggesting a 10 percent chance of rain on days where the heavens opened and left me feeling and looking like a drowned rat. I looked to the skies, constantly on edge as I fanatically tracked this most peculiar and unpredictable weather front like a paranoid prisoner of war.

148

What descended on the city that day wasn't the fine rain that Peter Kay complains about either (the one that soaks you through). It was the kind that turns the place from a sprawling metropolis of life and activity into a desert of bedraggled destitution in less time than it takes you to reach for your phone to ring your dad and beg him to allow you to buy that brolley you've been bringing up in conversation of late.

Either way, a brolley is no good on a bike, and once you are wet you are staying wet. You're like a giant sponge dropped in water then taken out to slowly dry out over the next few hours - or plunged back in during regular intervals depending on the duration of the rainfall. But there's nothing in the centre of Manchester that will dry you through, pat you down and make you feel slightly better, aside from the kind of remedy you might find in a few grubby side streets next to Chinatown.

As the rain pelted down all around me, and being unable to concentrate on anything else but water percolating through every conceivable pore, the next four hours of my life passed by like a feature-length form of medieval torture. If I had to rank all the weather conditions I've experienced or heard about during my time on this planet, Manc rain would be right at the top (or perhaps the bottom) of the pile. The monsoons of Mumbai, Skiddaw snow, Haiti storms or even the dreaded Scotch mist are nothing by comparison.

But then again, I had never had to endure these other weather conditions for any more than a few hours at a time. So you can understand me being a bit dramatic now I was undergoing twelve-hour shifts in poor weather conditions with minimal cycling apparel as my only protection. The rain was sometimes so horrific, on one occasion I was given 26 quid in tips over a three-hour period, a generosity unheard of in the more arid Northeast. Luckily, the majority was in coins, otherwise it may simply have dissolved in the deep recesses of my pockets, unable to be used as legal tender ever again.

Usually, your tips come from the older customers, who are more accustomed to tipping from days gone by. They are mostly irregular customers who may only have a takeaway every other week or even once a month, and who often live in the suburbs or council estates, where it sometimes takes more than twenty minutes to deliver the food. Or sometimes, it's those sky dwellers on the top floor of a tower block, where a temperamental lift or near-vertical flight of concrete stairs is the only way up or down. These are where your tips generally come from in this line of work, not from the new-school clientele of wealthy international students or the healthy old-school pool of domestic students. The regular customers normally don't tip.

To such customers, getting things delivered is seen as a daily right rather than a regular treat. They've just spent a tenner getting a Chinese herbal drink delivered from literally across the road, so the risk-to-reward ratio really isn't in your favour. And that's cool, as most of the time these orders keep you in full-time employment. Zero fuss or hassle. Central locations, with no flights of stairs to climb or lifts to squeeze into with your largely annoying and largely protruding backpack in order to complete the delivery.

The students appear outside, smiling and grateful for your effort, and as quickly as you can deliver the goods you have your next job assigned to you from the next hungry student at the same block of flats, picking up from the same restaurant or herbal tea outlet just across the road. Thank you and goodnight.

I knew the night was going to be a feature-length version of the prison breakout from *The Shawshank Redemption*, as the heavy rain descended to empty the city of anyone who had dared to venture out. I pulled up to a deserted block of student flats, which would normally have been buzzing with a campus-like vibe. I was charged with delivering a tasty-looking beef burrito to a Russian student who had only just arrived in the country. His English was a work in progress, but I fully comprehended where he was going with our initial ice-breaking conversation.

"Fuck zis shit, man. I travel from Moss-Cow last week, and better than zis shit."

I attempted a semi-defeated laugh through my soaking clothes, skin and face, but the rain had a weird distorting effect on the noise that emanated from somewhere deep in my soul and meandered in his general direction. I strode towards him head down, dragging my sorry self under a small shelter tucked away next to the entrance of the student accommodation.

"I'm sorry to bring you out to zis, fucking bad rain now. Even I not leave for food."

Fuck, I thought. If a Russian wasn't willing to venture out in the deluge for a mere burrito, I wasn't going to last long if this kept up. I naively engaged with him, in that self-deprecating way British people have, a trait that is practised with equal enthusiasm by our cousins to the East.

"Get used to it, mate. It always pisses down in Manchester," I offer. Come to think of it now, this may have been a subliminal message to myself, but in any case the Russian took pity on me and reached into his pocket.

"Here, man, take zis, you fucking earn it now bro."

He pulled out of his wallet a freshly printed crisp ten-pound note for my troubles – the newly laminated polymer type, too. I told him I had no change, but that it was a nice gesture. He could tell I didn't really want to take it, but he also instinctively sensed I would most likely be dragged through Dante's nine circles of Hell that evening. He insisted, I buried it in one of the waterlogged swamps that passed for pockets and wished him well for the rest of term. Solid bunch, the Russians, though not quite solid enough for the late September rain in Manchester.

Of course, I'm bound to say this, but you should always tip your rider if you can. Especially during such horrid conditions. A quid is more than sufficient. It acknowledges the struggle you've faced in getting the order to them in the face of adversity of one kind or another. It restores your faith in humanity and keeps you going throughout the difficult days like the one I've been describing. I delivered a cheeky Nando's that very same night to a Man U legend. Very cheeky indeed, as it wasn't his name that appeared on the app, unless he's had a name change since hanging up his boots.

I nearly went back and asked for a photograph with my childhood footballing idol, but the moment had been and gone, without so much as a thank you, without any kind of tip for the effort I'd made in getting his food to him that miserable evening, and with the door slammed unashamedly in my face for my troubles. The legend I had always imagined him to be had quickly disintegrated. Never meet your idols, they can only disappoint. I guess that's the thing with the gig economy – some Giggs are better than others.

That night was also the first night I ever chose to knock off early during my time in Manchester. Every man has his limits, and there came a point when I decided I couldn't take any more torment, no matter how well recompensed, from the constant heavy rain lashing down on me, penetrating my very soul, it seemed. It got so bad that I was unable to focus on anything other than the next droplets of rain running down my pitifully pouted face, down the contours of my nose and onto my defectively drenched phone. And when the phone started cutting out halfway through the deliveries, and then not responding at all due to water getting inside and onto the screen, I decided enough was enough.

I realised that night I'd had it pretty easy up until then. A part-timer in a drier part of the country, I'd switched to full-time hours in what was famously the wettest part. I got home, showered, sat down despondently next to the radiator for half an hour, heat-treated my tips so they would still be accepted as currency at a later date, and went to bed dreaming of better days and drier climates.

Still, there is still a certain satisfaction in working these horrendous days, so it's not all bad. I normally used up so much negative emotion on the horrible conditions I was faced with on those cruel nights that the relief of being home and dry made me far more positive than I had been all day long, and I went to bed happy and content! Yin and yang.

My old man is exactly the same, shouting so ferociously at *Channel 4 News* most evenings, so that when he goes to do his shopping at Morrison's the next morning, he's a complete pacifist. I shake my head, laughing at him somewhat sarcastically at the difference I witness, unable to fathom that the man who had offloaded his pent-up frustrations onto Jon Snow the night before could be so warm and engaging with the checkout assistant swiping the items he has bought for the evening ahead, when once more he will vent his spleen at the

TV as he puts the world to rights.

We all do similar things left to our own devices, and I was no different when faced with such testing conditions. Swearing intermittently at the rain pelting down on me most days, hands up waving aggressively towards the taxi driver cutting across me to take more of the road ahead and pushing me closer to the large puddle and the broken bottle I was trying my best to avoid. Head in hands at the lift not working, looking despondently up the seven flights of stairs I was now faced with in order to complete my last delivery of the night.

Venting is a natural part of life, and you soon become very proficient in the art of it when faced with tough conditions like these. Once you've arrived home, cleaned yourself up and defragmented, you start to appreciate the simple things in life again, which normally you take for granted. Warmth. A Mattress. A cup of tea. Bedsheets. And downtime.

But it's not just the weather that affects you. Another rather unpleasant side effect of doing the job full-time is the social aspect, or rather the lack of it. Be prepared to kiss goodbye to your once very social self. If you don't normally socialise outside of work, then this doesn't apply to you and life may well continue as normal. Cycling fifty-five hours a week leaves you with very little enthusiasm or energy for those few pints you once treasured on a Friday night, or for anything else you used to love throwing into your body at the start of a well-earned weekend break.

Besides which, it was proving nigh-on impossible to take a night off over any given weekend. To earn the right to work full-time hours, you now needed to work nearly every Friday, Saturday and Sunday evening between 7 and 9pm. In Manchester, the competition for shifts between riders was ferocious, more than I had found in Newcastle at a time when Deliveroo was first penetrating the market and had an initial undersupply of riders to work most hours of the day.

Deliveroo had initially sold the job as offering freedom and flexibility, and it certainly did just that in the very beginning. There were only a small number of riders back in 2017, handling an increasing number of orders as demand grew exponentially, when Deliveroo was starting to gain a foothold in the takeaway market.

However, a drive to recruit many more thousands and thousands of riders soon led to changes in the hours and shifts that existing riders could obtain through the app. Very quickly, there was a huge number of riders signed up and working full-time, resulting in fierce competition for shifts as riders vied for the ability to work all the hours they wanted on a weekly basis. After all, I'm probably not the only one stupid enough to want to cycle all day, every day!

You needed near-perfect statistics to be able to pre-book your weekly working hours. These 'stats' would include your attendance, i.e. the percentage of booked 'sessions' (working hours) that you've actually 'attended' (actually worked); late cancellation, i.e. the percentage of bookings (working hours) you've cancelled with less than twenty-four hours' notice; and super-peak participation, meaning the number of sessions (hours) you've worked during the busiest times (Friday, Saturday and Sunday nights, 7–9pm).

Of course, this implicit pressure meant those super-peak sessions were never the busiest time of the week to be a rider. They were certainly the ones available for most riders to work. So while they were the busiest in terms of the overall number of orders placed on the system, because nearly every available rider wants to, or in my case had to, work these hours, they become the bane of your life to work – at the end of a long shift, when you needed these extra two hours on weekend evenings to make your stats sufficient to access these priority shifts the following week and by doing so to qualify for the full-time hours you needed.

Especially if you would rather be at home with your feet up, or down the pub with the rest of the asylum on weekend release. These extra weekend shifts you were forced to work in order to access full-time hours the following week are what got in the way of being able to relax and enjoy a free and unencumbered weekend once in a while. Recognising an arrangement that basically sucks, the rosy tint in the glasses you've been wearing all this time slowly starts to fade.

For nothing is ever as good as the ad campaign or glossy promo makes it seem. Just like an exhausted DJ after the first big summer season in Ibiza or a footballer after a gruelling season, you need to listen to your body. If you don't, things start to get pretty ugly, pretty quickly. My problem was that I was trying to do it all. I have never been one for sitting around and smelling the roses. New city, new challenges, new opportunities, new girls, new clubs, new surroundings.

Add a dash of job applications and interviews into the mix and you can see how it all becomes a little too much to manage or prioritise. Applying for new jobs wasn't the difficult part; applying my brain to complex tasks was the difficult part. This didn't present itself as too much of a problem during my time doing the job part-time while I was studying. If my brain was overloading, I could always trim the hours I was working, sleep a little more, eat a little more and adjust my lifestyle so that I could function properly in whatever I was trying to do.

Anyone who has ever cycled a full day on a bicycle will know the feeling at the end of it all when you ditch the bike and finally get to relax. All the feel-good chemicals and happy drugs produced by this marvellous, mysterious upstairs organ of ours are swirling around after a day of intense exercise, bringing on a high that tells you your body has been working hard and will need to come down to properly regulate itself again. I was always hyper after working long days on the bike, with the high usually lasting half an hour to an hour after I got home, while the wonderful concoction of chemicals which had been coursing through my system all day looked for somewhere to escape.

Some folk get these highs from the gym, from drugs or alcohol, from endurance training of any sort, from closing a big deal, from trading on the stock market, or from walking up an imposing mountain. The problem arrives when you do too much of it at once. Any of those highs that people chase can be dangerous when taken to extremes, each in their different ways. Cycling for such long sessions over an extended period can start throwing up a few nasty side effects along the way, if you aren't recovering properly or putting the right things into your body, and even when you are, though to a much lesser extent.

Pro cyclists have a dedicated team around them seeing to their every possible need, be it diet, training, recovery, fitness plans, relaxation stations, a few needles or some experimental pills in brown envelopes to help inject some much-needed life into those beaten-up bodies. The two daft Geordies I lived with were my support system. Dean, a used-car salesman with a passion for all things hedonistic, looking to create a new life for himself in a fresh and vibrant city that was full of opportunity. And Michael, working full-time as a quantity surveyor, and studying evenings and weekends for a masters in Construction Law. Like myself, Michael had largely grown out of the need to spend his weekends hungover and was much more focused on forging a new career and spending his downtime doing anything but getting drunk.

It was a low-budget Northwest version of *Auf Wiedersehen, Pet*, as if the original wasn't bad enough! One was keen to go out and blow his wages every single weekend without fail, while the other one focused on his work and his studies. I was somehow seen as the centre ground. The influencer. The middleman. The swing voter. This presented all sorts of problems to a keen cyclist who ought to stay home, drink water, eat healthy food and recite his Hail Marys before settling down for the eight or nine hours of good-quality sleep that was an absolute necessity every single night of the week.

On the other hand, I had a pub on my doorstep offering two-pound pints, which is something even Newcastle's public houses would struggle to price match. Add to that a housemate who would part the Red Sea to make sure there was a weekly afterparty at the house you all shared, and it was becoming apparent that the luxuries afforded to most pro cyclists, or to most normal and rational human beings for that matter, would be strictly off the menu as I tried to manage life as a full-time cyclist in a new and exciting city. Luxuries like sleep, recovery, peace, tranquillity and a clean and comfortable house. Forces beyond my control were frustrating my intention of cycling as many hours as I could, week in, week out.

* * *

A hangover in your teens or twenties is a manageable beast. One day to recover, then back to work like the good upstanding citizen you ought to be. A hangover in your thirties, however, dear God. Clear the schedule for the next two weeks. Ditch your healthy diet, get on the blower for a different takeaway every night to help replace the 'lost salts', don't interact with absolutely anyone outside your home the whole time, and make sure you tell everyone or anyone that will listen that you'll never do it again. Ever.

Koop, the dysfunctional vinyl pusher on *Human Traffic*, sums it up better than anyone ever could. 'When the comedown outweighs the good times, you know the party's over, man.' This had been resonating with me for quite some time. Now it was quickly becoming the first commandment.

These are the generally accepted laws of nature for a hangover such as most people are likely to encounter in early adult life. I was firmly in this camp - in fact to a greater degree than most, because of all the cycling I was now doing. While job hunting and trying to enjoy myself a little in the process too. But a hangover in your thirties, while a nasty experience for most people, is a different beast altogether when you've been riding your bike all week and your muscles are craving water, electrolytes and food to help repair and replenish themselves. In fact, it doesn't even merit discussion, just widespread acknowledgment that it is what it is. But, just for the record, and as you'll find out later on, it's a horrific experience.

My new housemate, Dean, was in the top one percent, however – the elite of hangover artists. The type who seem able to outrun any chance of suffering a hangover. Those who simply keep going until they have to clock in back at work and pretend like nothing has ever happened. They're an unbelievable breed, made for being rockstars and DJs – purpose-built even.

In another life, he would have beaten Bez to the role of the Happy Mondays' mascot, but he was only a little lad from Blyth at the time. He was born in a similar era to myself, which made him my problem, my own mascot, rockstar and DJ rolled into one. Living in the very poorly insulated house we now called home.

Rolling the years back was top of his agenda. Having it large in Manchester, bringing the party to our dingy-yet-detached rental property, with its paper-thin walls and his newly acquired powerful studio speakers, was to become a regular feature of weekends in our homespun Hacienda. I tried sourcing a FAC51 sign on my travels around the music shops in the city, to add some authenticity and glamour to it all, but always came up short. It probably would have been pinched anyways.

In reality, the second summer of love – the birth of the rave scene from 1989 – that Dean was trying to recreate in the hollowed-out house in Fallowfield turned into a winter of discontent and lost sleep for me. You roll with the punches – he's a mate after all – but the lack of sleep starts to quickly eat away at your sense of well-being and overall clarity. The quality of your sleep diminishes, too. If you've had a fairly easy day in the saddle, nibbling away at food intermittently like you're supposed to, and have also gone easy on the caffeine, you'd normally be rewarded with a fair night's sleep, everything else accounted for.

If you've lost a few hours' sleep the night before due to Eyeball Paul (or Dean, as he's more commonly known) having

Kevin, Perry and the rest of the motley crew over for another ultra-endurance social gathering, then the following day you are going to have to compensate for the lack of sleep in order to stay upright on that very unsteady bike of yours for a ten-hour shift on the Sunday.

Sometimes the lack of sleep is purely down to the amount of intense exercise you've subjected your body to. There are nights when you wake up abruptly, alert and restless due not to a lack of exercise but too much of it. Overdoing it at the gym can bring this about; high-intensity training late at night has a similar effect on a lot of people. The same goes with too much cycling. It's not so bad if you don't have to get up early for work the next day, which I rarely had to. Read a book or magazine, gaze at your phone bleary-eyed for half an hour, slowly letting your body readjust to the hyperactivity from the previous day, and you are normally back asleep in no time.

Problems only persist when you're woken by the boom of the club-quality sound system downstairs – *again!* – making sleep impossible, especially when people start screaming over the increasingly loud subwoofer bass, each voice competing for attention as the party shifts through the gears to the point where only the hardened ravers are left standing – like proud, bold masculine lions feasting on whatever leftovers the party can provide for them. The weaker have clocked off, passed out, skulked off home or are currently propped up on the kitchen bench, listening to a complete stranger tell them how they've mapped out their whole life for the next few years. Hollywood-style boasting in the humble Manc suburb of Fallowfield.

I've lived through those years, and enjoyed them too. Talking complete shit to strangers all night, not a worry in the world – one- and two-day hangovers making you feel invincible. I'll do it again someday perhaps, too, though not with the same late nights and heavily intoxicated states I once found myself in. It was just that my current circumstances allowed for little of that sort of footloose frivolity, especially on a weekend, when these parties tended to take place. I was always working the weekend hours required to allow me to work full-time hours the following week. I needed sleep. But it was not going to be given to me on a plate. I was going to have to beg and beg and then beg some more for it until my housemate and party supremo ran out of steam. Like that could ever happen.

* * *

So you keep going. Working, eating, sleeping, waking up. Trying to crank down the afterparty on weekends. Hopefully getting back to sleep at some point during the early hours, just as the morning light starts to protrude through the middle creases of your bedroom curtains. Michael had lost it with Dean a few times by now. A habitual early riser, he was sick of coming down to the leftover remnants of the previous night's hedonism.

I had simply started going to work much earlier on such occasions if I could not get back to sleep by a certain time. I started doing the breakfast runs (crawls really) when I couldn't bear the thought of being in the house when the party was still going strong in the early hours of a bleary Sunday morning. It would be like playing the part of an extra in *Two Pints of Lager and a Packet of Crisps*, except sober.

It didn't always go to plan, with weeknights spent catching up on sleep and collective moans about the next instalment of party liaison coming our way. But then life rarely does go to plan, and is just as likely to throw you another curve ball, seemingly out of nowhere. Like a job interview, an actual positive response to one of the many applications I'd been putting out there. Christ! This was not what I needed right now. I was barely keeping it together at the best of times. I had just been pricing stabilisers for my bike one early Sunday morning, to keep me going in a straight line after another night of missed sleep – and now this!

I have already mentioned that overloading your body and brain with too many tasks all at once is not a good idea. But this was precisely where I was at, without ever really realising or acknowledging it. I was running on fumes, and was going to have to make my way down to London while trying to look and sound presentable, professional even, for a decent job in the big smoke. I was either hyper during or just after work, or completely knackered the rest of the time. These were the two states I had swung between since starting full-time hours with Deliveroo in Manchester. There was no middle ground whatsoever.

Like most things in life, balance is the key. I may have been working all day, every day on the bike, but I certainly wouldn't have described my health at the time as optimal or even ideal. Working to such extremes, burnout was inevitable. I had just been delaying the burnout for an extended period of time until something else came along. Much like newly graduated doctors do working such long shifts, sooner or later it all becomes too much, but you rationalise any thoughts and feelings you experience as part of the job, and part of the gradual learning curve.

Too much of anything is bad for you, and long-distance cycling certainly falls into this category, especially with everything else that was happening around me at the time. I could barely read a few pages of a book or play on the computer for longer than half an hour on my days off without falling asleep on the couch or getting back into bed – wherever I happened to find myself in a relaxed state.

Although my resting heart rate was now around the 50 beats per minute range – a strong indicator that the last year and a half on the bike had been good for my cardiovascular system – I was starting to feel the delayed effects of overdoing it since my time in Manchester. After twelve-hour days with the heart rate of a hamster, this lower resting heart rate was probably what was needed to balance out and remedy the caffeine-fuelled pressure I was subjecting my cardiovascular system to.

I had also been spending hundreds of pounds on Voltarol (the extra-strong pain relief gel) to help soothe the pain I felt in my neck and upper back most days. In fact, there were constant aches and pains coming and going on days off, leaving little room for doing much outside of working, other than sleep. Later, I was able to diagnose much of this pain as the result of wearing bib shorts.

For the uninitiated, these are tight Lycra shorts, designed for road cyclists, that are worn over your shoulders to keep your body in a low, aerodynamic riding position. They do this by keeping the crotch of your shorts firmly against your own crotch. They are not designed for cycle couriers who are up and out of their saddle all day, stood in restaurants waiting for orders to be prepared or for customers to come and pick them up. You live and learn (so please learn from my many mistakes!).

I had barely found the time to ring my gran back home to report on the monsoon-like conditions and weekend induced techno-militias orchestrated by Dean et al I was experiencing in Manchester since moving down. All this time I had developed a somewhat subconscious laser-like focus on becoming an ultra-endurance cyclist, keen on getting my resting heart rate to those levels demonstrated by Tour de France cyclists of something below 40 beats per minute (Lance Armstrong's was 32bpm, Miguel Indurain's 29bpm.)

I only managed a resting heart rate of around 44bpm, despite my best efforts; but now my heart was beating slightly faster as I pondered the task of preparing for a new, altogether different challenge. Now I was supposed to be capable of putting together a coherent business proposal as to why Her Majesty's Government should offer me a full-time, well-paid, respectable job as a trade trainee with the Department for International Trade for the next chapter of my life. The wind was against me.

I had worked flat out since I had taken my first ever shift in Manchester. I'd only taken a couple of days off in the months since then, mainly after a few pints, and always after working an entire weekend of twelve-hour shifts. Between 45 and 55 hours a week, partly for the money, but also because I wanted to squeeze as much out of this opportunity as possible. It wouldn't last forever, was what I told myself once again - so why waste the chance to earn some good money and take in the energy and dynamism, the sights, sounds and the smells, that Manchester had to offer?

The three weeks I had allowed myself to prepare for the

interview didn't seem nearly long enough. At the time I thought it was possible still to work most days, just for a few hours, as a chance to get away from the intense pressure I was now under for the first time in months. Working from home wasn't proving to be the most conducive or inspiring place to try and crunch the numbers and think of reasons why I should be accepted for a position in politics and trade.

It was, however, the first job that had properly struck me as being right for me at the time. Working on trade deals and travelling, putting to use some of my interests and the things I had learned during my master's in international politics, and satisfying the curiosity I had at the time of moving to and working in London. It was an itch I'd begun to feel since leaving behind my previous career, but whether London would be a good fit for me or not, I really didn't know. But there was only one way to properly find out.

The desk in my room resembled a French farmer's milking stool during the Battle of the Somme. More a shelf to store my sleeping pills, ibuprofen and Voltarol, for easy access come the weekend, than somewhere I could wargame the different scenarios I might encounter as I made my pitch for a high-profile career in London. So off to the library it was then.

Manchester Central library – beautiful, elegant, iconic, inspiring and impressive all at once. The complete opposite to how I felt, trying to muster some strength or energy from deep within me for one of the biggest challenges of my life. Trying to prepare for a three-hour assessment and interview along with working a few hours on the bike when I could. It was an unmitigated disaster.

Trying to eat, drink, concentrate, read, write and prepare to be grilled, all within an eight-hour period, won't work for most people and certainly didn't work for me either. Prudently, in the second week, I knocked the cycling on the head altogether. The first week had allowed me some limited time to scribble a few incoherent pages together, something akin to the inner thoughts of Charles Manson. Not exactly what was required for the battle I was preparing to fight in the Big Smoke. The final week wasn't much more successful or productive.

The problem you have when you stop cycling every single day is that your brain and body scream for all the things that you've denied them over the past few days, weeks or months of near constant abuse of overdoing it and not listening to your body when it really needed a break. You soon understand that to feel anywhere near a normal, functioning human being able to go about their daily chores, you will somehow need to substantially increase the number of calories you take in, just to have the energy merely to stay awake, never mind trying to squeeze anything else out of your unproductive day.

You now understand the struggles faced by Ricky Hatton and Tyson Fury, punching machines primed during training and fighting camps, normal humans outside of it all, with all the temptations your body has had to do without for so long. When you haven't got the gravitational pull of fitness and exercise in your daily routine, after a few pints and doner kebabs, all that hard work can start to unravel fairly quickly.

At a time when both brain and body needed an undisputed break, I was trying to get my brain to perform tasks it had not faced in months. Critical thinking, long structured sentences, dialogue longer than the usual "enjoy your food" and "have a nice day", and trying to memorise long lists of competencies I had proficiently acquired throughout my short working life, along with additional information I also needed to digest and regurgitate at will. Challenges that are hard enough for most, even with a clear head.

As Doomsday approached, one late afternoon in Manchester Central Library I sat hunched and hurting, both physically and mentally – head in hands, desperate for some natural light and oxygen to fill my lungs and inspire my inconsequential thoughts. But nothing was sinking in, to the extent that I couldn't quite believe how much of my mental capacity had been shredded by the hours of relentless cycling I had subjected my body and mind to in recent months.

I was struggling with longer sentences as I spoke out loud, never mind the level of verbal fluency that would be demanded in order to answer in great detail the competency-based questions set by the panel of people who were interviewing me. This gig would be a million miles from the one I was currently doing.

Of course, overloading your body to the point of exhaustion is detrimental to your brain, too. Studies have shown, based on analysis of MRI scans, that overloaded athletes have slower response times on account of reduced activity in a part of the brain known as the lateral prefrontal cortex, which is important for decision making. From this, it's natural to conclude that you don't make the same good decisions when your brain is in a fatigued state. [41]

Perhaps a cheeky Nando's could persuade them I was the right person for the job. Is food considered bribery these days or plain good manners? It was a little late to throw in the towel now, however, as I was travelling down to London the next day, so I went home and tried to sleep away any anxious thoughts and the nervous disposition I found myself in.

I woke slightly fresher than normal, but still exhausted from the months of abuse I had put myself through in the saddle. I boarded the train, tried to sleep some more, and then woke and stared despondently at some notes I'd been making at the library over the previous few, slightly more productive, days.

I felt so out of sync with the 'real' world, it frightened me. A world of spreadsheets, databases, meetings, emails and office politics. Had I changed so much over the past few years that I could no longer see myself in that parallel, unfamiliar world on the other side of the plate glass walls of the office blocks I'd been delivering to for what seemed like forever? My brother had worked his own way up the Civil Service career ladder over the past decade, and having went through a similar process for a promotion himself just months earlier, I called him the day before the interview, when I'd arrived in Central London.

I was sitting – feeling cramped and lethargic – at a small, two-person coffee table in the corner of a cold, bland, featureless Costa Coffee store on Bethnal Green Road, with endless notes and interview answers, looking blankly into the warm, glowing screen of my laptop. He went through some practice questions for the Higher Executive Officer (HEO) role, and I felt so far out of my comfort zone, it was as if I was playing the part of a blind, deaf and dumb contestant on *Dragons' Den* with no business pitch after a fortnight in Benidorm with Johnny Vegas. Or perhaps I just felt like Johnny Vegas.

The next morning, I woke up, grudgingly, in my small dingy top-floor hostel room a few hours before I would normally do so. I knew I wouldn't get back to sleep, such were the nerves and the adrenaline, so I scampered down to the basement-floor kitchen to quickly shove a few imitation Weetabixstyle biscuits splashed with thinly-disguised milk, and some lukewarm filter coffee, into my dilapidated system. Not the greatest of starts to the day, but it was something to fire up the engine while I raced through all the notes I'd been taking over the last few manic days of preparation.

I went for a casual stroll to nowhere in particular, trying to block all the external distractions building up from all the interview preparation. It was very rare that I ever went for a walk, and was probably some kind of a substitute for the lack of cycling, but I was craving the calmness and tranquillity of the closest possible park to help calm my nerves and slow down an overactive mind so that I slowly start thinking a little more clearly. I arrived back and got ready at the hostel. Having succeeded in calming myself, I started to relax a little after the walk. I blasted myself with a cold shower, to cool down from the walk and to cool myself for the day ahead, but also to shock my body into action.

Having walked the three miles to the interview location on Victoria Street, a few hundred yards from Westminster Bridge, I was starting to get rather hungry. Well, I was suffering from a growling stomach, which meant hunger, nerves or quite possibly both. The onset of extreme hunger had featured prominently on days off over the past few years. Very rarely did this ever occur to me on the bike, as my stomach was nearly always bloated. So my body had simply learnt to redirect blood and oxygen away from my digestive system and towards my legs and lungs instead.

This constantly bloated stomach had become a near permanent feature over the past few years, gradually becoming more prominent and protruded as my hours had increased since finishing university. I had never really given it time to settle and recover properly. Only, when having a rare week off from work, or a few days off in a row, would my stomach start to resemble anything like the washboard of a stereotypically fit cyclist. No one would ever have believed that I was cycling for such long periods of time if they had closely inspected my waistline.

Even when I went on dates, I would have to allow for a few strategic days off beforehand; not only to help my brain begin to formulate enthusiastic, elongated sentences after long periods of little communication and dialogue outside of work and the comings and goings in the house, but predominately to help my stomach shrink down to an acceptable size so that the large size shirts that were hanging in my wardrobe would fit somewhat more comfortably around my torso.

I even managed to make this a lot worse during a particularly tough spell in Manchester, when using creatine as a placebo in order to sustain my full-time hours when I was struggling during a particularly brutal two-week period in December. Getting home and showered, I would have the appearance of someone who is heavily pregnant. This feeling lasted the whole time I used it, so I quickly came off the creatine, as it really isn't suitable for someone cycling 55 hours a week.

It is much more suitably designed for people needing to develop explosive power, for weightlifting or short sharp exercises requiring significant power. Not for an idiot cycling around town, trying to find any conceivable shortcut to keep himself going for longer, rather than the tried-and-tested approach of rest and recovery.

You may have heard of 'fight or flight' – the adrenaline-based state we enter when faced with particularly stressful challenges. This is also known as the sympathetic nervous system, and prepares our bodies (all of our organs) for a fight, or physical challenge; or for flight, by preparing to retreat. The other side of this is 'rest and digest', the parasympathetic nervous system which slows us down and prioritises blood flow to our internal organs and reduces our heart rate – and your body isn't able to do both these things efficiently at the same time. When you're cycling, blood flows away from the gastrointestinal tract and into your muscles and lungs. The harder you ride, the less blood there is available for digestion. Research shows blood flow to your gut plummets by 80 percent when you're at maximum effort.[42]

Normally, around 25 percent of your overall blood and oxygen is being pumped to your digestive system, so that it works efficiently. When you're cycling, your intestines don't get as much blood flow as they normally would, which ultimately means your digestive system doesn't move food as quickly. Things stay in your colon longer, which can lead to more gas.[43] That gas builds up in your abdomen, leaving you looking like anything but the very fit cyclist like you really should be.

Breathing heavily when cycling can also lead to the same bloated feeling, as you suck in a lot of air as you exert yourself consistently over the length of a shift. Your body uses more oxygen, producing more carbon dioxide as a result. Instead of air going straight to your lungs, it can make its way down to your digestive system, leaving you feeling bloated and puffy.[44] Drinking lots of water is also known to lead to bloating, and as you sweat and your body temperature rises, fluid retention from a lack of sodium can also lead to a swollen feeling.

These symptoms usually occur together, not separately, if you work more than four or five hours at a time without sufficient breaks or rest periods. A flat stomach is not something I have ever had during my full-time career as cycle courier. It's much flatter as I sit week-after-week at my desk and write this book, having taken a prolonged break from cycling to get it done, but don't let that put you off cycling.

So, on days where I would skip breakfast and get something once I had reached the city centre, or having had breakfast after quickly getting ready and onto the bike, my stomach simply wasn't capable of digesting the food I had hastily put into it. Your blood and oxygen are being redirected to other parts of the body that most need it due to the constant and continuos state of all day cycling.

Waiting an hour (or longer, ideally) after eating largely solves this problem, allowing your stomach the time, blood and oxygen it needs to digest the contents of a meal – something I never properly adhered to when working long shifts that I had booked through the app, waking up just in time before having to cycle into town for the day. Which helps explain why I couldn't squeeze into my more formal clothing when I wanted to go out and enjoy myself!

* * *

To solve the growling stomach problem, I headed towards Westminster Bridge and into the nearest Tesco Express. I had an hour to spare, so more than enough time to fill my face with any assorted treats I could find on special offer to feed the beast, by which I mean my stomach. A carrier bag full of biscuits, Haribo and smoothies helped in this respect.

Then after finding the nearest public toilets to help release the pressure and ease the bloated stomach, which CHARGED you for the privilege to use them (that's neoliberalism for you) – I was ready for battle, in a government building next door to the Churchill War Rooms.

All the instant sugar certainly helped during the intense three-hour interview process. It had felt very unfamiliar and way outside my comfort zone to have to engage my critical faculties so arduously for three long hours - in a way that I simply had not done at all for the last few years, outside of debating in class. Much like getting a couch potato trying to do three hours of cycling, it was engaging a completely different set of faculties that I had tended to underuse in everyday life.

But I made it through the next three hours, pride intact, and celebrated by meeting an old housemate, Sam, for a few too many; I was still high from the feeling of getting through the afternoon without any major slip-ups, or perhaps from the excess bags of sweets I'd consumed just before battle had commenced.

I found out six weeks later that I had not been successful for the role of trade trainee at the Department for International Trade. They thanked me for my interest in the position and for staying awake during the whole process, which was kind of them. In fairness to myself, it went as well as it could have done, but I had set myself pretty low standards after the three weeks of preparation I had haphazardly put together – while my body had screamed at me to rest and recover during the whole process. In my head, in the weeks between waiting to find out and the interview, I had fully prepared myself for a new life and new career doing a job related to my master's degree, but in the end I came up short.

Once I had got over the crushing disappointment of missing out on the chance of a stable career somewhere new and different, I quickly rationalised my current predicament of still working as a courier after weeks of imagining a new existence and working in an office with all the added pressure and responsibility that this would entail once again.

Cycling quickly helped to dispel the overwhelming sense of disappointment I was feeling after having put so much into preparing for the interview. It was my reward system for when things had gone well, such as after my essays and dissertation during my time back at uni, but it was also my way of processing bad news – such as being rejected for an imagined, so-called dream job – so that I could get through to the other side in better overall mental health.

Cycling has provided me with the ability to escape and seek answers to such problems all my life, and I needed its restorative features now more than ever as I dealt with another setback in life. This was probably interpreted as cycling away from my problems, which is exactly what it was. My brother was more disappointed than I was when I phoned up to tell him the bad news. He perhaps feared that I would be put off from future applications for similar jobs.

And for a while I was, as for a few weeks I used cycling as an escape, a comfort blanket, my pat on the back for trying and failing. It was my own personal way to process the rejection. After he had helped me immensely with the job application – for weeks he had put so much effort into preparing me for every eventuality – I now felt as much guilt towards him as I did despondency for not getting the job itself.

It was time to go full-out post-fight Ricky Hatton now. The disappointing feeling of not getting the job – the pent-up anxiety and then finding out after an excruciatingly long wait – combined potently with the overriding relief in knowing that I could still ride my bike for a living. All of this blended with the overriding feeling that I had fought my best fight, and that maybe cycling so much was turning me into a different creature altogether - something I had perhaps subconsciously foreseen during my time back at university. There were so many questions, but only one answer.

It was time to rewind the past six months and party like it was 1989. The winter of discontent had passed. The summer of love was approaching, well, Valentine's Day anyways. Dean had bought tickets for a club night at the White Hotel in Salford. Think of the Phoenix Club managed by Brian Potter (after it was burned down) and you are getting close. It was exactly what I needed in my life.

Dirty, raw, unadulterated, unpretentious fun in a dilapidated nightclub (certainly no hotel!), with people to actually speak to rather than those standing curating pictures and videos of themselves all night long. A proper night out. A Manchester night out. Propped up by the housemate from hell, Dean, throwing more potions my way than came out of Harry Potter's final exam. A weekend that helped me truly release the pressure valves. I got well and truly rat-arsed.

The week previous to that Valentine's Day massacre, I'd experienced an almighty setback. My trusted bike had been stolen right in front of my very eyes as I had walked into the KFC on Oxford Road. It's one of the busiest roads you could ever wish to commute through on your way into or out of Manchester. I still had a somewhat naïve, rose-tinted view of life in the city, so here was still one of the places I would leave my bike unlocked right in front of the glass-fronted shop, as you could see the bike the whole time as you entered and left the place. Plenty of other riders did it, too, as you were in and out as quick as you could throw the food into your square backpack.

I learnt a harsh and costly lesson that day. Complacency breeds failure, and only the paranoid survive. These were my thoughts on that long bus journey back home to Fallowfield, equipped with only my cumbersome backpack, like a despondent tortoise with only his hard shell of an exterior to protect him against the slings and arrows of outrageous misfortune. In retrospect, the thief who managed to get away on the bike did me something of a favour. It was in worse condition than I was.

Going uphill the chain slipped off every few metres, while the brakes were non-existent, and the wheels moved with the same poise and elegance as the Arkansas Chugabug on *The Wacky Races*. I had worn my bike, as well as myself, firmly into the ground. I looked after neither with the level of commitment or care required in this kind of work.

I had only been in KFC for twenty seconds tops. Yet Dick Dastardly had managed to scoop up my bike, cock his leg over it, keep the chain on it while pedalling away and successfully steer it down the nearest side street in the time it took me to pack up someone's bargain bucket meal and turn around. I rang 101, the crime-reporting number, told them my bike had been stolen, then waited for the call handler's apathetic groan, confirming it was nothing too serious, before being politely informed that as it wasn't strictly an emergency it would take a bit of time to get someone out to take a statement.

I was put on hold, and as the rain started making its presence felt for the umpteenth day in a row, I thought it best to head home and lick my wounds rather than get caught in another Pennine deluge, waiting around to justify to a Police officer why I hadn't just locked my bike up in the first place.

I had auditory hallucinations of Muttley's mischievously high-pitched wheezing on the bus home as I browsed the web on my phone for a new bike to keep me in employment. I arrived home forty-five minutes later, crawling through the busy traffic out of the city centre on the so-called magic bus packed full of students and workers – all looking round suspiciously and wondering if I was perhaps completing deliveries using the slowest possible bus route in and out of the city centre. It was only marginally slower to walk home than it was to use the magic bus at such busy times of the day, but I was in no mood for any of that as the rain trickled down the passenger side window of my seat, perfectly complementing my current mood.

The fine folk at 101 were still keeping me waiting as I flopped myself into the dreary-looking house - Dean's club speakers and empty vodka bottles the only things to welcome me back as I closed the door behind me - so I decided to cut my losses and admit defeat. What chance would they have of catching someone able to manoeuvre my battered old bicycle away from right under my own eyes and actually pedal it away in a straight line.

He must have been Special Forces – that or endowed with superhuman speed by whatever substance or beverage (special brew) he'd been consuming that day. I had a nap to help ease the crushing disappointment, then jumped out of bed, made a cuppa and sat in front of the computer screen looking for my next cheap-but-cheerful partner in crime.

Still, at least it meant a few days off work to help me recover from the past few months of full-on, flat-out riding. Four full days off to eat, sleep, recover, let my stomach learn how to properly digest food again, and most of all treat myself to a shiny new bicycle. To be honest, any excuse would have done, as it really did need replacing.

So after a few twelve-hour sleeps, with time to properly reset both hardware and software, body and brain, I went from Windows Vista to Android, from a 1.3 megapixel camera to a Nikon, from a worn-out rusted, busted figure incapable of formulating proper sentences due to complete exhaustion to an altogether more upgraded version of myself - ready for a full weekend of debauchery with Manchester's newly self-appointed night tsar, Dean.

My fresh new bike was delivered early on the Friday morning of the Valentine's Day Massacre. My immediate instinct was to take it around the block for half an hour, showing it off and wearing it in. Much like getting those new trainers or football boots you'd begged your parents to buy you for the previous six months when growing up, either as a condition for passing all your exams or for simply going back to your bedroom and pretending to do some homework. That feeling of getting something new and shiny never changes, no matter what age you are, though I admit that it's a million times better as a kid, because you didn't have to work your arse off to pay for it in the first place.

Well, I had, and it felt like upgrading from a Fiat Panda to a Fiat 500. It was a newer model, slightly more expensive, slightly less shit, but not something you'd really want to be seen in as you pass your mates in town. But at least it was something Dick Dastardly wouldn't be too bothered about getting his hands on down Oxford Road again if he found it chained up next to a shinier, more appealing mountain bike or electric jobbie.

Yes, *never* buy too good a bike for the job of a cycle courier, amigos. You're a sitting target. A moving target too, as some people won't mind jumping you for your hard-earned vehicle if they think they can make a few quid from it. Some people make a living from this vein of thievery, though probably not from my old bike. Perhaps the thief might have got four tins of homebrew for it if he had known how to haggle at the highest level.

But the new steed, despite its somewhat lacklustre perfor-mance, was still a shiny, fully functional, smoothly rotating, brand-spanking-new workhorse, which enabled me to start making money again. Unlike my ex, it was at least able to go in the direction I wanted it to without too much effort and to also glide along effortlessly without the continuous angle-grinding sound my stolen bike had started to make of late.

It seems sensible and pragmatic advice to clean your bike every day to help keep it running smoothly. I could never find the enthusiasm or energy to do so at the time. I would simply end up replacing parts rather than clean them most days to keep the bike in any kind of functioning state. I was treating my body with a similar disregard. Ignoring the warning signs. Letting things build up until something finally snapped or simply became unfit for purpose.

So off to work I went, rather than sit at home and relax before clubbing, safe in the knowledge I would be returning a few hours later, in time to finally let off some steam for my first big weekend off in Manchester. When things are busy and you get in the groove, you completely forget about time and place. Remember Csikszentmihalyi and his concept of flow.

Manchester is a very busy urban zone, with small distances for most deliveries, most of them inside the city centre, an area bounded by the ring road. Unless, that is, you are one of those masochists who are happy to travel a further two miles out to the inner city for an extra fifty pence. If you are, good luck to you, but we have nothing in common.

It was getting late, and I'd been waiting around fifteen minutes for an order from TGI Fridays, which wasn't too unusual for a busy Friday night. I was willing to wait, as I wasn't in the usual laser-guided, every-second-counts mentality: to make as much money as possible from every second of the day that passed. I was wearing in my new bike, so was in a great mood for the festivities that lay ahead of me that night.

Places were busy, staff are overworked, chefs are swearing their tits off at the fact that they are now cooking twice as much food, for both diners and delivery firms, yet are still being paid the same paltry wage as five years ago. Restaurant staff bearing the brunt of changes to increased custom to Restaurants, without reaping any of the additional rewards. We get it, really we do.

Inspired by that good old Friday evening feeling from days gone by, I left the restaurant with the newly prepared food and headed down the street onto Deansgate. It was cold and crisp, a typical February night, but most crucially it had stayed dry. A rare late-winter night that had been good to me, I thought, as I was gently guided by the continuos streaking effect of the blurring lights either side of me down towards where the customer would be gleefully waiting, cap in hand.

I looked up at Beetham tower pulsating panoramically at the end of Deansgate, like a vibrant disco mirror ball exploding out of the ground below, pulling me instinctively towards it with a mesmerising aura of reflective energy and purpose, the giant glass skyscraper a decadent reminder of the weekend ahead and a feeling that anything is possible.

I was approaching a fellow Deliveroo rider as I cruised more intently with a few heavier pedal strokes, head slightly over the handlebars and out of the saddle, to my final drop-off for the night. Call us roo riders, rooers, rookies, guroos, rood boys – however you like to live your life, I suppose. I gave the customary nod as I went to overtake him, an acknowledgment that we were both engaged in the Friday night rush-hour struggle together, brothers-in-arms. Then I looked down towards his bike, like all keen cyclists do with fellow cyclists, like all keen car fanatics do when they see similar cars on the road.

I noticed it was a similar bike to my ex. Same colour, same make, different back wheel, but it looked as beaten and bruised as the same bike I'd had stolen the previous week. It couldn't be mine, I thought to myself, instantly dismissing the idea as the traffic lights ahead turned red and we both thought of slowing down. No one would have the brass neck to do the dirty on one of their own, surely? But as I analysed the rest of the bike, it was slowly starting to sink in that this was indeed my bike.

There was one huge giveaway. An anomaly that would make it a cinch to pick out in any police identification parade of the usual suspects. The royal-blue plastic bottle cage, standing out like a Tory at uni. If it hadn't been for that two-pound bit of plastic Chinese crap that I had welded onto my bike to have something I could shove my water supply into, I would have passed by with just the mandatory nod and been on my way to make my last delivery of the night. This was personal, however, and I was damned if I was going to let my battered, beaten and slightly blue ex-partner leave the scene of the crime without me fighting to get it back. Loyalty to my bikes runs deep, even the ugly ones that have been through the wars with me – perhaps especially them.

Me and this bike had history. It had seen me through the past few years with little to no drama, and as a result I respected it like a farmer does a sheepdog. I screamed at the lad to pull over, waving like a madman while yanking out my earphones; the tranquillity of the atmospheric techno mix I was listening to would not suffice for confronting the altogether more serious situation I now found myself in.

The next hour was a bit of a blur, but the poor lad I had screamed at to pull over on my old bike barely spoke a word of the Queen's English. Having said that, I can barely speak it myself when incensed. It's sometimes hard not to revert to the most primitive and barbaric version of yourself when confronted with difficult or hostile situations. Such language is rarely fit for public consumption, if you consider yourself a half-decent human being most of the time.

On one side of the scale, you have the practised and polished professional telephone voice, the one your friends can never imagine you using, having known you in a completely different way their entire lives. This is the kind and gentle side of humanity, the Dr Jekyll manner, which as a professional person you are obliged to tune into and refine as you go through life. The other side is Mr Hyde, the belligerent savage, aggressive and unprintable when challenged or threatened in any way – the type many Brits quickly turn into on 'Black Eye Friday' each Christmas season.

I was trying my utmost to keep it together. No need to be a complete and utter twat, I told myself. The happy drugs flowing in my brain would hopefully keep this encounter from spilling out into an unnecessarily bitter confrontation of any kind. Try to be a caring and considerate human being, even when shit does hit the fan. Don't reach straight into your top pocket and become the more primitive version of yourself.

What would Jürgen Klopp do in such circumstances, I often thought to myself at times of great difficulty and turmoil, as a proudly adopted Liverpool fan. Probably hug them into submission, give him fifty pounds to get the bike fixed up and send the guy on his way with tickets for the next Liverpool match. That wasn't going to cut it here. Not in Manchester. I would have to take more of a Roy Keane approach to proceedings this time. So I rang the police. Ha! I'd probably be waiting longer than when the thing was first stolen. I'd go through the proper channel this time, though, meaning 999.

It could be a while, I was politely informed once again. It's a Friday night, and there's other, more serious, devious and mischievous crimes to solve, and lots of very drunk people to round up – all of which are more urgent priorities than dealing with the petty theft of your bike. I would have to bide my time. So I rang Deliveroo. While it was waiting to connect, I had a mini panic attack thinking of how I should articulate the reason why I couldn't possibly deliver this food to the paying customer just a few blocks down from where I was now standing, stationary, with another rider.

How was I going to spin this one? It would sound like

184

complete and utter bollocks if I actually explained to them the exact predicament I currently found myself in. With no police at the scene of the crime, and chances being fairly unlikely that any would ever turn up until a community support officer happened to stumble past on a random patrol down the street, I would have to do some Alastair Campbell-style improvising to convince the Deliveroo call handler that I couldn't travel a mere four hundred yards down the road to drop off a well-earned hot supper for one of their loyal customers.

I got through to rider support. I explained that I was involved in an ongoing situation where somebody's bike had been stolen and I was a witness, and that I was very sorry I wouldn't be able to deliver this poor individual's food at this point in time. I had tried to make amends by suggesting the customer come down the road to meet me for it, but Deliveroo understood and accepted what I had relayed to them.

They told me simply to complete the delivery, log out, and they would restart the order and let the customer know on my behalf. I swiped for the order to be completed, feeling a massive pang of guilt, as I could see the block of flats a short distance away. The unfortunate bugger had tipped me too. I felt an overriding sense of guilt coursing through my tense, troubled body, looking to escape through any available orifice or pore on its way to the surface.

By this time the other rider was also getting restless. He, too, was also likely to be in the middle of an order. I enquired passive-aggressively how he had managed to get his hands on my bike. His broken English was just good enough to explain that he had bought it from a friend of some sort. Well, that friend had likely stolen it from me, I informed him, slightly calmer, but with my hands waving violently like Mussolini during a rallying speech. He looked blank and despondent. Not hugely guilty, but then again it would be difficult to shape the specific contours of your face to look completely innocent in such circumstances.

I told him that I wasn't going to let him keep the bike, and he was slowly starting to understand where the ferocity of my raging rhetoric was coming from. All I could do was keep a hand on the bike, and the guy wasn't making a big struggle of it anyhow, but was in the process of calling somebody himself, to explain the predicament he now found himself in. I didn't have a clue what my next move would be. My critical thinking had slowly degraded since I had made the step up to full-time hours in the job, to the extent that I now had the cognitive ability of Homer Simpson when faced with any kind of complex dilemma.

How could I feasibly stop this person from going on to complete his delivery? How could I pass the time waiting for a copper to come and referee the situation I now found myself in? How could I even get the two bikes home with me once or even if this situation was fully resolved? My brain was coming up with all the ways this extraordinary event might play out, and I wasn't taking any comfort in having to engage in such an invidious stand-off.

I rang my ever-so-reliable housemate Dean. He owed me a favour or ten after all he had put me through during the winter. He would be finishing work around this time, I dearly hoped, and with any luck he wouldn't be starting the weekend too early without me by his side. In fairness to him, he grumbled some incoherent sentences to the effect that this wasn't how he wanted to spend the start of his weekly pilgrimage to Never Never Land.

Me neither, but I wanted my bike back, and some backup if things went south. He said it would take him a while to come to my aid, and I made some heat-of-the-moment promise to the effect that I would party with him all weekend just for the inconvenience I had just caused him.

Talk about making a deal with the devil. After the hostile hospitality of the homemade Hacienda in my humble abode for the past six months of near-constant weekend parties, I still somehow found myself in his back pocket. It's not like I could do anything else with two bikes, apart from a very long walk home. That would take about three hours, and the weekend had already landed. Something I wasn't willing to sacrifice once again for the sake of my total obsession with cycling.

I messaged him with my exact location, told him to step on it and went back to Defcon 1. The guy with my old bike was getting impatient by now, as was I. He was explaining in slightly clearer broken English how he had acquired the bike, from some dodgy back-lane shop near the Arndale Centre. I was playing the role of Judge Judy, a touch less flamboyantly or certified, trying to get all the facts together. I was in no mood for the back and forth, I just wanted the old bike back and to be on my way. I scanned the road, up and down Deansgate, for any sign of divine intervention.

I was in luck. A police car was coming towards me. It was a busy artery of the city centre by any stretch, but like most things in life, they usually only come around when you least expect it. Nothing was going to stop me from exercising my inalienable right to reclaim my property that Friday evening.

I ran out into the road, waving my hands and shouting like a madman - partly to get the attention of the police car, partly to let the proud new owner of my battered old bike know that I meant business. Or that I had just escaped from Broadmoor. Either way, it had the desired effect on both parties. Stand tall, I thought. Keep it together, and engage your critical faculties, and you'll be reunited with it in no time.

The young police officers who emerged from the flashing patrol car were slightly confused but nevertheless reassuringly understanding. I showed them evidence of the legal online purchase I had made on my iPhone. The perpetrator started to employ his English language a little more skilfully now, arguing his case, but it all came down to the little blue bottle cage on that trusty old workhorse of mine. Luckily, I had a picture of the bike and the quirky blue bottle cage somewhere in the deepest archives of my phone photo library from a few years back.

A vault containing old flames and acquaintances from the past decade or so of my random cycling trips, near and far. Every time I scrolled through the reams of photos on my phone archives, it brought back those adventures I'd been on through the years and made me fully appreciate the times I'd had. I'd done most of the trail centres in the North of England and Scotland, and a good few three-day Coast to Coast and Coast and Castles tours, when I had reignited my love of cycling with a bunch of lads I used to work with at the leisure centre.

Some bicycles were better than others. Some gave you nothing but bad luck, and some made you wonder why you stuck it out with them all these years later. But you paid your money and took your choice, of course, and in that regard, there was also the odd photograph of what you'd bought when it was still sleek, polished and naturally alluring, when you were both still in that special honeymoon period, when nothing goes wrong and you don't have a bad word to say about one another. For better or worse, I romantically reminisce. The bike was on the scrapheap, but it had seen me through my first few years as a cycle courier, so there was a deep unwavering loyalty that meant I would fight tooth and nail to get it back.

Remonstrating outside the newsagent's on the corner of St Ann Street, I pleaded my case, managing to string a few semi-coherent sentences together. After all, I had been off for most of the week, so my brain was allowing me the privilege of well-chosen words in just the right order, after not having been able to string together much that was coherent over the previous few weeks and months. The accused stood his ground, arguing he had merely bought the bike from a friend of a friend near the Arndale. Without sufficient evidence of purchase, or being willing to ring his friend to invite him to defend himself at the scene of my citizen's arrest, the case was settled. Claimant collects.

The accused walked away empty-handed, much like I had a week earlier. A cold, broken, beaten, defenseless, crawling misery of a tortoise, still with an order to deliver. He would have been going through all the same emotions as me, no doubt, if his story had checked out as he had argued. His only comfort was the hard shell of a backpack, dragging along like the ball and chain of conscience. He would have gotten away with it, too, if it hadn't been for that pesky blue bottle cage.

* * *

The weekend had now undeniably landed. The screech of worn car tyres echoed with the sound of ruthless purpose in the very same direction I had come from on my half-completed journey just a short time ago. It could only be one person. Window down, car as rickety as my old bike was, Dean was approaching in his black, beaten-up but still turbocharged Mazda. It was a huge relief to see him. Fifty different shades of black-tinted paint reflected off the city lights down through Deansgate, as I waved him down to my squatting location on a quiet side street off the busy main road.

He was probably begging for a big scene, something to warm him up for the weekend ahead. All he got was the elated and ecstatic figure of a cyclist sat at the side of Deansgate, checking over the old bike for signs of abuse and gloating at the fact that all the stars had fallen into place, as he shepherded his prized possessions to get them home and show them some love. The bikes were flattened and compressed into the hatchback boot of the Mazda for the journey back.

Dean had also been on a journey of sorts, picking up his weekend prescriptions, and mine, too. We were both competing for each other's attention on the drive home. One excited over his reclaimed bike and the free supper he would get to enjoy on arriving home; the other over a journey to the heart of darkness to source some decent gear and the debt I now owed him for being such a good mate.

I wasn't listening to him with any real purpose or attention, far too excited by how the night was now panning out. It was going to take something special to bring me down from this nirvana of good fortune. Luckily, that had already been accounted for. Dean's in sales after all, my chauffeur for the next half an hour, until the party really started.

He knows his customer base. Knows how to press the right buttons at the right times. If he had started out his career out with the student loans company, he would have changed repayment plans to coincide with the first big night out of term. Catch them at their best. Catch them on the way up. But always catch them.

We were both coming up naturally in any case. He had just escaped the humdrum Monday-to-Friday world of sales, eager to put himself about around the city, to help blank out the monotony of everyday office life. I was keen to get out into the wider world and tell anyone who would listen that I was now involved with two steel-framed partners, after a recent messy split with the oldest and less attractive of the two.

I brought the bikes into the backyard of the house and gave the old, reclaimed mistress a quick spin around the block to see how decrepit and dysfunctional she still was. Turns out the wheels had been changed, upgraded even. It was fairly sturdy again! In the week since the bike had most likely been flipped, it had been brought back to being a semi-functioning vehicle. Like a payday loan for an item that you wish to repurchase at a later date, but better. All with no hidden charges, other than the next forty-eight hours of my life.

Luckily, there was a massive bag of food to devour before the madness of the evening transpired. Sticky wings, ribs and a bagful of French fries to help us ease into the festivities. I ate most of it, as I would need it most after all. Since it couldn't be crushed up into a line and inhaled through his nostrils, Dean mainly stuck to the more Colombian delicacies on offer that night.

Fast-forward a few hours, and I was now an extra in the

weekly repetition of the after-party clubbing mayhem I'd become so accustomed to over the past few months at home, usually from the discomfort of my own bed. I was now participating in the summer of love in '89. I was 30 years too late, of course, but better late than never, I suppose.

Problem was I was only three years old in 1989, and now I was feeling as naive and vulnerable as a three-year-old child as the party prescription from the night before started to wear off. I wasn't going to be able to bow out gracefully, as it was only half-time after all, and what I really needed was a few buckets of cold water and some fresh oranges to see me through the second half and possible extra time.

Instead, I received a few doses of what is normally needed to knock out a large stallion. Keeping myself upright most of the weekend, I somehow managed to carry out the terms of the agreement I had struck with my housemate during the frenzied drive home on Friday night.

I wouldn't get back on my bicycle until four days later, a complete and utter mess, with barely enough cognitive function to get my leg over it. Throwing up twice, and completing just one delivery during the whole ordeal, I headed home defeated after just 30 minutes on the clock. It was the first time I had ever thrown a sicky in my beloved job. It would cost me dearly, too, knocking me off the hallowed top-priority spot for the hours that you can choose to work.

Cancelling your hours at the last minute meant that your statistics became sub-standard compared with those of others in the app-based system. If those statistics weren't near-perfect (99 percent plus in Manchester), there was always someone waiting in the wings to take that most-prized position away from you. It meant being put back on the late slot.

Next to no guaranteed hours, apart from five or six measly hours spread over the course of the weekend. From hero to zero, and all for a weekend of fun and frivolity. Punished in every sense for my weekend of dubious shenanigans. Talk about riding the white pony. Much better to be riding the bike.

Like they always say – never again….

7

The Ugly

'Everything changes because nothing stays the same.'
Unknown

The good times couldn't last forever.

Once a hobby changes from an amateur pursuit to a full-time profession, or obsession in my case, it's to be somewhat expected that good won't carry on rolling for long. Any economist will tell you that if you're willing to pay people pretty good money and give them a certain amount of autonomy to ride their bicycles for a living, there will quickly be an oversupply of willing and able riders. This recruitment model is how Deliveroo and the other tech-platform delivery businesses have grown so quickly from the ground up.

The lure of good pay when you're first starting to operate, not to mention flexibility, freedom and the chance of being your own boss. Who wouldn't want all these benefits wrapped up in one manageable job? Current riders get their friends and family to sign up through the referral program, earning themselves a few quid in the process, saving the companies huge amounts of time and money in recruitment drives for new and willing riders. Fairly rapidly, there's a vast oversupply of riders to service the demand for orders in any given city or town. Herein lies the problem.

In what other profession do you start by earning an acceptable living wage, but then progressively over time earn less and less money? Every day you are getting better at your profession, at the same time as the number of customers and the size of area that Deliveroo can deliver to also keeps increasing. Ever since the company was first founded, the fees paid to riders for completing jobs have decreased at an alarming rate. Roughly speaking, the fees are about 25 percent less than when I first started (and only likely to drop further as Deliveroo looks to cut costs and increase overall profitability).

This is the reality for thousands of couriers who rely on Deliveroo for a sustainable wage to get them through each month. Once again, there's no sick pay and no holiday entitlement. If you don't turn up, you can't earn money. Rain, sleet, snow, family emergency, vehicle issues, phone issues, network issues, app issues or last-minute plans: all of these factors and many more can stop you from earning a steady income.

If you've had a big one like I described in the previous chapter, and you don't cancel your shift with at least twenty-four hours' notice, or are unable to work your allotted hours, even if incapacitated in some way, then your position in the pecking order will change pretty quickly.

Having near-perfect or perfect statistics is what gave you access to priority shifts. Anything else meant having to fight for a few measly hours outside this top-priority group. In my experience this could transform your weekly earnings of around five hundred pounds into a mere fifty or perhaps one hundred pounds if you're lucky. And there was nothing in between.

Those in the top-priority group were desperate to work as many hours as they were allowed – to earn as much as possible but also to help maintain their perfect statistics – while the ones at the bottom of the priority system were left fighting it out for random hours which happened to appear on the app at times of increased demand, bad weather or when shifts were dropped by those in the top-priority group.

When you were displaced from this elite group, and you still wanted to work on your days off, this meant chaining your phone to your side, waiting for notifications to ping you into life. It was a case of hoping for extra hours to become available and dropping everything when they did. When the phone alerted you to these additional hours, this led to a mad rush to click a few buttons before someone as desperate to work as you were got there first and snapped them up. Sometimes you were the one who got lucky from randomly scrolling through the app and being first to the punch.

Looking back, this was something of a mixed blessing, as you always needed the time off to allow your body to repair itself. Sometimes having a full week off would only just about allow me to start feeling anywhere near human again and recover some of the more creative side of my brain, which had simply shut down when I was overdoing the hours.

It can be a myopic existence at times. Studies have shown that overexercising not only leads people to be far more impulsive, but a specific part of the brain – the left side of the middle frontal gyrus (or MFG), known for its role in decision-making – is much less activated. [45] Reading, any other kind exercise or activity, and applying for jobs only became easier to do when I had given myself enough time off to unwind and wake up the bits which had shut down after long bouts of cycling.

Since the job had become so addictive, it almost hardwired my brain to become dependent on the constant exercise and the feel-good endorphins, to allow it to function as normal. Again, think back to Tyson Fury and Ricky Hatton. That lack of structure and constant expenditure of energy, and the endorphin release it leads to, soon changes how your brain processes the monotony of daily life outside your high-intensity routine. You start to oversleep, overeat, overcompensate for the lack of feel-good signals being processed by your brain when in recovery mode.

I recently read an article describing how Tyson Fury was masturbating seven times a day ahead of his heavyweight rematch in order to keep the 'testosterone pumping'.[46] While I wasn't quite up to heavyweight standards in that department, it gives you an idea of what your body is doing behind the scenes during and between bouts of extreme and prolonged physical exertion.

Not knowing when you are going to start earning a full-time wage again adds to the pressure building up in the cauldron, and things can unravel pretty quickly unless you keep a lid on things. It feels much like I imagine depression must be to those with naturally low serotonin levels. As essentially that is exactly what you are doing to your body in order to constantly feed it the high-intensity exercise you feel you need to keep those happy chemicals pumping around your brain.

To climb the ladder back up to the top-priority group, you needed to work as many additional hours as possible, work every single peak shift that becomes available, and hope somebody like me has been stupid enough to overdo it and drop some hours in the process. You pray for the chance to prove yourself once you've managed to get back to the top with those elite couriers, busting a gut, day in, day out, to carve out a living.

It really does take over your life in ways that you eventually begin to realise are actually the opposite of the dream you've been sold of becoming your own boss - doing things on your own terms while making a decent living - along with all the benefits of having a seemingly flexible work/life balance.

The ability to unite and take collective action is something that has brought many working in the gig economy closer together. The first strike action I was made aware of was during my time in Manchester, a few weeks into the drought period when I wasn't able to pick up many hours and felt chained to my phone as a result, praying for more hours to become available on the app. And eventually the app did start to release a lot of hours not normally available to anyone outside the top-priority group.

Great, I thought. A chance to start working more hours and moving my way slowly back up the Deliveroo ladder. Full-day shifts were becoming available too, which were much more preferable to the cold, wet, miserable intermittent nights I'd become accustomed to since the Valentine's Day Massacre.

Feeling suitably revitalised after a few weeks away from the intensity of all-day cycling, I headed out to start the adrenaline-fuelled delivery rounds all over again. After completing a few successive double deliveries (which by this point was quite rare during the day), and realising that work was a lot busier than the normal Tuesday afternoon shift I'd become accustomed to, I started wondering what had happened to all the regular faces I was used to seeing darting in and out of the city at this time of the day.

In fact, there were hardly any roo riders about at all. At Five Guys, while waiting for a double order with a backlog of other orders not being picked up, and sensing something in the air, I asked the restaurant manager why there were way more orders than usual for what was typically a much quieter weekday in the city.

"Everyone is striking," he barked, gravely signalling to the terminal bleeping at him and his staff, demanding they make more and more orders as they came through at a rapid pace.

"We were only told this morning by Deliveroo," he conceded as he smashed several more patties down onto the grill.

"First I've heard of it as well," I say to him, now understanding how the extra hours I've managed to obtain have been gifted to me by those currently on the picket line, which must have started gathering somewhere out in the city. I was faced with the mother of all dilemmas. While I supported the causes of the strike being organised, and wanted to join in out of solidarity with my fellow riders fighting for better conditions, I also needed to make some money to help pay my rent.

And I couldn't drop these hours without twenty-four hours' prior notice, as that would knock me off the top-priority spot once again – relegating me to another few weeks of paltry pay and being chained to my phone waiting anxiously for extra shifts to appear. That paltry wage wouldn't even cover the copious amounts of food I now needed to keep me moving over the course of any given week, never mind the rent.

As I left Five Guys and navigated St Peter's Square, the central hub in and out of Manchester for many working in the city, I caught a first glimpse of the striking riders as they gathered in this busy artery to make their voices heard. Like a proverbial rabbit caught in the headlights, and facing the prospect of being labelled a scab for the rest of my career in the Northwest, I sprinted like hell, hoping to avoid the awkward situation I now found myself in.

It's not like I had anything to feel particularly guilty about, having only been working full-time in Manchester for a matter of months and being unaware of any groups or unions representing delivery couriers at the time. The Industrial Workers of the World Union (IWW) had helped organise the strike on behalf of the forty-odd Deliveroo motorcycle riders, representing 80 percent of Deliveroo's cohort of lunchtime couriers. They were striking over lower fees and a change in the priority system that meant riders with motorcycle accounts weren't allowed into the city centre. [47]

Still, the fact I was able to regain my hours while others were out fighting for better conditions left a bittersweet taste in my mouth. The rest of the week was spent trying to avoid eye contact with any of my full-time comrades when I was out and about. I was fearful of the repercussions of not joining the strike action, while also making a pretty solid week's earnings at last, spending a good few hours on that Tuesday afternoon playing real-life Tom and Jerry trying to avoid being spotted by the striking crowd on their commendable protest through Manchester city centre.

This was to be a sign of further disruption to come in the longer term, as Deliveroo continued to grow exponentially from city centres to inner-city areas, suburbia and far beyond.

As a result of the huge growth in demand, the original shift-booking model did in fact change to accommodate the greater number of riders that were being taken on - new faces seemingly popping up every other week when out and about doing the rounds. No longer would this system be based on booking in scheduled hours, depending on overall demand levels throughout the day and week, with priority given to those riders with the highest overall scores within this statistics-based meritocracy.

Something had to give, as the more riders that came through, striving for perfect stats to work full time hours, the more likely it became that the system would be rendered useless once everyone, sooner or later, was attaining perfect stats: by working full-time hours and not taking any time off whatsoever and repeating every single week. As it came down to the number of hours worked overall, it would always be those full-time couriers who attained those maximum hours from the previous week – desperate to maintain their maximum allotment of hours for the following week, and therefore their spot at the top of the system – who would be completely unable or unwilling to take additional days off or any holiday time whatsoever.

The system had become completely inflexible to those working full-time hours and largely inaccessible to those who weren't. Deliveroo could now use this inflexibility to their advantage and to the detriment of all those riders who had worked their way to the top of the priority system, fighting tooth and nail to maintain their statistics.

Most areas now changed to being a 'free login zone', a concept which had already been rolled out in places like London, Brighton, Oxford and Cambridge, where riders competed for large numbers of orders. UberEats operates on the same principle - essentially anyone with an account can work, which makes earning a steady or consistent income with UberEats almost impossible. Stuart (a logistics partner of Just Eat) operate in a similar way, with the same problem faced by couriers as UberEats.

Essentially, this enabled anyone with a Deliveroo account to be able to work whenever they wanted, night or day, without pre-determined hours booked through the app. In theory this was Deliveroo championing the flexibility card once again, offering riders the chance to work whenever they wanted. Most importantly, from a legal perspective, it meant sidestepping and future proofing themselves against the possibility of its riders being seen as employees and not self employed contractors - as riders were now choosing the hours they wanted work rather than working to a fixed schedule, and were now able to deliver with other platforms while still working for Deliveroo at the same time.

In practice it meant a much larger pool of willing and able riders flooding the area, driving down the number of jobs that any one rider might be able to obtain. This in turn drove down average earnings for many full-time riders, as the large influx of riders was far greater than the overall demand for orders being placed. Gone were the days of having a constant stream of jobs being offered to you morning, noon and night, where a limited pool of riders could pick and choose from a glut of potential deliveries available to the cohort that was working a particular set of hours, as with the previous booking system.

This shifted all the remaining power from the riders to Deliveroo. A lot more riders were out now, working every hour of every day as they were now entitled to, competing for a limited number of orders between an increasingly growing pool of available labour. This translated into much longer waits between deliveries, as well as much further distances to travel as the zones became ever larger, to accommodate more customers and thus to generate more orders overall. The longer distances meant longer getting back into the central area before being offered another job. This chipped away further at your weekly earnings, as Deliveroo had cut down on delivery distance fees paid to the rider - knowing with the large influx of riders on the new system that these jobs were much more likely to be accepted and delivered.

As a result of all these changes, earnings plummeted. Distance-based fees were lowered further still, based on overall distance travelled to the restaurant and customer's address, and also the time it would take restaurants to prepare the food, which was nearly always much longer than the app (or algorithm) told you. Deliveroo assured its loyal riders that they would continue to make consistently high earnings, stating that the new system would actually benefit the majority of its riders.

Riders were once again very sceptical, and such widespread scepticism was largely justified. In a very short space of time, the job went from paying a fair wage (bearing in mind the lack of any entitlements) to being a minimum-wage job with no guarantee how much you could earn in any given period.

Lots of new riders emerged, seemingly as enthusiastic as I had once been when I first started. Lots of existing riders had also worked their way up the Deliveroo hierarchy from bicycle to E-bike to scooter and also car. Many riders who start out on a bicycle save the money from working long hours to upgrade to wheels that are much faster, more comfortable, less tiring and therefore usually making more money from being able to work longer hours as a higher priority vehicle. It's part of the natural evolutionary cycle (pardon the pun) of the courier, which helps those who wish to make more money, while spending less time massaging sore legs and less of their weekly wages on food in order to carry on working the following week.

I had bucked that evolutionary trend and stayed true to my roots. Stubbornness is a difficult trait to shake off. Convinced I could maintain my aspiration to be a full-time cyclist while earning enough money to fund my increasingly anti-social lifestyle outside of work, things were nevertheless starting to look bleak.

My much mellower housemate, Michael, was looking at relocating as part of his new job to Belgium, which would mean moving from the house in Fallowfield to somewhere new. It would be very short-sighted of me to consider a place on my own, as I was only ever one accident, illness (or hangover) away from not being able to pay the rent and bills on time.

It would be disastrous if I got a place with Dean, who was by now getting into the full swing of life in Manchester, and was spending a lot of time with a girl he had recently met. Not that he's the settling-down type whatsoever, but previous experience had taught me that being a third wheel in a house of two is as close to a living nightmare as it gets. I'm sure many know that same feeling. You feel like a stranger in your own home. Far from ideal.

Maybe this would have translated into fewer house parties in the long term, but I had my doubts and couldn't hang around to take that risk again. I was also worried that another winter in Manchester, living with Dean or not, focused solely on cycling most days rather than other aspects of life, would leave me in a similar (if not much worse) state to the one that I had only recently emerged from, beaten and broken both mentally and physically.

The money I had earned over the winter period had been the best that I had ever earned with Deliveroo, but with little free time or energy to enjoy the fruits of my labour. I was in desperate need of a prolonged period of time off from cycling, and a move back home could provide me the perfect excuse to give myself that break.

I had thoroughly enjoyed my time in Manchester and met some great characters while out working in the city. A few seemed to work as often as me, too, each one sharing the lived experiences of pain and pleasure that they encountered while out most days. Each one recounting the life they had left behind to start all over again, going it alone as a cycle courier. Aspiring authors, musicians, entrepreneurs, photographers; ex-insurance and salespeople, factory workers, students and dozens of others – all out trying to change the course of their lives while they still could.

Each one different and unique, but united by a mutual understanding of what cycling means to them, a passion made stronger by what they were now doing. A shared appreciation of the challenges we faced in fighting through the worst that Manchester could throw at us all on any given day. There's always magic happening on the ground during times of great struggle and social change. *Auf Wiedersehen*, our kid.

* * *

So I moved back to Newcastle, where I was able to have the first proper break I had allowed myself in several years. I finally allowed my body time to slowly start repairing itself from the damage that had been inflicted since first going to full-time hours. From all those aches and pains that you dismiss during periods of earning good money, to the intense demands you subject your body and mind to, week after week.

Your body accepts it. Your mind almost dismisses any feelings of pain as it is constantly being flooded with happy drugs that act as natural pain relievers during such prolonged periods. It feels like an unconscious state of autopilot when putting your body through the grind like this. Drip-fed by caffeine and sugary products throughout the whole ordeal, partly for morale, but also energy, reward and to help numb the pain you dismiss as simply being part of the job.

There's an expression related to the dopamine fix you crave in such circumstances, where *the chase is better than the kill.* It sums up very succinctly the mindset of the dedicated cycle courier.

A few weeks off from work, and another new house share in Jesmond – where I had lived during my master's degree – now living with people who spent their weekends relaxing, helped rebalance my attitude from the one-track mentality that is the inevitable result of non-stop cycling. I had just emerged from the most intense period of cycling I had ever done – six months of ten- and twelve-hour days, six days a week.

Poor interrupted sleep; a pretty poor diet of eating mainly when I was cycling in the city; a terrible recovery routine consisting of lying in bed, sprawled out on the shoddy 'two-man' thinly disguised couch in the living room; attempting to read anything more than a few pages of a book I'd picked up before I fell asleep; and the fact that deep down I had also started to fall out of love with cycling, too.

Being back home close to family and friends meant I had good reasons to leave my bike alone for more than a few days at a time whenever I needed. To recalibrate a little. It took me a few weeks to reconnect with cycling, because at the time I really didn't want to go back to work. I had massively overdone it and was sick of the feeling of being constantly tired and lethargic and unable to do anything outside of being a cycle courier.

As mentally exhausted as I was physically, I was unable or unwilling to delve into other, more sociable, creative activities as and when they came up. I couldn't go mountain biking anymore as I didn't have a car, but perhaps unsurprisingly, the idea of recreational cycling as a way to unwind from full-on couriering had rarely entered my head over the past few years.

Once I'd made it home to Newcastle, I could quite happily have taken three months off from the job, and perhaps this would have been enough time for me to start enjoying it once again, properly refreshed and relaxed. I didn't have that luxury, however, as I was paying rent again and needed the regular income to have some kind of living standard, after blowing a good chunk on food and coffee to keep me in an upright position most days.

The precariousness of my situation was starting to hit home. A few weeks off from work, even with holiday pay, is dangerous enough for many. A few weeks off in this line of work, with no benefits to speak of whatsoever, and the well-earned reserves you've built up from the busy winter period quickly evaporate. I realised that if I didn't start to budget properly, I'd be soon moving onto the instant coffee.

I walked into Newcastle one late afternoon for a coffee and to catch up with a friend. I was still unwilling to go anywhere near a bike until I started to re-humanise again. I read a good few books, applied for the odd job, and distracted myself in any way possible rather than getting back on the bike and back to work.

I noticed many new faces, mostly unfamiliar, as a new cohort of Deliveroo riders raced past me in both directions on the brisk walk from Jesmond down onto the Quayside. While I'd stayed loyal to my trusty bicycle during the time spent in Manchester, everyone else and their grannies had been progressing up the Deliveroo ladder of life – the natural hierarchy or internal promotion to higher earnings.

Riders I recognised back in Newcastle from when I had first started, who had once upon a time declared themselves as dedicated to cycling as myself had been just 18 months earlier, were now flying around the city on shiny, L-plate-covered scooters and E-bikes that would leave me in their dust. Each one I now looked down on with contempt. How dare they!

Now only the clinically insane or the stubbornly single-minded among that initial early group of cyclists were left using pedal power, fighting for the leftover deliveries at the bottom of the proverbial food chain after all the higher-priority vehicles took the majority of the orders on the new vehicle-based system. Cars and scooters were now being prioritised for orders, as these are the fastest vehicles and have to pay insurance to get a licence to do the job. Cyclists were now at the bottom of the list, despite having helped the company to establish itself in the first place with the eco-friendly approach that was so widely praised (and rightly so) back in 2013.

I finally got back on the bike a few days after that leisurely stroll into town, though now I had little enthusiasm, energy, passion or even much idea what lay in store for me. Watching all those other riders zoom past as I settled down near Eldon Square – a natural waiting location and meeting place for many couriers in the city scattered with plenty of benches and a Greggs nearby – I wondered what had happened in this short period of time to change my perceptions of the job from a dream come true to a nightmare on Northumberland Street.

Like a decrepit old antelope among the lions, I was starting to feel completely out of my depth, or simply out of sorts. Waiting for something to come my way while knowing my place in this most unforgiving of ecosystems. At the mercy of bigger, stronger and faster players all around me.

Manchester had been the city of the cyclist: the dedicated tram lines cutting through the heart of it make it near-impossible for motorised vehicles to get around. Newcastle was another matter, full of hills that make cycling more of a challenge and give powered vehicles an even greater advantage. No wonder those who had started around the same time as me had either upgraded to a motorised vehicle or to an electric bicycle, discarding their once-cherished bicycles, leaving me firmly in the rear-view mirror. My earnings had dropped off a cliff and, since coming back to the city, I was bringing home less than the minimum wage for many of the hours that I was now working.

It felt like the beginning of the end, and what would likely be the huge anti-climax of bidding farewell to the job if I managed to find myself something else anytime soon. In fact, I was even starting to regret my decision to come back home, largely for financial reasons, as Manchester also provided the perfect territory for a cyclist to flourish and earn a decent living too.

No hills, a great bunch of dedicated yet idiosyncratic cycle couriers, great independent shops to peruse while working, and a constantly busy zone to work in – despite the increasing number of riders recruited to serve the growing demand. In fact, I realised that this situation had been spoilt only by my living arrangements and my compulsion to work nearly every single day without fail. And the weather, of course.

Back home I had now been pushed to the periphery, and the motorised vehicle had become king. It was the Easter Bank Holiday weekend, and my third day on the job since moving back. Daunting, as I really didn't want to be back at work yet, but unconsciously I had entered into a contractual coalition with cycling way back when. *For better or worse. Get back together, you stubborn, ungrateful bastard. You'll never find another one like that.*

The Easter weekend was usually a very busy time indeed, like most bank holiday weekends of course. I had dragged my sorry, semi-functioning carcass out of bed, ready for a full ten hours' cycling to right the many wrongs of the previous few weeks. Why I couldn't just choose to work a few hours to ease my way gently back into cycling is still beyond me, but I thought a shock to the system would prove sufficient to bringing me back to life – back to the norm of cycling every day that my brain and body had become accustomed to.

I'm not religious in any sense, but I was starting my days with a few metaphorical Hail Marys as I slung a leg over my bike, hoping to bring my cycling career back from this nadir. Once in the city centre, I could sense that today would be a busy day. It becomes instinctual after a while - or else just plain common sense. If there aren't groups of visibly animated riders sat around the usual busy areas of a given zone at any given time on any given day, you are normally in luck.

These groups normally resemble a meeting of the United Nations, with seemingly every nationality present and very heated discussions going on all around. There's usually some kind of unofficial chairperson, trying to keep balanced debates going between members. Politics of some sort is bandied about, with people dropping in and out of debates as jobs allow. New members stand at the periphery, sharing their enthusiasm for this newfound way of making some sort of living. Old stalwarts discuss the good old days when you had the run of the town, recalling how good the money was at a time when children respected their elders.

These committees and subcommittees can be found in every town, city, area or zone if you look hard enough. They are normally a reliable place for newbies to get a good idea of the busy areas within each zone, with riders congregating in such areas according to the availability of orders and popular restaurants close by.

With no such groups gathered around the city on this particular day, I assumed things were looking up. Twenty minutes went by, which is an awful long time to be waiting for an order during a *quieter* period in the city, and even more so when everyone is at home hungover, enjoying a few days off, or watching *Ben-Hur* on the telly - unwilling or unable to cook a satisfactory meal of their own. Something was amiss, and for the life of me I couldn't quite work out what it was.

Maybe the move from Manchester to Newcastle had knocked me back down to the bottom of the so-called priority list, alongside the fresh-faced cycling newbies. Maybe my free food exploits had flagged me as a dangerously irresponsible, greedy and guilty member of the Deliveroo fraternity, as nothing in life is free, after all. Maybe my performance levels had dramatically declined without me noticing, my cycling ability now far below the par set by those fresh young faces who had just started working through Deliveroo.

I rang the company to try to work out what was going on. The zone was marked in the app as 'Busy', meaning that the rider should expect to receive regular offers of deliveries without too much delay. That was the jargon anyways.

"You're through to rider support. How can I help?"

"I've been in town for twenty minutes now, everyone else around me is receiving orders, and I'm getting nothing. What is wrong with my app?" I blustered, half-disheartened, half-angry and frustrated.

"Your app seems to be fine, sir. Please stay connected and you should receive orders in due course," came the reply, with all the charm and charisma that anyone can muster when they have to repeat that same phrase to countless other cyclists twelve hours a day. I hung up the phone and sunk my head in my hands, wondering if this was to be the end of my short-lived cycling career. Maybe it was time to get real, time to finally get a proper job. To re-enter the world of spreadsheets and small talk around the photocopier. Hang up the helmet at last.

A tear started forming in my eye. I sucked it back into my face, and started thinking of other kinds of work I might be capable of doing. Work that involved using my critical faculties, coming together with other humans in conversations that were not related to cycling, even wearing formal clothes again.

It was a lot to consider, but it seemed certain that I wouldn't be able to make much of a living anymore from cycling, as I had for an all-too-brief-yet-happy period of my life. Did my long service to Deliveroo mean nothing beyond soundbite reassurances read from a pre-prepared script of the kind I always came up against whenever I rang rider support?

Darren, one of the remaining cycling loyalists from my first winter in Newcastle came up to me as I considered all these life-changing possibilities. I imagine at that moment I cut a truly lonely figure among all the couriers dashing in and out of restaurants as I stared at the floor disconsolate. Sensing my disillusion and the look of impending doom in my eyes as I met his gaze, he offered the most popular of ice-breakers among couriers (one that became mainstream through taxi journeys - and Peter Kay, of course) as he pulled up and checked his phone for orders.

"Been busy," he offered.

Unsure whether this was a statement or a question, I tried to muster some kind of articulate response. I could sense the positive intent in his voice, but it wasn't enough to stop me bringing the discussion down a few notches to the bitterness and resentment I felt at falling so far down the pecking order.

"Haven't been offered anything, I've been here about half an hour and been on the phone to Deliveroo to ask what's up," I sighed, with little dignity or self-respect remaining.

"I started three hours ago and already made forty quid," he threw back at me, like a red-hot branding iron being pressed into my face.

"I just don't get it, it never seems busy anymore when I come out, and everyone seems to be getting orders while I'm sat on my arse," I complained, checking my phone at the same time, hoping that someone somewhere would heed my prayer on this most holy of holidays. Thoughts of abandoning my atheist beliefs and doing a backdoor deal with God entered my thoughts for a brief lapsing moment.

"You still got a cycling account?" he asked.

"Of course," I retorted. "I'm a cyclist!"

"You need an E-bike account," he countered, looking to his phone as another job was offered to him, which left me feeling even more defeated, still waiting for my first job of the day.

"I haven't got an E-bike, man!" I exclaim, my frustration breaking through the surface in the form of Geordie dialect, threatening to turn this brief friendly exchange into a more hostile encounter altogether. It is generally the case that the angrier a local gets with another local, the stronger the regional dialect that is thrown into the exchange to reinforce the level of animosity involved.

Sensing my errant emotions bubbling to the surface as he rejected yet another delivery that I would now have traded a kidney for, he understood the situation I found myself in and offered his twopence halfpenny-worth to help me out.

"You don't need one. You just need to submit a photograph of one, along with a written note of your rider ID, name and date of birth. You'll get priority on orders above cyclists. Hardly anyone has a cycling account now since you've come back to Newcastle. That's why you're getting nowt. I switched months ago and get non-stop orders again." In the course of his speech, my posture changed from near-foetal position sat despondently on the park bench to hyperalert meerkat. "Ah, really... Cheers, mate!"

He left smugly – or what I perceived to be smugly, as he hadn't been sat around for the past half an hour, freezing –

while accepting another delivery, as I processed the information he'd just offered me. I tried to engage my critical faculties once again. Like wading through mud, I slowly started to trudge through the options at my disposal. I didn't actually know anyone with an E-bike I could take a photo of, to enable me to upgrade my account.

I could maybe enter a bike shop with a pre-prepared card and quickly take a photograph of one. But that would be kind of difficult to do with staff circling like piranhas, hoping that you're actually there to buy something - and with the price tag dangling suspiciously from the handlebar it would be a somewhat difficult task anyhow. I wasn't in the mood to play real-life *Metal Gear Solid* on a day like today. Not with the appearance of a clinically depressed Ninja turtle.

Then I realised there was someone I might be able to ask. A true wildcard option, the Crazy Turk – as I had affectionately dubbed him after a few brief encounters in the city – was always full of beans and wired to the moon anytime you conversed with him. Ayhan, his real name, was someone I'd started talking to as we passed each other between deliveries, usually only very late at night.

He was always animated and never calm, like the steam from a pressure cooker always boiling away in the background. Whenever we seemed to cross paths, he was always bringing up his ability to build E-bikes, never letting me get a word in edgeways, and always eager to speak about his next ambitious project.

He was just the type I always seem to attract, someone who could engage in long bouts of conversation – well, monologue – while I just stood there, seemingly unable to make my excuses and pedal away for a breath of fresh air. Our working relationship had so far consisted of short bursts of polite pleasantries about his prolonged bouts of erratic gambling, his near-obsession with spending money on constructing E-bikes, and his total obsession with shipping a Thai bride over to help him with the cooking and cleaning he wasn't overly keen on doing himself.

He had also tried on multiple occasions to lead me on a two-man crusade to various casinos that he hadn't yet barred himself from in the city. Claiming it as our Christmas party, Ayhan wanted me to join him to help change his luck of the past twelve months. Since I had worked at a betting shop in the past, he was inclined to believe that I was privy to information he hadn't quite figured out himself. Like the house always wins, perhaps?

Every chance encounter we had on the street acted as a form of therapy for him, as he disclosed how much he had lost in various casinos and betting shops on his travels. I suggested that barring himself from all these places would mean he wouldn't be allowed back in again to lose his weekly wages, but by the time the words had even left my mouth he was already getting ready to counter them with something much more important and dramatic than any advice I could offer.

Having sensibly swerved the idea of the two-man Christmas party, partly to hold onto the little pot of money I had accumulated over the winter, and partly to try to steer Ayhan towards a more sensible investment of his hard-earned money, such as a foreign-born bride, I eventually reached out to see if he would be willing to send me a picture of his E-bike, so that I could get back to the daily grind of regular deliveries to help me pay my bills on time.

It seemed every time I bumped into this colourful character, he had a larger arsenal of mobile phones than a staffroom full of teenagers on their first day at McDonald's. Three phones, three delivery apps. No wonder he was able to blow such a considerable amount of money on things I had not had the luxury of doing in years.

I bumped into him, for the first time ever during a day shift, picking up a shopping order for Deliveroo in Marks and Spencer's. Up until now, I had always presumed he was unconditionally nocturnal, having only ever seen him late at night with multiple layers of thick old clothing on. Dressed like a Norwegian fisherman, with the same heavyset features of someone who screamed antisocial hours and everything they entail, I asked him why he was out so early. It was the equivalent of seeing a solo distressed bat on the afternoon school run.

"Money", he abruptly replied, shielding himself from the artificial light streaming out above him, as I quickly started wondering if he slept upside down when not at work. I hurried to the counter, asking the older woman who stood there smiling if my delivery was ready to pick up. I considered getting Ayhan away from the topic of finances. Luckily, as I turned back to enquire about his natural sleeping habits, he was staring intently into the screen of his phone.

He turned the phone around, slightly less animated than before but speaking in his mother tongue, putting me on video call to what seemed like his elderly mother while we were both waiting for our orders at the back of the store. She was lying in bed, looking quite poorly, and I was put on the spot to formally introduce myself to her while I waited for some shopping to be picked for my next job of the day.

"Your mam, yeah?" I enquired.

He stopped, thought, then said, "My mother, yes."

Speak English, Ryan, I reminded myself. "I hope your son is looking after you... and tells you how bad the weather is in this part of the world."

She grinned, slightly confused but happily engaged as she raised her good hand and put her thumb up to acknowledge my swift yet incoherent introduction. I put my left hand around his shoulder and with my right hand used my extended index finger to make small circular articulations near the base of my temple.

"How did such a lovely woman... create such a crazy man?" I tried to tell her through the phone in the most formal English accent I could manage. She pointed her right finger up towards her own temple to make the same international cuckoo gesture, signalling someone with a screw loose, pointing towards the screen and her own son.

We all laugh, and Ayhan told his mother in his native language that in Newcastle, most people considered him a little crazy. She nodded her head ever so slightly and Ayhan translated her words back to me as she sat up from her bed to take a sip of tea.

"She says to you", Ayhan says, smiling, "that anywhere I go, I am considered crazy!"

I waved goodbye to her, and left the shop in a joyful state that continued for the next ten minutes as I made my way to the next customer. I was thinking of all the similarities different cultures share around the world, which effortlessly unite us. Everyone is slightly deranged in their own, uniquely tailor-made way, I reasoned. Just some people are more comfortable showing their more raw, authentic human side than others. People say the Geordies are a passionate bunch, yet the Turkish are right up there in terms of their warm embrace and equal intensity.

* * *

I tried to reach out to Ayhan a few days later on one of his many mobile phone accounts, hoping he would let me speak first before he started to reel off his weekly gambling profit and loss statements.

"I need a picture of an E-bike with my rider ID, name and date of birth on. Can you help me out at all?"

"Bro, I work now, message later what you want," he said before hanging up. Talk about Turkish charm.

Just as he suggested, I messaged him later on through WhatsApp, when I saw he had come online. I got nothing back. Normally when I reached out to him, I got bombarded with profiles of potential partners he had found in one corner of the internet or another. He usually wanted to know my thoughts and opinions on each one, leaning on someone he must have thought of as more responsible, who could offer slightly more sensible and pragmatic advice to mitigate his own tendency to make such impulsive decisions. I normally responded to these intrusions on my privacy with a thumbs-up or thumbs-down emoji, which I suppose he interpreted as a lack of enthusiasm on my part.

On the day in question, when I finally needed something from him, I put the lack of a response down to him being tired. He was among the more manic of the couriers, and based on appearances was even more extreme than me in his work/life imbalance. Darkened eyes, fluffy hair, unshaven for weeks, same clothes worn for work every single day of the week.

Battle scars on work clothing to show that he's been at the deep end of long hard nights spent in the saddle. Not a fair-weather rider out to get some fresh air or a bit of exercise. Think Jack Nicholson towards the end of *One Flew Over The Cuckoo's Nest*. Then picture him on a superfast E-bike after five double espressos and a few lines of superstrength cocaine. Now you're getting ever-so-slightly warmer.

A few days later he messaged me to say that on one of his phones the camera didn't work, another of his phones had no data with which to send the photo to me, and the other he had lent to a friend who needed to work, and he wouldn't have it back for a few weeks yet. So that was the wildcard option exhausted then. I should have known better really.

Scrolling through Facebook one afternoon, waiting for an elusive delivery to fill the time between being idle and feeling useless, I stumbled upon some juicy pictures of my uncle Stephen's E-bike being used on a family getaway. I reached out and asked if he would be kind enough to send through some pictures of the E-bike with my details attached to them, so I could earn a little extra money while still doing my job. He acknowledged the request, somewhat perplexed, and sent through the photos I needed so that I can change my account status to that of an E-bike.

I think in the delirium of it all I may have offered a few beer tokens in exchange. Uncle Stephen, just for the record, I haven't forgotten your most selfless act of charity towards your distant northern nephew. Next time I happen to be passing through South Wales, I will honour my end of the bargain and buy you a pint or two. Only a global pandemic has stopped me from completing this task any sooner, but I'm sure you already put two and two together on that one.

Back to earning a living. It felt good to finally hear the familiar beeping noise of regular orders coming through on my app once again. Thoughts of signing up for Just Eat and Uber Eats had long been boiling away, but due to the longer distances involved, and not being able to see where deliveries were going before accepting them, I pushed those ideas aside for now, as I could now go back to making a living using just Deliveroo.

Going into a busy McDonald's has made me feel more and more nauseous the older I've got, and as the majority of orders riders receive on the other two platforms tend to come from McDonald's restaurants, I thought it best to avoid them for now. I have the same issue with Primark – far too overwhelming an experience to ever consider going in for a 99p bargain.

For a variety of reasons, leaving the city centre for deliveries never appealed to me. There was the safety in numbers you find in the city – the presence of other people on the streets – while outside that zone, there was an increase in broken glass and hooded menaces, and also far too many hills around Newcastle for my older, increasingly weary legs to cope with over the course of a day of constant wheel turning and pedal grinding.

It was basically much harder work for not much more money. I would leave those jobs to the Lycra lads, the much-younger, fitter, faster and leaner cyclists of the Deliveroo fraternity hoping to beat their personal Strava scores and increase their heartrates to over 160 bpm just for the hell of it. Lads with fresher legs and super-slick road bikes, built for hills and pain. I was 33 by now, but felt ready to retire.

These hard nuts were in fact the most likely to be working for much shorter spells, after college or uni, getting as much bang for their buck as possible. The first few months of the job I had done just as they did, accepting any type of delivery to any location. The road bike prioritised speed over comfort. I was never of the mindset just to take my time during those early days – always treating the experience like a game of *Mario Kart*, eager to find any possible edge or dastardly shortcut to beat the rest of the competition (or just myself perhaps).

But once you step up the hours you work, and you realise you need some fuel left in the tank for the next ten-hour shift the following day, you soon learn to prioritise the easier and shorter deliveries whenever you can get them. Maybe what I really needed was an E-bike, not simply an E-bike account. *For better or worse, Ryan, for better or worse. Stop complaining.* I was now in it for the long haul, with little interest in applying for other, 'proper' jobs since being back in Newcastle and getting regular deliveries again.

I needed to conserve my energy, to drink coffee at regular intervals, to eat handfuls of nuts and dark chocolate whenever possible, and to pace myself for the long days I was now becoming accustomed to yet again. But trying to avoid the steep gradients I had successfully avoided while in Manchester – as there they didn't exist – is very difficult in Newcastle, a city that slopes up steeply from the Tyne.

Choose your battles carefully, that's the name of this game, for days can become long, hard, lonely, draining affairs when you're out in the saddle. Sometimes the briefest of friendly exchanges between restaurant staff and customers can be the only mental stimulation you receive all day. Sometimes this can be a blessing, like the times when Ayhan had been unloading his multiple stresses deep into my subconscious at regular intervals for days on end.

However, the group interaction of working together as part of a team in a nice, warm environment is something you can really miss on long, dark, cold winter nights, when it's only you all alone battling the elements to deliver someone's well-earned little treat within an acceptable timeframe.

It can be difficult to build up meaningful work relationships as a courier. No two riders have the same, structured routine or work the same set hours. Each person works their own individual schedule, so going to the pub at the end of a shift, or the much-anticipated Christmas party, doesn't exist in this line of work. You sometimes meet a fellow rider for a coffee in the middle of a shift, or stop for five minutes in between jobs to share a collective moan or a story on a rude restaurant you have just picked an order up from. But many riders are simply there to make a living. As a cyclist, having an extended lunchbreak can also knock you off your stride, so a lot of the time it makes sense just to carry on and delay the hearty meal until you arrive home later on.

You start to appreciate the struggles faced by Travis Bickle in *Taxi Driver* a little better. The solitude can get to you during those late-night shifts battling the elements. I wasn't quite ready to shave my head and cleanse the streets, but the graveyard shifts bring with them a certain feeling of existing outside the normal rhythm of daily life.

At least Travis had a roof over his head. In fact, looked at objectively, things really weren't that bad for him. If the film had been made through the lens of a cycle courier, on the other hand, the main character would surely have deteriorated a hell of a lot quicker than what resulted from driving a taxi around the city.

Take the constant need to find a suitable place to empty your bladder. Gravity can hit at any time when stood upright after dismounting from the bicycle every few hours, so it's important to remember to use the toilet when you are near one and feel the need. This may seem like a simple remedy, but when you cycle for very long periods without ever really stopping, it is all too easily dismissed. I very rarely followed this rule for the first few years on the job.

A king-size breakfast when I woke up, followed by a strong espresso with plenty of honey or a litre bottle of Lucozade, would usually set me up to fire on all cylinders for the day ahead, only occasionally stopping for a loo break if a restaurant waiting period allowed me enough time. The human body can be remarkably adept at tricking you into blocking the urge to urinate when you are unable or unwilling to visit the little boys' room.

Think of long car journeys. Faced with the overwhelming need to relieve yourself, you somehow miss the turn-off and carry on past the services, but stubbornly resist the urge to turn around and lose time. Despite noting that the next services are fifty miles away, you persevere with the journey, and after a few minutes you have somehow forgotten your discomfort and suppressed the urge to pee, despite your inflated pot belly telling you otherwise. It's exactly the same on a bike. All day long I could go without a loo break, despite numerous pitstops at Greggs for savoury and caffeinated goods.

After a while, however, it would start to weigh me down. Feeling that extra baggage between my hips I would soldier on regardless, trying to block it out, much like those long car journeys on the motorway. Anatomically, this effort of suppression is aided and abetted by the remarkably robust detrusor muscle, covering your bladder, a smooth muscle under voluntary and involuntary nervous control that comes in very handy in preventing your bladder from suddenly exploding in such circumstances.

Of course, going hours on end without relieving yourself does have consequences. Even a young man's bladder is not immune and an occasional release of pee to save yourself from potential internal ruptures is not uncommon. These mishaps can be made more likely by things such as coffee, Coca-Cola or alcohol. *Gulp.* Over time, I had learned to limit my caffeine addiction to double espressos, flat whites and filter coffee throughout the day, in that order.

Most accidents occurred with just enough time for me to flop my little friend out to prevent me from truly peeing my pants (or thermal leggings), and they usually occurred at the very end of a long and gruelling shift, just as I was getting out of the saddle and into a more upright position, reaching into my jacket pocket for the keys to the back gate. In these moments, gravity would almost instantly take over.

All hell could break loose, like a dam bursting, the breaking waters flowing all the way along the backstreet, destabilising wheelie bins and delicate ecosystems alike. A collective sigh of relief followed as I watched as much as a gallon of caffeinated urine (it certainly felt like that much!) on its fast-paced journey to find a drain to descend into.

On occasions I would even time myself. This came with a

habitual sense of euphoria that my bladder had still not burst despite the strain my fluid intake had subjected it to, and the realisation that my detrusor muscle must now be stronger than those of most regular folk on the planet. Not that you can use that kind of boast on a first date to impress a potential partner. Occasionally, my bladder would suffer from the very smallest of involuntary spasms while I was riding, resulting in the leakage of a very small amount of pee in my underpants (the only part of me I've never been able to fully waterproof - yet).

I can assure you, however, for the purposes of health and safety, that no burgers have ever been harmed by these unfortunate accidents. As this can also happen to Tour de France cyclists during long periods in the saddle, I put this newly developed condition down to utter dedication rather than the sheer stupidity and short-sightedness that others might rightfully see it.

Physical therapy and yoga can supposedly help with this condition, as can regular toilet breaks, of course. I am slowly learning to build the latter of the these practices into my schedule, releasing urine at regular intervals throughout the day and hopefully easing the muscles protecting my bladder along the way. It ought to be a regular concern for those couriers who care far more about how much they earn than how far they can stretch their bladder.

If you ever look or feel pregnant while cycling, then, please, get off and take a leak. You can also think about cutting back on alcohol or coffee, too, though I realise that this will be considered a bridge too far by the vast majority of the courier community, myself included.

* * *

Once I had regained the ability to control my bladder over a long day's shift, things were starting to look up. Summer had passed with little drama – long, laidback sunny days eventually merging effortlessly into passive, painless, peaceful nights. All day spent in the saddle, the blessing of sunlight making cycling so much easier at most times of the day, while I tried my best to avoid the peak lunchtime hours between 11am and 3pm which on much warmer days could be particularly draining.

The summer months were quieter periods for most couriers around the country, but much more satisfying for not having to battle the harsh winter elements. Students leave the cities en masse and, along with the rest of the population, try and escape on some kind of a summer holiday in warmer temperatures and new surroundings.

I assumed once again that this could be the last summer doing what I so dearly loved doing, so it wasn't going to be wasted in warmer climes trying to relearn the fine art of drinking to excess. My engine only accepted caffeinated and sugar-based liquids now. Like petroleum in a diesel car, when I tried to drink alcohol by catching up with friends and on nights out, the results were truly horrific.

Call it getting older, call it cycling for long periods every week, but if you place regular, stressful demands on the body, it will start to demand the right fuel to keep going. Put the wrong fuels in and you simply can't perform to the same high intensity for such prolonged periods of time, day in and day out.

This all sounds like common sense, but having enjoyed

a relatively hedonistic lifestyle during long periods in my twenties, it took time and effort, full of trial and error, before I started to fully comprehend what my body really needed. In a nutshell, the better you look after yourself, the more hours on the bike you'll be able to manage, and the quicker you'll recover afterwards. Still, all the free food helped balance out this incessant need for fuel to keep the engine in good working order.

Burgers, sushi, fried chicken, pizza, pasta, burritos, Thai, Chinese, Indian food. It all gets devoured when you're working so many long days in the saddle. Once upon a time when indulging in such rare treats there was a guilty tendency to have to work it off in the gym or by doing a fitness class, or simply limiting such meals to once a week or only on special, one-off occasions.

No longer was this the case. I wasn't blessed with a superfast metabolism by any stretch of the imagination, but a few years of riding my bike all day and every day had taught me to see adequate calorie intake as a necessity and no longer the rare luxury after the kind of superlong ride I used to take on my days off when working at the leisure centre. All these bonus free meals were quickly consumed without coming up for as much as a breath.

Sometimes they were eaten in the course of a shift when energy was low and you couldn't go the distance without some soul food to help. Usually, however, these free treats were saved for when a shift had ended, when both the build-up of anticipation and the mental reward for making it through the excruciatingly long day made the reality of that free meal a mouth-watering prospect.

No guilt. No food coma following the meal. No need to

worry about how to burn off the monster banquet you had just been gifted by some poor soul who hadn't turned up in time to receive their food. Just no-strings-attached, freshly prepared, free food. It was utter heaven, or so the story goes.

I had tried to heed the lesson from the bonking episode in Manchester, and it was still fresh in my mind how gaunt I had started to look and how awful I had started to feel when not riding the bike. Days off in Manchester had been miserable, monotonous, tiring affairs – largely spent trying to consume enough calories for the next day I was working.

Days working weren't anywhere near as fun as they used to be, so I knew I had to recalibrate my work/life relationship in order to get some much needed balance and enjoyment away from the bike. If you only derive pleasure from one source – be it work, exercise, a creative outlet or anything else, for that matter – and you are suddenly unable to do that one activity, then it becomes difficult to derive pleasure from anything else. I trimmed back the hours I'd been working of late, and spent days off reading more books and doing other things that piqued my interest.

Winter was now approaching. I thought back to the previous winter in Manchester – rain and pain. I knew this coming winter would be much easier weatherwise (and sleepwise) and thus easier in most other respects, too. Drier and slightly colder, but you can dress appropriately for the cold, far less so for constant heavy downpours of rain.

Besides, as a result of my Manchester experience, I had amassed a weatherproof, water-resistant, storm-ready wardrobe that would stand me in good stead for the coming winter season, or for any inhospitable place on the planet, for that matter. Third time lucky, I told myself.

I now laughed in the face of the rain coming down in my hometown, as I embraced my third winter doing this job that had become so deeply embedded in my psyche, my soul. There were short heavy spells, passing showers and drizzle, but nothing frightening. In fact, I was beginning to appreciate that Newcastle was a much more forgiving place to ride a bike, hills aside. Not that it couldn't lash down occasionally or even frequently, just much less frequently than the daily monsoons which had plagued the previous winter in Manchester.

This miserable experience instils in you an almost rock-bottom expectation of fair weather going forward. As disgruntled couriers passed with resigned, weather-beaten faces, complaining about the Northeast drizzle, the first thing I always said became a signature catchphrase of mine as I started to appreciate the much fairer climate of my home region. "I've just done a winter in Manchester, this is a piece of piss," I would boldly declare, never failing to get the attention of those around me as I reminded my fellow Geordie riders that things aren't ever as bad as they could be. That the poor folks to the west of us have it far, far worse.

Still, the rainy days do exist and must be planned for appropriately. Your summer road bike with skinny tyres and featherweight frame isn't the most appropriate choice for this more hostile time of year. Bigger tyres, more grip and more stability are the name of the game if you want to stay upright through the many difficult days of a wet and windy winter. A hybrid or mountain bike will be more comfortable for the winter season, when comfort is more important than speed.

In any case, in a part of the world like Newcastle, snow will also slow you down, while frost will stop you in your tracks completely. Only a few cyclists can negotiate the icy conditions that bring the country (or perhaps just the Northeast) to a standstill for a few weeks every year. Normally, these hardy souls are in fact living within the central zones and don't have to brave the treacherous roads in and out of the city. Inside the zones while working in such conditions, it becomes easier to walk between short jobs when cycling becomes simply impossible.

You are only ever one minor or major slip, crash, or fall away from not being able to work. So it's important to understand the risks you are putting yourself through. Many couriers have been left in a precarious financial position after having an accident while working in such conditions and being put out of action for a time. After all, there is no sick pay, even if the 'sickness' is something you've picked up as a result of hazardous working conditions, so it's not like riders have a choice whether to take time off or not when like most other folk they have bills to pay.

On one occasion I was approaching the end of one of these treacherous days, which had been much like any other during the peak winter months when the courier can actually earn a decent living. A ten-hour day with minimal breaks, my bladder stretched to its physical limits once again. Regular caffeine injections at restaurants kind enough to supply them free of charge. Sporadic lashings of semi-aggressive rain. A change of gloves every hour or so.

Shake yourself off like a drenched dog on entering and leaving dry and warm outlets – hoping the temporary warmth counteracts some of the rain that has saturated your clothing and body, shrivelling your skin to the texture of mouldy bread. Rinse and repeat until you finally arrive home to blast yourself with a comforting warm shower and even warmer food. You go to bed only slightly warmer, hoping your skin has de-shrivelled in time for the next day of ultra-endurance.

The rain was testing my mental strength once again, and I was tempted by the prospect of finishing earlier than normal, and trying any extreme method that would warm me up and dispel the frost that was starting to accumulate around my lips and eyebrows from being out for so long. As my teeth clattered into a slightly faster rhythm, I was ready to call it a day and look to arrive home with most of my bodily functions still in working order. My bladder was pulsing, but after such a prolonged period of near-constant abuse, I had to hope it would hold out for a few more minutes while I navigated my way home among the Friday night revellers.

An order popped up for a fancy Indian restaurant. The customer address was on my way home, and I was passing the restaurant anyways. Perfect. Usually I was unwilling to wait more than five minutes for an order to be made when in the laser-guided mindset I adopt when I log on and am busy, but this was a rare chance for me to empty my bladder before the distinct possibility that I would end up in Accident and Emergency with the rest of the drunken delinquents that night.

I shook off the excess raindrops and freshly forming frost, which felt like small speckles of dust disintegrating when hit with the warmth interior of the restaurant. These were familiar elements which had started to congregate around every nook and cranny of my exposed skin since the previous delivery; this shakedown had become a well-rehearsed action that was second nature on nights like these whenever I approached an entrance of any kind where people on the other side were warm and dry.

232

"Ten minutes for the food, sir," I was instructed in the most welcoming of manners as I stepped boldly into the restaurant, being ushered into a small corner of the entrance away from paying customers. I shook the water from every orifice onto the plush pile carpet beneath my feet, with all the grace and distinction of a German Shepard dog emerging from a lake and diving straight into the interior of a brand-new luxury car. It was clearly annoying for the staff to have to mop up the mess I had brought into the restaurant. But on this occasion I didn't have time to be apologetic or self-conscious, as there were more pulsating issues to deal with.

A look of familiar, institutionalised pity emanated from the diners in my immediate vicinity, as I dropped my backpack and shuffled to the toilet as graciously as I could manage in such circumstances. I hoped and prayed that the water falling from my lower half and onto the hallway landing was a clear colour and not the coffee-stained yellow which felt ready to erupt any second now, though luckily it was impossible to tell by simply looking down towards the ruby-red carpet.

Finally, I burst into the pristine décor of the men's toilet and let out sighs and howls of relief that only fellow strugglers can appreciate as secret code for an unbridled, unstoppable waterflow. In the hope of setting a new record, I started counting the seconds, to compare this near-miss to my previous calamitous inundations. Ten seconds in and I'm rudely interrupted by a drunk in the cubicle next to me, with only the locked wooden door between us helping to disguise our shared indignities.

"Sounds like you've had a few pints there, mate," he howled as he was plunged into a sit-down battle with the toilet bowl. It's a common occurrence in curry houses across the land as the heat of an ambitiously attempted vindaloo forces a break for the loo before you have even finished your meal. Something drops into the bowl and fills me full of dread. I'm talking a solid stool that would usually mean some kind of damage limitation for those forced to share a toilet with him. He was obviously using the chance to engage in friendly conversation as a way to hide his shame at the agony of what he was evacuating from his back passage.

"Something like that," I managed to bleat as I gasped for the last remnants of clean air. I exited the toilet in a state of panic, without fully emptying my bladder, or cleaning my hands for that matter, but merely patting myself down quickly for the return journey home. Annoyed at being unable to record my time for research purposes, and being forced to forgo a proper wash, I left the restaurant with a bagful of Indian food ready to drop off to one lucky punter on my way home.

Arriving at the block of flats to make the delivery, having already phoned ahead and left a voicemail to say that I was arriving, I was at least somewhat thankful I had managed to relive some of the waterworks in the little boys' room just minutes ago. My stomach had begun to resemble that of a full-time cyclist again. I looked down with an overwhelming sense of relief towards my phone.

There was no message or call-back from the customer yet. But that was OK. Lots of blocks of flats have a poor signal, or if not the customer could simply be heading down in the lift, probably with the same look on their face right now as when I had managed to release my overflowing bladder just minutes earlier - pure joy and elation.

As is the case when you have already called and messaged the customer on the app to tell them you've arrived at their address, you then wait for the countdown timer to pop up. Going on instinct, you usually know after a few minutes of waiting whether the customer is coming for their food or not. Finding some metallic building railings to chain my bike to, I rang the flat number provided.

Sometimes the customer is simply not next to their phone when you arrive. Sometimes the customer simply expects the food to be delivered directly to their door, refusing to answer the phone and hoping you will buckle under pressure and go the extra mile for them. I pressed to start the five-minute timer, informing the customer they only had a brief period of time left to come and collect their paid-for goods.

It was still raining, and the alluring warmth of the flats was calling me for my last good deed of the night. But there was no answer on the flat entry system either. It might be that they had only just got the message and were heading down now. Either way, there were four minutes left for them to get their food. I messaged through the app that I had tried ringing their flat but got no response, my senses now sharpening at the chance of a free meal to redeem what had been a pretty shitty day weatherwise.

'You'll have to be quick. I've already tried ringing your phone and your flat, no answer. Please get in touch ASAP,' I frantically type as the rain trickles with clockwork precision from my nose down onto the phone screen, making it near-impossible to type coherent messages without each one looking like the scribblings of a six-year-old dyslexic. Two minutes left. It wasn't looking good for the chances of this customer receiving what felt like a pretty substantial Indian banquet.

The smells permeated the bag, allowing me briefly to salivate over the prospect of sampling this fine cuisine when I finally arrived home. And why not, as the odds were now firmly in my favour that what looked like a sumptuous set meal for four would soon be mine and mine alone. In fact, it would probably feed two very hungry human beings relaxing after a long hard week of compulsory labour, with possible leftovers. Better still, it would make a mighty feast for one ravenous human being who spends the majority of his time rotating his two long, weary legs for a living.

One minute remaining. Now it really was crunch time. The *Countdown* clock music bubbles up again from deep within my subconscious, as it instinctively does in every same scenario from when I had first started the job, replaying over and over until the longed-for end note, *dum*. I was daring to dream, but I also had to keep it together, on the outside chance the customer now magically appeared. Pulling up in a cab, fresh out the shower perhaps, or annoyingly taking the many flights of stairs rather than the lift, because their pedometer or fitness watch seemingly controls every movement they ever make. Any of these situations could have snatched my fantasy meal from out of my hands.

I tried the flat entry system one more time. It just kept ringing through again, with no one answering on the other end. If someone entered or left the building, you could normally get into the block of flats, leaving the meal outside the customer's front door with a little message on the app letting them know you've been able to get in and leave the food for them. It was one of those typically harsh nights where people simply aren't willing to leave the warmth of their flat to venture out for anything.

The seconds ticked down. I unchained my bike and

mounted it in delirious anticipation, hyperalert now to every noise and movement in the immediate surroundings. People passing by. Cars pulling up in the street. Fellow delivery drivers whizzing past. Time slowed down as the last few seconds counted down reluctantly to zero. I'd made it! I clicked *Order not delivered*, then made a note on the Deliveroo app of why this customer hadn't turned up for the meal they had paid for, though of course I didn't know why and didn't mind so much that they hadn't.

I turned away from the scene of the crime and looked forward to receiving my unanticipated monthly bonus for all the hard work and dedication I'd put in, toiling away in such wretched conditions. It helped turn an otherwise incredibly tough night into one worth savouring. The rain running down my face now combined with the warm saliva forming around my frostbitten lips as I raced home to enjoy the spoils of my labour.

And that's how quickly a night can turn from being complete dogshit to being the dog's bollocks in this line of work. Just like that, the previous ten hours can dissolve into oblivion as you realise the pain and the elevated heartrate you have put your body through for mile after weary mile will now be duly rewarded by a meal that is piping hot and ready to be consumed immediately upon arriving home.

There's a certain satisfaction that comes from arriving home having endured the rain all day. If you've ever been caught in monsoon-like conditions, you'll know that same feeling of relief and satisfaction that washes over you after being caught in a downpour. That overwhelming feeling from having suffered something bad to get back to something good. The calming effect of having made it back despite adversity and having finally escaped the outside elements brings with it a liberating feeling of safety and contentment.

A warm house and a warmer shower quickly washes away the nagging thoughts and feelings that have weighed you down all day, and you feel a certain satisfaction in making it back in one piece, exhausted but rejuvenated in equal measure. Then a quick blast of freezing cold water from the showerhead jolts you back into life, stiffening the muscles, telling my body to begin the process of recovery after long hours of stress and strain.

On this occasion, I let body and mind come down from the previous ten hours spent battling the worst that Newcastle can throw at a cyclist in the winter season, a task that demands a certain degree of resetting and rehumanising amid the comfort of the mattress. This process takes longer in the winter, as the days feel longer and the time passes more slowly as you battle tougher conditions to complete most jobs, in sharp contrast to summer, where the light breeze and warm rays of sunshine make the work a far less daunting prospect.

Finally, suitably relaxed, on this evening after the narrowly avoided catastrophe in the toilet of that Indian restaurant, I was ready to refuel, and snap out of my semi-vegetive state, to become a much more sociable human being altogether. I walked downstairs, eyeing the Deliveroo bag I had left near the front door, hoping the steam escaping from the sizable package as I unzipped the thermal bag would help revitalise the senses. Like every free meal I had ever earned (or been gifted by default), I approached the aromatic package like a giddy child on Christmas morning, impatiently tearing into the main present of the year.

Having checked the receipt, I examined the contents, trying

to guess the overall value the meal would have had to the poor punter who didn't turn up in time to receive their goods. A good fifty pounds' worth of food, I soon realised. Good lord. Even in my ravenous state it would most likely take me two sittings to consume even just the majority of my work bonus. Nothing too hot or spicy either, which meant tomorrow's shift in the saddle wouldn't be as tormenting or explosive as it might have been.

I make a start on the food, oblivious to the collective huddling of my fellow housemates, who look on in envy. They had learned by now not to request any of the leftover spoils if I was able to finish a free meal within my usual twenty-minute window of self-declared entitlement. Anything else I would usually leave as recompense for having to endure my occasional late-night antics in the communal fridge – on those occasions when I was so hungry I ended up pinching their food – or the constantly dirty bikes I dragged into the house, or the 500 strands of hair that were left to clog up the shower drain most days of the week.

I could go on, but old housemates are fully aware of my many flaws in and around the house. At least the ice-cold bottles of water didn't feature as prominently in the winter as I switched to cups of tea instead. Maybe on this occasion, I begin thinking, I would leave a meal or two for them all to scavenge when I was done. But first, I needed to calculate the calories needed to replenish lost energy after a hard day's work, followed by a further hoard for the long day ahead tomorrow.

Much like a forward-planning squirrel storing nuts for the winter ahead, just with far less grace and dignity. This is always a difficult thing to calculate, as a lot of the time you really aren't that hungry when you get home, having outlasted your hunger streak, or simply because you're too tired to eat and would rather go to bed for some much-needed rest than force-feed yourself just because you think you should. Hence why you occasionally end up with your face in the fridge at 4 am, acting like you're trying to unpick the lock on a bank safe without being caught by infrared sensors or CCTV in all directions.

The first set meal slips down comfortably enough. Sitting-room guests look on intermittently in hope, silently acknowledging that this probably isn't going to be one of those rare nights for complementary leftovers. I tuck into the next meal that has been carefully stacked into the neatly organised carrier bag full of Indian cuisine. A minced, meat-based dish, with a side of flour tortillas which have hardened in the time it has taken me to get around to them. Combining the two, I quickly start on them as I eye the third meal by the side of me.

Like a dog with two bones, impatiently I bite into the tortillas I've made from the next meal in front of me, suddenly hearing and feeling a forceful crunch sound that shouldn't normally resonate from such a dish. The extra-hard tortilla drops onto the plate, like fragments of glass from a broken window, along with two front teeth, as my brain tries to process what has just transpired. Dental implants I'd acquired after a drunken assault I'd been the victim of at a Courteeners concert eight years earlier, they are now extras on my plate as I root around in my mouth to confirm a large gaping area where my two front teeth had previously been.

I looked at my housemates with an expression of resigned horror and received only bewildered chuckles and expletives in return. They scrutinised my free banquet with very different intentions now, keen to examine the failed dental implants which had dropped out of my mouth, leaving the gaping hole I could now see when I reluctantly gazed into the mirror. It was a depressing sight, with only my tongue appearing in the gap as I began again the whole process of learning to speak fluently. Equipped with a newly acquired lisp, I trudged up to bed, defeated in every sense.

The next morning I mopped up what was left of the food, having to learn how to chew it only at the sides of the mouth and tilting the head back aggressively in order to slowly chow down the leftover banquet. I sent an open-mouthed picture message to my brother to gauge his initial reaction to the state I found myself in, to which he simply replied, 'You look like complete shite, and I'm not talking about the missing teeth.'

I instinctively knew I was overdue another extended break from all the cycling and the long gruelling hours to which I had recently been subjecting myself to. Sometimes you are simply blind to the reality of your current predicament until someone near and dear bluntly spells it out to you. I did look like shit, and I did need some time off. But I dismissed such feelings every morning when I woke up, seeing it as my duty to get up every day and grind it out like everybody else.

I just convinced myself that there was nothing better to do than to get up and go to work and subject myself to another ten hours of delayed pains and sores of the kind my body was now experiencing once I got home. Take a few ibuprofens and ride it out, I told myself most days, ignorant of the abuse I was putting myself through during those cruel winter shifts.

After the initial embarrassment over my changed appearance had subsided, I reluctantly started working again. I had taken a prolonged period of unpaid leave during December, staying in bed most of the time, reading and minimising contact with the outside world except over Christmas. Using a snood to cover my gaping hillbilly features, I learned how to maintain a smile-free face for a few long months, while I saved up enough money to cover the expense of inserting two new, small white stumps into my mouth, to make me look presentable in public again.

Having just mastered control of my tongue, which also meant avoiding any elongated 'S' words, it was time to get the new implants fitted. Explaining to the dentist the situation that I had somehow got myself into that cold winter morning, he smiled graciously with that warm, professional demeanour that only dentists have. As he continued drilling deeper into the front regions of my face, I threw up anxious arm to stop proceedings and take a small shot of the magic pink juice by the side of me – partly to help remove the plaster now stuck to the inside of my cheeks, partly to swill around in my mouth to counter the metallic sparks which had been flying out of it for the past few minutes.

Also, momentarily, to stop the Black & Decker drill going further into the deepest recesses of my gums, as he worked quickly to remove those remnants of the old implants still embedded in the deepest crevasses of my upper gums. I tried to slow the sadistic dentist's journey into what felt like the substructure of my nose. As he reached into his war chest and looked intently for various drill bits, I informed him that this time approximately two months earlier saliva had been running down my chin, as I had sat down to enjoy my free Indian banquet, the one which had caused all the damage. Nothing. My heartbeat and breathing intensified further as we approached crunch time, so to speak. The assistant passed him back the Black & Decker.

He finished his drilling campaign and mechanically tilted me into an upright seated position, after twenty minutes of fully funded facial torture. I started aggressively scrubbing the plastered-on saliva which had dried onto the bottom half of my face. Once I had chipped away what was there, I pondered how in my next life a career as a stonemason working on Donald Trump's ugly mug on the side of Mount Rushmore might be a slightly more fruitful and less destructive living than that of the cycle courier.

The dentist turned proudly with the portable mirror and pointed it towards my distressed mouth, showing me the results obtained for the small fortune I was just about to cough up, and to gauge what I really thought of my newly reconstructed smile. I placed my tongue in its new position behind two perfect-looking front teeth, and tried to formulate a coherent sentence to justify the twenty minutes of skilled labour I was paying for.

He swiftly put his hand on my shoulder and gently imparted some words of wisdom: "Just goes to show, there's no such thing as a free lunch, is there?" Even if I had wanted to conjure an appropriate response to this profound observation, my displaced tongue, new teeth and the anaesthetic coursing around my face wouldn't allow me to do so. I raised my eyebrows compassionately and mumbled under my breath a despondent thank you for the excellent clinical work but also the philosophy lesson he had just provided free of charge.

I settled the debt and left the building as quickly as I could. That lovely free lunch had ended up costing me fifteen hundred quid in new dental implants. Karma in its purest form.

8

The Pandemic

'The best rides are the ones where you bite off more than you can chew, and live through it.' Doug Bradbury

So I learnt to adapt to a world that could understand what I was saying again, while not having to cover my face in every conceivable public situation any longer. A few months later this would come full circle. An unexpected event, a global chain of events as momentous as anyone can remember, meant that absolutely everyone would be covering their faces for quite a long time indeed.

Having just regained full control of my tongue and the ability to speak fairly fluently again, and thus a time when I wanted to show off my face to the world and maybe even smile at strangers if I was having a particularly good day, Mother Nature stepped in and it was time to cover my face for the foreseeable future yet again.

A global pandemic ripped through most of the planet. Covid-19. The masses retreated from their offices to the confines of their homes, leaving city centres desolate. Only a small number of people remained out wandering the streets. The odd bobby on the beat, homeless person, taxi driver or courier was now left with the city all to themselves.

Every busy back lane now deserted, every bridge across the river vacant, every shopping centre abandoned, every main road silent except for the occasional wail of a siren from an ambulance or police car attending to some emergency whose cause we tried not to think about. As close to a real-life scene from *The Walking Dead* as you could ever possibly imagine.

Time slowed down completely. Life became more primitive than anyone could ever have envisioned just a few weeks earlier. I rode around the city centre in complete awe of what was unfolding before my eyes. Not a single soul out. Not a single sound audible, except those of Mother Nature. The air as I gazed up to the sky now completely clear of pollution. Views for miles around the city that I had never been able to fully appreciate, due to the constant flow of traffic that coursed along its main arteries, the haze of toxic emissions clogging up the skies all around it as a result.

It was the countryside merging with the city. The circumstances were harrowing, but it was also a beautiful, poignant reminder of the world we share with other living things. Never before had I heard birds chirping so loudly in the morning as I cycled into the city centre; something that in normal times I would only expect to hear on breaks to the Lake District or rural Northumberland. But now there was no manmade noise whatsoever, just that of the creatures with which I was sharing this fresh, clean, serene, uncluttered, uncomplicated environment.

There was even a deer spotted on CCTV roaming the city

centre early one evening in May 2020, enjoying a peace and tranquillity you don't normally associate with a metropolitan area. It had instinctively made its way to the Bigg Market area, the main party destination for stag and hen dos descending on Newcastle from far and wide. Northumbria police got in on the act, sharing a video that went viral, with one tweet reading, 'Even lockdown couldn't stop this stag from enjoying a night on the town.' [48] Clever bastard. Now get back to work.

I even stopped using my headphones as a distraction when cycling, choosing instead to tune in to the natural world all around me. Unsure of how long this phenomenon would last, I strove every day to appreciate this new environment to which, like everyone else, I was responding with an enthusiasm that surprised me. As time slows down, so do people. There are multiple reasons why people may be generally more friendly, receptive and less hostile when you leave the city and venture into the great outdoors.

A less frantic lifestyle and more time spent outdoors usually makes for a happier and more wholesome human being. The average westerner spends approximately 90 percent of their time indoors, but merely being exposed to nature helps slow the heartrate and boost our immune response, and is likely to lead to a reduced stress response, too.[49]

Working long hours is often a prerequisite for young adults starting their chosen careers living in a big and expensive city, as everyone around you seems to be deep into the career rat race. A recent Timeout City Index survey found that a whopping 55 percent of Londoners and 52 percent of New Yorkers reported that their city can feel like a rather lonely place. [50]

It's also a numbers game. When people are born, grow up

and grow old in the same places, it is likely that they have a more cohesive and familiar sense of community. In cities, where people are a lot more fluid and may never settle for long periods, this sense of community can be harder to develop and sustain as city folk grow older and move out to the suburbs or further afield.

Getting to know your neighbours with any sort of familiarity in a block of high-rise flats can be a lot trickier than it is for those living in a cul-de-sac or street. Especially as those neighbours may be coming and going every six to twelve months, as opposed to those buying their first home and planning to stay there a long time.

There's a much greater incentive to get to know your neighbours when you are staying in the one place for a prolonged period of years and maybe decades. But the population mobility typical of cities means many of us don't even know our neighbours, as many people never really settle into the community or area where they live when starting a new job, or else they sign a short rental agreement in their new space on the understanding that it will suit them as much as their landlord that they can move on at very short notice.

This is a far different kind of life to what countless generations of ancestors have been used to throughout history, where people have tended to thrive inside smaller, family-based tribes rather than the artificial environments we now pursue for career, educational or financial reasons.

Constantly being surrounded by thousands of people we don't know can sometimes feel like being inundated by dozens of the same product in a supermarket. Online dating apps rings a bell here, too, giving us much more information than we were ever meant to process. Like being at the supermarket

248

staring at a shelf full of the exact same items but slightly modified, this is an example of a 'paradox of choice', a term introduced by Alvin Toffler in his 1970 book, *Future Shock*.

This paradox of choice, according to Barry Schwartz, is the negative consequence of having too many options to mull over, an overabundance that can lead to anxiety, indecision, paralysis and dissatisfaction.[51] Rather than being faced by one or two people when outside tending your garden, if there were ten or twenty people coming and going on your street, it would be much harder to engage with these additional people, or pressures, the great variety making it hard for your brain to adapt.

This leads to the idea of negative politeness. This is the tendency people have to ignore social niceties when they are in large crowds. As we feel like we are imposing on other's space, we avoid the small talk and friendly hello that we would normally be inclined to in smaller, more personal groups. It always takes me a few days when back in Northumberland, cycling along the coast or out for walks, to adjust to this more friendly and personable way of life.

Like a kind of dimmer switch slowly turning in my head, I adjust to the idea of people walking past and greeting me, smiling and saying hello, compared to the much colder and less personal nature of living in the city. By the time I make my way back to the city, having only just started to feel suitably relaxed and at ease again, back goes the dimmer switch cranked back up to city mode. Again, I have to readjust to the fast-paced nature of a different space, of a different life, without realising that I am even doing it and participating in this contrasting game of personality and societal traits that depend on where you happen to be.

There are many complex and divergent reasons that contribute to the feeling of urban isolation experienced by so many city dwellers. A transient population, for example – a large population of non-nationals can make people feel ungrounded. It's something Britain has struggled with for many years, as the EU expansion in 2004 brought many hundreds of thousands of arrivals into the UK from eight former communist states in central and eastern Europe. A third of leave voters said their main reason for voting for Brexit was to control immigration. [52]

Technology plays a role too. While our phones and computers allow us to stay connected to friends and family as we move more freely, this can come at the expense of connecting with our own neighbourhoods. As many city folk are single, live alone or indeed in cramped house shares, this can magnify the need for technology – a way of escaping our immediate surroundings – to quell this loneliness, a problem undoubtedly exacerbated by the Covid-19 pandemic and the social distancing this enforced, as well as in general by increasing individualisation within society.[53]

Cities can now be very lonely places to live and work in. Some people in Tokyo even hire a 'friend' from an agency to feel a bit more human and mitigate the alienating experience of being alone for prolonged periods of time in these increasingly atomising urban environments.[54] This problem is only likely to increase, unless city planning allows for dramatic and progressive changes in uses of, and far greater allowances for, green spaces; as well as many more appropriate and necessary communal spaces of the kind that can make city living more pleasant for all.

The merging of the country and city seems an almost

impossible dream. However, there were promising signs during the first lockdown of the Covid-19 pandemic to suggest that this doesn't necessarily have to be the case. As people started working from home, leaving their cars largely redundant, many soon realised a need for the great outdoors. Those precious public spaces scattered around many cities – parks, denes and riversides – helped many people escape the monotony of endless Zoom calls and Netflix binges while being stuck indoors.

The spring weather was kind to the outdoors type, as a rather utopian society emerged from its millions of locked-down bunkers to spend precious free time out walking, running, cycling or playing football, and generally getting more acquainted with the outdoor spaces that were normally reserved for joggers, dog walkers or the mothers taking youngsters to the playground. The city was slowly learning how to adapt to the new normal.

As the frantic pace of life slowed to a halt, it was possible to converse with people in a way that would have been difficult beforehand. When everyone is so consumed in their own problems, working so hard to keep the boss happy and the rent paid on time, it becomes very easy to dismiss the need to interact with your fellow city dwellers, the people with whom you share the same urban space and, at least for that reason, something of the same experience.

It's a condition of modern living, this process of individuali-sation, of atomisation. The eroding of community and human connections. The gig economy is the very embodiment of this in many ways. No boss. No chain of command. I can't even receive a reference from Deliveroo for any job that I might want to apply for. It's just you against the world - along with any other fellow gig economy workers you happen to pass on your way between jobs.

What a difference it can make to your overall sanity, being able to stop and come together with people, rather than being caught up in the hyper-speed capitalist system we are usually enmeshed in, whether we want to be or not. That togetherness was something like the spirit of the Blitz brought into the modern era. A chance to remind everyone of the genuine and tangible obligations we owe to our fellow human beings, the need to help one another and to try to be more accommodating whenever possible.

Of course, during normal times people are too often consumed by their own daily struggles to stop and smell the roses. The pandemic should act as a wake-up call that the current structural inefficiencies of working forty hours a week in the office are inconvenient and unnecessary for many workers. Once people have realised the flexibility and convenience of being able to work from home, it will become common practice for many in rebalancing their work–life relationship going forward.

The average daily commute time in the UK is 59 minutes; that's five hours a week that could be spent more productively – whether sleeping, having a good breakfast, getting outside, exercising or doing additional work (cough). No one enjoys the morning commute, stuck in slow-moving traffic or staring blankly at your phone surrounded by coughing and sneezing strangers, reading more terrible news, setting the tone for the rest of the day. If you enjoy this part of your day, you should be certified insane. Unless you walk or cycle to work, of course.

In terms of the environment, people working from home is fantastic news. There is less pollution due to fewer cars on the road. CO2 emissions dropped by at least 25 percent in February 2020, leading to the number of 'good air quality' days that month to rise by 22 percent. Estimates suggest that around 77,000 lives in the UK may have been saved due to reduced air pollution.

If those with remote-compatible jobs worked from home just half of the time it could result in saving 54 million tons of greenhouse gases – the equivalent of taking 10 million cars off the road in the UK. [55] This would be great news for those of us using outside spaces, who would benefit from breathing in much fresher air. Many millions more would reap similar benefits if this became a permanent change.

City centres and the office environment will always attract a young and vibrant mix of people and ideas, much needed for businesses to thrive. But, much like the pandemic has persuaded most people of the convenience of shopping from home, city planners and business leaders will have to adapt to the changing priorities of the people that live, work and visit the big conurbations if such places are to continue to grow and attract people to set up shop there.

Being stuck in a small, dark dwelling with little natural light or outside space will not have been much fun for those poor souls cooped up in flats and apartments throughout the pandemic, especially those living alone. Some 30.9 percent of remote workers say that they struggle with loneliness when working remotely, and 62 percent of the same group want employers to provide technology that helps them stay connected with their colleagues.

A lack of human connection that existed before it has been exacerbated by the pandemic is becoming all too common in society, and much time and resources should be given to considering how to rebuild these fraying living conditions. Tiny steps can make a huge difference – like leaving books out in blocks of flats, and also in residential areas inside beautifully constructed neighbourhood book boxes. Such small initiatives warm the heart when I'm out doing deliveries, as it's the little things in life that matter, after all. Sharing books, along with music, is one of life's simple but most fulfilling pleasures. Building connections is what people crave, whether they show it or not.

More than a fifth, some 22 percent, of telecommuters say that 'switching off' after work is their biggest challenge.[56] With many young people using their bedrooms as makeshift office spaces, it can hardly come as a surprise that so many struggle with the disconnect from work to leisure time. Nick Littlehales, an elite sport's sleep coach, says the bedroom is exclusively for sleeping and sex, nothing else. A decluttered environment for sleeping is essential,[57] and having the office set up in the bedroom tells your brain that you are sleeping in the office, not relaxing in your detached sanctuary before getting your much-needed rest and recovery.

The pandemic has accelerated many trends that were already taking place. As people began to work from home and leave their cars on the driveway, they also began to realise how many of their everyday essentials they could have delivered to them at the click of a few buttons. A much larger share of the deliveries I now do are from supermarkets and convenience stores, with city folk able to get their everyday items delivered within half an hour. Once people have developed the habit of having their milk and eggs delivered to them without ever leaving the warmth of their own home, battling the elements to pick up a few everyday items on a wet spring afternoon or cold winter night becomes a much-less-appealing prospect.

Twenty years ago, if I wanted a pint of milk, some trainers, or a newly released book, I'd have got a lift from my parents or taken the bus into town to pick these things up, much like everybody else. Cutting down on what by today's standards are fairly unnecessary journeys is again good news for the environment, whether you are aware of it or not. As the likes of Deliveroo, Amazon et al. look to electrify their vehicle fleets, directly or indirectly, encouraged and incentivised to go green through lower costs, carbon tax credits and ESG (Environmental, Social, and Corporate Governance) credentials within investor prospectuses, most of these last-mile logistics will be better for the environment. Your carbon-producing car stays on the drive and a green vehicle comes along and drops off your food, drink, trainers or the freshly printed book you've been looking forward to for weeks.

Whatever emerges from the new blend of working from home and getting back to office life, people have become accustomed to ordering more meals on the popular delivery apps for the past few years, accelerated more so by the pandemic and people being stuck at home, and latterly by those worried about the prospect of going out to eat and drink again in a post-lockdown, learning-to-live-with-Covid world.

Such habits will stick, justifying the growth strategies pursued by the likes of Deliveroo, Just Eat and UberEats. A brutal battle is currently being fought amongst the tech delivery firms, and newly emerging rapid delivery firms, for increased market share of home deliveries - and that market will only continue to grow as people realise the benefits of staying at home and doing convenience shopping from the comfort of your sofa or swivel chair.

Food delivery app downloads in the UK boomed by 33 percent during the pandemic,[58] with the global food delivery services market growing from $115 billion in 2020 to nearly $127 billion in 2021. The market is expected to reach $192 billion in 2025 at a compound annual growth rate of 11 percent.[59] The race to enter these developed and developing markets around the planet is also intensifying. Lobbying for access to these markets as many emerge from multiple lockdowns into a new normal should be low-hanging fruit for many of these companies.

Having started as a fast-food-only delivery service, Deliveroo now has supermarkets, convenience stores, pharmacies, pubs, coffee shops and much more besides to cater for a burgeoning customer base that has continued to grow rapidly during the course of the pandemic and is still expanding as the UK looks to get back to business as usual. The three lockdowns since March 2020 have completely transformed the company's fortunes, which continues to show strong growth from the lifting of the UK's lockdowns.[60]

Though the IPO at the end of March 2021 wasn't quite the triumphant arrival onto the London Stock Exchange that many had hoped for, and though it has yet to make a profit, nonetheless it is now a publicly listed company worth billions of pounds.

It has been a very different story for the couriers working during the pandemic, however, with earnings decimated as rider numbers increased dramatically due to anticipated demand from people staying at home and using food-delivery apps. The first lockdown in Newcastle (and beyond) saw many nationwide fast-food chains close for dine-in and takeaway deliveries, with only a few smaller independent places left open to compete for business. Many cyclists were left unable to work, with many who would normally travel from outside the city on public transport stranded at home.

Working most days for six to eight hours during the first national lockdown, I was able to make around half the money I had made previously, but was nevertheless grateful that I wouldn't be stuck in my small square bedroom, living in a house share that we would all be confined to for the foreseeable future. This was perfectly acceptable, I thought at the time, still being able to work while experiencing a completely different side of a usually sprawling, vibrant and eccentric metropolis.

The cityscape around me was strangely barren and new, and during those early and eerie days of the first national lockdown I made countless videos and photos to show friends and family how abandoned and lifeless it now looked. It was an experience I was never likely to get the chance to live through again – that of a whole city emptied, with only a few worker ants left carrying small numbers of passengers and parcels of food in and out of a suddenly becalmed urban centre.

Right at the start of the pandemic, I finally gave up job hunting, for obvious reasons. I had never really seen anything that took my fancy since the trade trainee job in London, so I finally just accepted the fact that I would be doing this job for a prolonged period of time. A switch went off in my head that just said Fuck it, accept things for what they are and just enjoy what you are doing. Many people were stuck at home climbing the walls, yet I could still go out on my bike every day for some fresh air and exercise, delivering bundles of joy to those unfortunate folks stuck at home staring into screens all day long.

Play your little part during the pandemic, and stop living for the future, for the next job application, for the next thing to happen in your life, for things you can't control, I told myself. Not that I had been putting much effort or time into job applications lately, but it helped ease the mental pressure that I'd put myself under on my days off when I really needed to relax and recover from long spells on the bike rather than look idly at the computer screen for the right kind of job to jump out at me.

This pressure could build up and become very intense as my mood swings changed with the amount of time I spent cycling, week after week. Some weeks, I would love the job and be on top of the world. Other weeks, I quite simply hated the fact that I was cycling for so long, hoping and wishing to hear back from one of the jobs I had half-heartedly applied for in some faraway fantasised destination like Dubai. I could spend all day or all week in the saddle imagining a new life for myself somewhere new and exciting.

These negative thoughts and fantasies would normally occur when I was completely shattered, and were most likely a coping mechanism for the stress I was putting my mind and body through at the time. Instead of just taking some time off and unwinding from it all, I would normally just power through for the sake of it. Bonkers really when I look back and try to understand my mindset at the time. Throughout most of my life, I had used cycling as a force for good to help me deal with most things that occurred in my life, positive or negative.

I had now turned it into an excuse to deal with anything that was not going smoothly, to the point where I simply abused cycling as a means to try to get myself back to a better state altogether. Mentally, this had not been great for me lately, and physically I would simply end up crashing and burning as the weeks wore on. I had to change my relationship with cycling, and the first lockdown provided me the opportunity to do just that.

I took a week off, wrote down what I wanted to do differently, opened up my laptop, stared at it despondently for about ten minutes, then typed out the title for this book. The chance for me to focus my energy on something else would help massively, take my mind off working, but also help while out working when thinking of ideas for what I was actually going to write about. I hadn't engaged the creative side of my brain since the job assessment and interview in London, and before that was probably when I was writing my master's dissertation.

I had quite simply completely worn myself out over the course of the previous two years of such long hours, but now I had a chance to do things differently, as everything around me slowed down or ground to a halt. I bashed away at the keyboard for progressively longer periods and let my body slowly recover until I felt suitably refreshed and ready to re-emerge on the bike.

I also realised that I would have to hedge my bets, and started working for the other delivery companies, Uber Eats and Stuart (Just Eat). Students were leaving the city to go home early, so the demographic changed from that of majority students to professionals working from home. Those also who, unable to order in restaurants, were driving into the city centre to order food on apps, and getting it dropped off at the exact place where they had parked. Multi-apping on all three platforms meant I had a more reliable revenue stream than just through Deliveroo, where riders relied mainly on student orders to stay busy most days. No longer could I rely on the one delivery company to provide a steady source of income.

The fine weather of spring 2020 made working much easier and enjoyable. With less happening in the world, I had the chance to do things differently. I was able to cut down the cycling for a while, and started scribbling down ideas for the book. I worked to a much more relaxed Mediterranean schedule – and in a much more peaceful, even beautiful environment – than I had ever allowed myself before.

An altogether slower pace of life unfolded, a gentler rhythm to work and cycling, reading a book between deliveries, and generally being a more open and receptive human being than I had been in the previous few years while working. It was an unfamiliar experience of city life that I had never really known, one that is usually the preserve of city cleaners, early-morning taxi drivers or those maniacs chasing sunrises for spiritual or selfie-driven-vanity reasons. I had worked the occasional early-morning shift, with an altogether gentler rhythm and less frantic pace, in Manchester on the weekends - which had been forced upon me by my housemate Dean's late-night/early morning antics.

I always found this the best possible time to work for the soul, if not so much the body, though increased caffeine doses usually did the job, and once out in the clean, crisp air, your senses soon come back to life after a few pedal strokes. The daylight gets the body started on producing serotonin, as the secretion of melatonin stops as we move from darkness into daylight. It's much like a switch being flicked internally, as our circadian urge to be up with the sun helps alleviate the tiredness we feel from being up earlier than normal.

There's something about a city coming alive in the mornings which strikes at the heart of most people who have ever experienced it. The smell of coffee percolating through the air as a shop owner puts out their display stands for the day. Shutters frantically opening with a familiar metallic swish and clunk as they shoot up to reveal the welcoming frontage of the latest hipster fad in the trendy part of town. Office folk striding past in smart formal attire, cappuccino in hand, walking with purpose to clock on for a day's honest toil. A new day emerging with an overwhelming sense of opportunity, the script as yet unwritten.

This was the attitude I took into the first lockdown. Every person I interacted with seemed more open and humane than before, much like I felt I was. During more turbulent times, tragedy always brings people closer together with a caring and compassionate undertone. Something that can easily be dismissed at other times, but nevertheless helps reveal the best side of humanity during such difficult days as we went through in the spring of 2020. Take the heroics of doctors and nurses who help others in their direst need every single day of the year. They are on the front line of life and death and understand better than most the fragility of life.

There's always someone, somewhere, a lot worse off than you. I'm convinced most people develop this attitude during times of great tragedy. It was an incredibly uplifting experience seeing a whole city coming out to clap for those who were helping to protect us. Whole blocks of flats outside on their balconies clapping, creating a feel-good atmosphere around the city, as I stopped and took it all in between jobs for those brief yet emancipating few minutes when so many showed their appreciation for the few who were getting us through the toughest times we'd known.

I was out in the streets cycling in what felt like a parallel universe, stopping and clapping alongside them, showing the immense gratitude we all felt for those risking their lives in the hospitals and care homes to care for others. It was a truly humbling experience.

* * *

As summer arrived, I was undeniably lifted by this communal spirit of getting through the hard times together. As places started to reopen, the 'Eat Out to Help Out' scheme made me raise my ability to work long days to levels I didn't think were possible prior to the pandemic. Twelve- and fourteen-hour shifts became the norm as I was lured by the temporary offer of half-price food courtesy of the state, and also to help plug the gap in my earnings as work stayed pretty dire throughout the summer months.

Out with the peasant's meal deals I would consume through-out the day, and in with the carvery dinners and Korean sticky-beef suppers that kept the engine roaring during those long summer days in the saddle. Paying as little as £3.20 for a full Sunday roast with all the trimmings, I indulged myself on an almost daily basis in between long bouts of cycling morning and night, with feelings of near-constant bloated stomach aches and pains that generally subsided by the time I had made it home late at night.

I reminisce with fond gastronomical memories of that strange time in our nation's history. Like most of the country,

I put a few extra pounds on my waistline, but saved a good few pounds on the slap-up meals I was enjoying most days too. They balance themselves out over the long term, I told myself, and by the end of the summer, I had gently weaned myself off the Sunday dinners onto a much stricter diet of coffee and sausage rolls for a few weeks of self-prescribed rehabilitation.

Only a really bad headache and muscle fatigue for a few days knocked me off my stride. At the time, these were not really considered symptoms of Covid-19, and with testing not being available to anyone early in the pandemic, I was none the wiser. As I never suffer from such things unless hungover (now a very rare occurrence!), I have come to the conclusion that it was more than likely to have been a small bout of the virus.

Still, the perfect storm awaited as the long warm days receded into the start of term for university students and the city came roaring back to life - after the tranquillity of the past few months faded into a distant, fond, fleeting memory. Most of the country thought normality was being restored after a summer of half-price food, and we seemed to be gearing up for a winter of business as usual.

The large influx of students from far and wide is surely a defining feature of globalisation in action. Close to 540,000 international students now come to the UK to study for higher education purposes. Universities are giant petri dishes during the best of times, with Freshers' Flu a common occurrence for many students as they settle into studying after meeting and mixing with fellow students in their first few weeks in higher education. Cities have quickly adapted, expanded and prospered with the increasing numbers of international students that have been welcomed into the UK.

In 1998 the total number of international students was around 200,000 a year, and by 2016 this was closer to 450,000. It continues to grow exponentially, with no set cap on the number of international students that universities can take. The last decade has seen the most dramatic change in the number of students arriving from China, up from 25,000 in 2006/7 to 66,000 in 2016/17. In every year since 2012/13, the number of Chinese students coming into the UK for higher education has exceeded the total number of students from all EU countries.[61]

Since Brexit there has been a 17 percent overall increase in the number of international students, driven largely by non-EU students, with 1 in every 3 international students originating from China in the 2018/19 cohort, up from 1 in 4 at the time of Brexit a few years earlier.[62] This is only likely to increase further as the UK looks to the rest of the world for trade deals and access to wider markets for its own products, hoping to lure these well-heeled economic migrants for many cities and universities, with all the jobs they help support and money that they spend.

Chinese students visiting the British Isles were wise to wearing masks long before it became mandatory during the Covid-19 pandemic. I used to look on in wonder as these hungry Chinese students skipped excitedly towards me, politely taking possession of their bundle of food, wearing these strange-looking and somewhat intrusive blue face masks. Maybe they had been warned by the Chinese government that the fog on the Tyne could penetrate their healthy skin cells while studying in Newcastle?

I was never quite sure exactly why they were wearing them when they were out and about in shops, travelling or standing outside their student accommodation waiting for their food to be delivered. More likely, the experience of living through previous virus outbreaks such as the Sars 2003 pandemic has taught many Asian cultures – where mask wearing had become common even before Covid-19 – valuable lessons in personal hygiene.

In some parts of Asia everyone wears a mask by default, as it is seen as personally safer and publicly more considerate to your fellow citizens. In mainland China, Hong Kong, Japan, South Korea, Thailand and Taiwan, the broad assumption is that anyone could be a carrier of the virus, even healthy people. So, in the spirit of solidarity, you help to protect others from yourself.

Some places go further, with some places in China arresting or punishing people not wearing a mask. In Singapore, which used to discourage citizens from wearing masks, it is now compulsory to wear one outside or you risk a fine. Being sick, having hay fever or the common flu, it being impolite to openly cough or sneeze in public, and also heavy traffic pollution are common reasons why other cultures choose to wear masks outside of global pandemics.[63] Makes perfect sense now, doesn't it?

Liberal societies were struggling to comprehend all these profound changes as we nosedived into wintertime. Students mixed and had fun, and of course infection rates began to soar as they had done in the spring. The rest of my winter season was spent delivering weekly shopping to students caged in their student accommodation, as universities replaced lectures and seminars with virtual classes and £50 food vouchers for isolating students unable to leave their accommodation.

Freshers' flu was now replaced with the very real and

contagious threat of Covid-19, reappearing in the west to make a mockery of the notion that we had learned from our previous efforts how best to contain it. I wrapped up every inch of my body to try and avoid catching it. Only my eyes were left exposed, to make sure I could catch sight of my unhappy customers' faces as they emerged to collect their food, before retreating back into their prison-like conditions until the next delivery arrived.

Some went even further than I did in the precautions they took. An excitable and enthusiastic Lithuanian student, Arthur, who I'd become friendly with while out working in Newcastle over the past few years, was wearing a gas mask to make his deliveries. In all fairness, this had started long before the global pandemic reared its ugly head. He'd first approached me when I'd been helping out as an extra in a promotional video for Deliveroo with Jack Whitehall, who'd been visiting Newcastle as part of his nationwide comedy tour.

He'd pulled up in tight Lycra cladding and a full-face gas mask, and I'd wondered why such a statement piece was necessary in the middle of Newcastle. At first I assumed he'd gone missing from a Greenpeace protest in the city, but once he got closer, removed his gasmask and revealed his steamed-up face, I eventually recognised him as a fellow comrade. I was pretty surprised at his wartime-courier-cum-Lance-Armstrong persona.

"What's with the gas mask then?!" I asked.

"The pollution here in Newcastle is terrible," he said, exhaling. "I've measured the air quality, and the mask filters out all the particles," he went on, gasping as he lifted the mask fully off his face. At this point, I was trying to get into character for my part in the short clip being filmed, and looked over tentatively to the production crew in the hope that they would cast me in the next available segment of filming to help me shake off the eccentric character I was now being distracted by just minutes before my small-screen debut.

"How do you even breathe?" I asked half-heartedly, edging closer to the production crew, who are now wondering why their paid extra is engaging in small talk with an extra from *Saving Private Ryan*.

"Out my mouth or out my nose," he offers in a crude and cynical tone, perfected by his dry, sarcastic accent. This kind of dark, sardonic sarcasm is something which people from that part of the world share with the British – effortlessly reciprocated in equal measure when probed.

Abstaining from sex and choosing not to shower were two of the things I soon found out we had in common. Not that I had abstained from sex by choice, it's just that I had barely found the time to engage in such luxuries between long spells in the saddle and long spells sleeping. I did manage to shower more frequently than he did, though you'd never have guessed it if I passed you in a restaurant to pick up an order. He had only recently finished reading the whole of the Quran over the course of a fortnight, and gave me chapter and verse commentary on what he saw as its glaring anomalies and inconsistencies.

My daily wages would plummet every time I crossed paths with this most engrossing intellectual, yet I was always fascinated by what he had to say, and the energy and intensity he exuded when saying it. He even built his own bikes, with parts he also made himself. He very rarely wore anything more than Lycra shorts and a compression T-shirt, even in the coldest, hardest winter climate that Newcastle can offer up. The sure-fire, fast-track way to becoming a proper adopted Geordie. Respect.

Late one night as we travelled back from a delivery drop-off a few miles out, he had even sat outside my house with me in such attire for an hour and a half, as I shivered and did star jumps to keep warm, even though I was layered up and wore gloves and a woolly hat. It was then he told me how the police had raided his house one night, as he had probed his university lecturer a few days earlier about several rare earth metals that were commonly associated with making explosive devices.

He laughed out loud, and I gasped wide-mouthed in the much colder late-night autumn air as he revealed to me how his university lecturer had had to disclose the contents of the conversation to Northumbria Police. Just to be on the safe side, of course. Several times during the course of that long conversation I had nearly asked him if he would like to come inside the house for a cuppa, desperate for the warm, friendly glow emanating from the empty front room I was gazing into from where I was sitting - compressed to half my original size - on the front-garden wall. But he was on a roll, and I was terrified at what he might be able to do with the remnants of the kitchen kettle once inside.

I bumped into Arthur again during the height of the pandemic in November 2020, as I arrived cold and walked over shivering to collect food from a restaurant late one night. Wearing layers of warm cycling kit under merino layers of base kit to keep some heat trapped inside my own body, I pulled up laughing out loud, praising my comrade on his consistently minimal choice of winter cycling wear. Shorts and a lightweight jacket were all he needed to brave the near-freezing temperatures at this time of the year, only downgrading to a skin-tight Lycra top during the more hospitable summer months.

He was also bare-faced, which did surprise me. So I asked him, "What's happened to your gas mask?" as he approached me, walking purposefully alongside his bike. The friendly warmth and embrace of a new conversation seemed to be enough to neutralise the effects of a winter night approaching zero degrees. Of course, it was partly a tactical question, as I was hoping I could spare myself the twenty minutes it would otherwise take him to explain the theory of relativity or whatever academic endeavour he had undertaken that particular week.

"Why would I need my gas mask? There is no traffic on the roads right now. It is very good," he countered, as he pulled out his phone and started proudly showing me an amateur video he had made of himself, sparks flying from across a bedroom laboratory, as I tried to narrow my cold-hardened eyes to fully dissect the contents of the video.

"Surely during a global pandemic, now's as good a time as any other," I offered back, playing my sarcastic card for the first time that evening. He looked at me nonplussed, as if I'd missed the point completely.

"I'm not worried by the coronavirus. I'm outside and everybody else is inside," he stated, with a flippant but inescapable logic, as he rejected a job offer for a delivery outside the same restaurant I was picking up from.

"You not taking that delivery? It's down the road and there's loads of orders ready to be picked up," I pleaded with him. I was called into the restaurant for my delivery, put the designated food parcel into my bag, hoping he wasn't going to keep me for another hour and a half, wondering how to politely rebuff the conversation he wanted to have about his homemade video. He always shows little interest in work and deliveries when he gets onto a subject he knows anything much about. Which seems to be pretty much any subject I or he brings up.

"Let me quickly show you this," he said excitedly, pushing his phone back into my face, even as I clicked my pedals into life and tried to look in the general direction I should have been going. By now I was worrying that my next customer might have passed out by the time I got away from the mad scientist and onto the mile-long route the app was suggesting I take to reach the destination.

The video showed a few loose sparks flying around Arthur as an amateur bout of bike welding seemed to be getting slightly out of control. I looked at him, halfway through the video, to gauge his level of pride and satisfaction at the work he was carrying out on his homemade Frankenstein bike.

"This is why I don't wear the gas mask, you see. The strap was burned when I was welding something onto my bike last week."

The tears streamed down my face as the irony hit me, and I patted him on the back, congratulating him on making me howl with such convulsive laughter in these disconcerting times.

"I've never met an Eastern European or Russian that didn't either terrify me, or make me laugh uncontrollably," I said, wiping tears from my eyes, eager to get away so that the customer had a fighting chance of eating their lukewarm meal sometime that evening.

"Which do I make you do?" he demanded from me with his usual bluntness, searching for the humour in the previous exchange.

"Both!" I shouted to him, as I mounted my bike and pedalled off into the darkness of the night, shaking my head in a state of disbelief - hoping the bitter-tinted tears streaming out quickly evaporate with the warmth exuding from within, and don't become a permanent feature on my cheeks with the frost planning to glaze over my facial features once again.

"And I've never met an English person with good teeth," he fired back, as he scoured the area for more comrades to whom he could show his home videos.

I turn back to the empty road, gently tapping my two new front teeth, hoping they were still there among all the fast-paced teeth clattering from the bitter cold and laughter. I prayed that he was only being facetious, as I anxiously checked to see if the two front teeth were still there. They were, as I breathe a heavy sigh of relief, hoping they would get me through another winter without using all my wages to pay for another set. I looked skywards and thanked God that he was only being facetious.

9

The Encore

'Sometimes you're ahead, sometimes you're behind. The race is long, and in the end it's only with yourself.' Baz Luhrmann

OK, amigos, I admit it. Maybe it was a pyramid scheme of sorts, after all. One in which all the benefits are accrued at the very beginning and gradually diminish over time. Flip the pyramid upside down, and that is how the whole experience has felt. Such is life, though the initial liberation you get from being on a bike never really leaves you. But doing any kind of activity for fifty-five hours a week soon becomes, like anything else in life, monotonous and self-defeating.

However, having racked up over 100,000 miles during my time in the gig economy, I can truthfully count the number of bad days I've had on the fingers of one hand. Well, maybe two hands - if you include the breakdowns and random bicycle issues you encounter on those rare occasions when going home to sulk is the only option. Most of these bad days have already been laid out in the previous chapters. On every other day, I have simply ridden my trusty bicycle until my problems either washed themselves away or I was simply too tired to remember what was wrong with me in the first place.

In that respect the job itself is fairly unique. If you are ever having a bad day, get on your bike and ride until it becomes a better day. If you are already having a good day, get on your bike and ride until it becomes a great day. Cycling has that unique and rather magical ability to cleanse the soul and lift the mood whenever you need it most.

The characters you meet while out working add colour to those otherwise black-and-white days in the saddle. And while every office has a larger-than-life character to keep us entertained through those more mundane periods, out in the city the childlike euphoria you feel while riding a bike turns us all into characters of sorts. A real mix of unique, eccentric, flamboyant characters that you could never imagine being confined within the boundaries of an office environment, when you consider their shared passion for being outdoors and on their bikes. Operating on the periphery of society, without ever being fully integrated into the conventional world of work, assuming there is such a thing or will be in the post-Covid world.

That's precisely what cycling does to all - man, woman and child: knocks down the conventional barriers that normally inhibit our ability to converse with our fellow human beings. Much like having a dog does for someone when they go out for a walk, cycling has that same inherent quality of bringing people together in something that is bigger than themselves, a social catalyst where conversation can flow along an infinite number of routes, just like the myriad journeys a courier might make on any given evening, but may end up back where you first started.

And while for me cycling now feels more like a full-time endeavour than a part-time passion, I still count my blessings to have been born at a time when I can be paid to ride my bike around town and make a living from doing so. Not so long ago, I most probably would have been stuck down a pit lumping coal and destroying my lungs in the process, all in the name of the Industrial Revolution, i.e. capitalist exploitation. These days it is the Digital Revolution that is gearing up to profoundly change the way we work, live and relate to one another; more than the previous industrial revolutions ever could, though there are still the same kinds of exploitation taking place at the expense of the workers. Some things never change.

All the moves I have made in the past few years have been to enable me to ride my bike for a living. Accommodation close to busy areas, upgrades to old bikes, gear to waterproof yourself through the great and the not-so-great British winters. Enough food and coffee to ensure your basic survival from day to day – oh, and a couple of teeth to replace old ones lost in battle, something I can smile about now! Anything that helps make the job easier and keeps you dry and moving through the unpredictable seasons of our temperate maritime climate.

I even built an E-bike to ensure I could still make a decent living as the wages plummeted further; the future is still uncertain as Deliveroo are still striving to turn a profit and keep their shareholders happy. I know the cycling enthusiasts will be projectile-vomiting their espressos onto the screen as they read this. Fifty-five hours a week on a bike week after week can break the best of us, myself included.

The E-bike means I hang on to the faint notion that I am still cycling for a living, though I am no longer fully committed to the lifelong career of a cycle courier. Psychologically, the E-bike allows me to justify doing the job as a side hustle while also pursuing other passions in the meantime (sleeping mostly). If I was ever to upgrade to a scooter or car, the job would lose the whole romance that comes with being out and simply riding a bike most days.

Will I change careers one day? Most likely. During times away from the bike I feel much like an aging rockstar ready to pack it all in and search for the next project in my life. Leisure time turns into time spent doing anything but riding a bike, which completely contradicts the relationship you enjoyed with your two-wheeled friend before you became a full-time courier; when you could not wait to escape for a few hours on a warm summer evening after work, to put the world to rights by resetting your physical and mental self.

The long, cold, dark winter nights in the city briefly allow you to fantasize about one day returning to a cosy office environment, but these thoughts are quickly washed away at the end of the night as you are brought back to a semi-functioning state by the healing warmth of a restorative shower and a hearty meal. Such thoughts also disappear completely during those long summer days in the saddle from sunrise to sunset. You wish these days would last forever, and appreciate them so much more after the winter you've had to endure to get back there.

Your thoughts and emotions change with the seasons, as do your facial contours and bodily functions. You become intertwined with the mood of the weather, which can both lift your spirits and send you into a state of complete disarray during the course of a single day. Those occasional moments of yearning for another life never last long, however, and most days I wake up ready to get out there all over again, my inner child eager to mount his carbon-fibre steed ahead of another day of new, unscripted adventures. No two days are ever the same for the courier, as different faces and different places keep you coming back for more.

The Deliveroo CEO Will Shu still goes out to make deliveries to this day, having completed the first-ever order for his start-up company in London back in 2013. If I was to ever change careers, I'm sure there would still be a little bit of me eager to get out and work a few hours as a courier, to get a breath of fresh air (well, maybe not fresh), see old friends and have a fun workout all at the same time; and especially to escape being confined in the same energy-sapping environment all day long.

Retention rates seem remarkably high for a job that offers little security or employee benefits. Only a few riders I know have left the work behind in search of better money and fairer conditions; the majority soldier on, largely thankful for a job that better reflects their core passions and interests – with many eventually switching their bicycles for faster vehicles once they have saved up enough money to do so.

Even those who do find alternative employment usually keep the courier work on as a way to make some extra money as a side hustle. Many miss the freedom and spontaneity that comes from being outdoors. The delivery firms know this all too well and are happy for there to be an abundance of riders on any given platform for the work that is available. The race to the bottom, in terms of wages, continues unabated.

So in looking for another career path to match the thrills

of riding my bike for a living, I have set the bar remarkably high. The freedom and flexibility would be very hard to give up. Following someone else's rules after a prolonged period of setting your own spontaneous, autonomous schedule even more so. The added value cycling provides me is somewhat offset by the seasonal, inconsistent and often poor pay.

Of course, over the past few years I have made various applications for jobs that seemed objectively up my alley but without any real conviction that any of them was something I really wanted to do or that the person doing them would be someone I wanted to be. And this epitomises my relationship with cycling. It is who I am and what I want to be all at once. Thoughts of careers and bigger ambitions simply evaporate when something you are already doing is so central to your being and purpose.

Not that a job has to define who you are. If you're in a job that doesn't fit with who you are, you can use the experience to help realise why you didn't like it so much, and what it is you actually want to do in the future. Equally, if you have a great job, or something you enjoy doing and get paid for, then use your free time to fulfil other parts of your life that the job you love doing cannot quite meet.

I've loved being a cycle courier, but as I have for most of my young adult life, like a lot of people I've always been looking for the next 'better thing'. It's ironic, but it was only at the very start of the pandemic that I really accepted what I did for a living without fully realising it. Knowing that I would be doing this job for some time all of a sudden made me give up the time-consuming task of job hunting – a somewhat misguided search for the next chapter I would take through life.

I shook off this internal feeling of shame and embarrassment that I should be doing something else, something with more gravitas, or simply something that would make my parents more proud of me. Accepting this was the point at which I started exploring other, more creative outlets that my job had deprived me of since finishing my master's degree. Crucially, all these creative outlets were solely for me and no one else.

Even with a job you love and look forward to doing most days, this cannot and should not be the sole focus of your existence or what you put all your energy and time into. It wasn't healthy for me, and probably wouldn't be for most other people - doing the same thing, day in, day out, for so many hours every week. Expecting your job or career, hobby or interest to provide you with all your happiness cannot be the sole reason for getting out of bed in the morning.

I tried this for two long years as a full-time courier and was left mentally and physically exhausted, to the point where I didn't want to cycle any longer. Cycling, when used as part of a balanced routine, like during studies or while I've been writing this book, can be a fantastic all-round means of feeling better, thinking clearer and learning how to unwind and de-stress. Cycling, when done to extremes, leaves you with little energy or enthusiasm for any other aspect of your life. The same is true of most things done to extremes.

Like most things in life, balance is of course the key. Focusing on only one aspect of your life is much like putting all your money into a single company on the stock market. Better to hedge your bets, likewise with your interests and passions in life. Not putting all your eggs in one basket should prove a much more reliable longer-term strategy - geniuses, visionaries and fascist dictators aside. There's never one job that can give you all that you want or desire from life.

But that doesn't mean you can't make up for those missing things in other ways. Adding those extra missing ingredients into your life can make all the difference, and make you realise that the dream job you aspire to one day isn't really the be-all and end-all. Or that dedicating the majority of your day to one repetitive task you are good at or enjoy isn't the dream you once thought it would be.

I'm a lot healthier and happier now than in my previous career, as I spend a large chunk of my time cycling, opposed to sat hunched over a desk or playing catchup with my sleep. I may have a few quid less in the bank at the end of every month, but I would take health over wealth any day. Days at work used to be spent wishing the hours away, until I could be reunited at the weekend with the outdoors and a sense of freedom attained from the drudgery of slaving away for most of the working week.

Rather than making what I earn my main incentive for happiness, I focus instead on making myself happy through what I do. I now work to my own schedule, when and if I want to. And because I love cycling, I do work a lot of the time. This concept of time changes everything. Now I have a far greater appreciation of time, purpose and my own future goals.

Money comes and goes. Time only goes. Time is finite. Money may be hard to attain, but time and health are much more important than status and wealth - when you zoom out and look more holistically at life. Look after your health and your time spent living will be richer than many others, whether wealthy or not. Time is a commodity like no other, it will never come around again. We need to use it wisely.

Think back to the things that made you happy as a child. Most of those things you did back then you simply may have grown out of, forgotten about, or stopped doing as you start working and take on extra responsibility. As kids, we have a profound sense of freedom and creativity that can easily evaporate as we neglect such hobbies and interests in later years.

The bicycle is normally the first machine we learn to master, and the first we neglect as we grow older and become more self-conscious, feeling the need to adapt to the world around us as we become young adults. The bicycle, like most of our hobbies and interests, is pushed aside, dismissed as childish or adolescent as we pursue the more 'grown-up' goals of a family, career, house or nice car.

It needn't be one or the other. Sometimes as we move through life it is vital to reconnect to those things that used to give us such joy, inner peace, creative passion and child-like pleasure. We can all reconnect to those precious pastimes if we allow some time and space to do so. After all, we aren't so different from the smaller versions of ourselves, who spent the summer holidays exploring new places and pushing existing boundaries. Some of these activities can even be transformed into a career, or a part-time paid hobby. Once you find a market for your passion, the rest is child's play.

I remember vividly when I was around seven years old, I received a Purple Ronnie (novelty stickman cartoon character) diary from my older sister one Christmas. Along with a few other, smaller, insignificant gifts, I left the diary in my corner cupboard for a week or so until I was getting ready to go back to school after the holidays.

I was becoming bored and had grown tired of playing with

the same few toys since Christmas Day, having built all of my Lego sets and put them onto a shelf to collect dust. So I started rummaging through some of the toys and gifts that I'd forgotten about or thrown into the bottom drawer to play with or discover at some later date.

I opened the diary out of curiosity, with no real intention of ever really using it. It had a 'Things to do' section right at the front. I went down into the kitchen and retrieved a half-chewed pen from the designated drawer full of miscellaneous, lost-and-found junk, then I sat on my windowsill for half an hour before writing down under 'Things to do':

Be rich

Be happy

A few days passed and I'd been thinking long and hard about the two short sentences I had scribbled down, and what they both actually meant to me. After waking up in the middle of the night, unsettled, restless, unable to get back to sleep and looking out the window towards the stars, I went back to the diary and opened it up to the only page on which I had written anything down.

I crossed out the top two words with the pen, and put a large tick to the right-hand side of the bottom two words, with a small smiley face sketched below it. I closed the diary with the elastic strap attached to the rear of its back cover, and it soon became hidden amongst some books and magazines, never to be used again.

When we moved house six years later, I rediscovered the diary amongst some random items of no worth or use, in a neatly kept old cardboard shoebox, and I asked myself the same question again. Then again at 18 when my parents moved and I finally threw out the diary, and again as I finish this book and ponder what might be the most profound question any of us will ever ask ourselves. And my own answer has never changed, merely the thought process that gets me there.

The thing that has changed are the little boy's experiences as he has travelled through life, unsure of what was coming next. I've never told anyone about those words I scribbled down all those years ago, but that seven-year-old boy who lay in bed looking up to the ceiling, contemplating life, then stared into the darkness of the night and the stars that filled the sky – well, I'm pleased with how he came to find that answer. I owe him a lot.

Much like the rockstar on his fifth world tour, I know that the reason why I still do this job is that it gives me something profound most other jobs or professions simply could not. A rockstar reconnects with a crowd of old fans, wherever the location and despite the dwindling pay packet, just for the thrill of performing again.

I simply reconnect with my bike and the city that I love, for the sheer thrill of it all, and to escape for a few hours on any given day or night. Eager to perform, and eager to derive some pleasure from the simplest of activities that helps keep me happy.

I stumbled upon the most wonderful quote as I finished writing this book. 'You can't become a craftsperson unless the process itself is the reward.' It resonates with most things in life, and highlights the competitive advantage you get from doing something that you love for a living. It makes all the difference. Tuning into the seven-year-old boy lying in bed, gazing to the sky, hopeful of the future and what it may bring. Despite the dwindling pay packet and the outside chance of being admitted to rehab sometime in the not-so-distant future, for aggravated assault in the bedroom during a bout of cycling-induced sleep in the early hours of the morning after one of my gigs.

So as long as I'm being paid to ride my bike, and I am able to do so, the gig isn't over just yet. The show must go on…

Notes

THE EARLY DAYS

1 Hunt, Lindsey. "Biking for Your Brain: The Neurology of Cycling." Duvine. 05-06-18. https://www.duvine.com/blog/brain-biking-the-n eurology-of-cycling/ (01-07-21).

2 Gray, Richard. "Regular exercise can improve memory and learning." The Telegraph, 19-02-12. https://www.telegraph.co.uk/news/health/n ews/9090981/Regular-exercise-can-improve-memory-and-learning.h tml (05-07-21).

3 Pollock RD, O'Brien KA, Daniels LJ, et al. "Properties of the vastus lateralis muscle in relation to age and physiological function in master cyclists aged 55-79 years." Aging Cell Volume 17. Issue 2. April 2018. https://onlinelibrary.wiley.com/doi/full/10.1111/acel.12735 (12.06.21).

4 Hunt, Lindsey. "Biking for Your Brain: The Neurology of Cycling." Duvine. 05.06.18. https://www.duvine.com/blog/brain-biking-the-ne urology-of-cycling/ (accessed 01.07.21).

5 Andrews, Linda. "Bicycling can sharpen your thinking and improve your mood." Psychology Today. 26.05.15. https://www.psychologytod ay.com/gb/blog/minding-the-body/201505/bicycling-can-sharpen-yo ur-thinking-and-improve-your-mood (18.07.21).

THE MAIN EVENT

6 O'Hear, Steve. "Deliveroo drivers hold protest in London over possible changes to the way they are paid." Techcrunch. 11.08.16. https://techcr unch.com/2016/08/11/deliveroo-drivers-hold-protest-in-london-ove r-possible-changes-to-the-way-they-are-paid (10.04.21).

7 Hunt, Lindsey. "Biking for Your Brain: The Neurology of Cycling." Duvine. 05.06.18. https://www.duvine.com/blog/brain-biking-the-ne urology-of-cycling/ (accessed 01.07.21).

8   "Can exercise really have the same effect as taking illegal drugs?" BBC. 01.07.16. https://www.bbc.co.uk/bbcthree/article/3259e81b-dc89-47 7e-ad80-793b06972b16 (12.08.21).

9   Hunt, Lindsey. "Biking for Your Brain: The Neurology of Cycling." Duvine. 05.06.18. https://www.duvine.com/blog/brain-biking-the-ne urology-of-cycling/ (accessed 01.07.21).

10 Can exercise really have the same effect as taking illegal drugs?" BBC. 01.07.16. https://www.bbc.co.uk/bbcthree/article/3259e81b-dc89-47 7e-ad80-793b06972b16 (12.08.21).

11 Littlehales, Nick. Sleep: The Myth of 8 Hours Sleep, the power of naps… and the New Plan to Recharge your Body and Mind. Penguin Life, 2016, p. 146.

12 Fry, Alexa. "Sleep, athletic performance, and recovery." Sleep Foundation. 24.07.21. https://www.sleepfoundation.org/physical-activity/ath letic-performance-and-sleep (03.08.21).

13 "Cycling and Sleep: What's the link?" Cycleplan. 27.07.18. https://ww w.cycleplan.co.uk/cycle-savvy/cycling-and-sleep (14.07.21).

14 Littlehales, Nick. Sleep: The Myth of 8 Hours Sleep, the power of naps… and the New Plan to Recharge your Body and Mind. Penguin Life, 2016.

15 Lilly, Chris. "Working from Home (WFH) Statistics 2021." Finder. 01.03.21. https://www.finder.com/uk/working-from-home-statistics (01.10.21).

16 Littlehales, Nick. Sleep: The Myth of 8 Hours Sleep, the power of naps… and the New Plan to Recharge your Body and Mind. Penguin Life, 2016.

17 Fry, Alexa. "Sleep, athletic performance, and recovery." Sleep Foundation. 24.07.21. https://www.sleepfoundation.org/physical-activity/ath letic-performance-and-sleep (03.08.21).

18 Fry, Alexa. "Sleep, athletic performance, and recovery." Sleep Foundation. 24.07.21. https://www.sleepfoundation.org/physical-activity/ath letic-performance-and-sleep (03.08.21).

19 Suni, Eric. "What happens when you sleep?" Sleep Foundation. 30.10.20. https://www.sleepfoundation.org/how-sleep-works/what-happens-w hen-you-sleep (02.08.21).

20 Suni, Eric. "Stages of sleep." Sleep Foundation. 14.08.21. https://www. sleepfoundation.org/how-sleep-works/stages-of-sleep (04.08.21).

21   Cronkleton, Emily. "How to treat and prevent diarrhea during and after a workout." Healthline. 17.09.19. https://www.healthline.com/health/exercise-fitness/diarrhea-after-working-out/ (16.06.21).

22   "Do you have hair loss or hair shedding?" American Academy of Dermatology Association. https://www.aad.org/public/diseases/hair-loss/insider/shedding (16.06.21).

23   Migration Advisory Committee Report. "Impact of international students in the UK." Gov.uk. September 2018. https://assets.publishing.service.gov.uk/government/uploads/system/uploads/attachment_data/file/739089/Impact_intl_students_report_published_v1.1.pdf (26.06.21).

24   Tidman, Zoe. "UK warned not to take appeal for international students 'for granted' amid drop in EU student numbers." Independent. 09.09.21. https://www.independent.co.uk/news/education/education-news/universities-international-student-brexit-report-b1916932.html (10.10.21).

25   Coughlan, Sean. "Overseas students add £20bn to UK economy." BBC News. 11.01.18 https://www.bbc.co.uk/news/education-42637971 (10.06.21).

26   Fast food capital of the UK." Fresh Student Living. 05.12.20. https://freshstudentliving.co.uk/2020/12/05/fast-food-capital-of-the-uk/ (15.08.21).

27   Lock, S. "Food delivery and takeaway market in the United Kingdom (UK) – Statistics & Facts." Statista. 03.12.21. https://www.statista.com/topics/4679/food-delivery-and-takeaway-market-in-the-united-kingdom-uk/ (15.06.21).

28   Curry, David. "Food delivery app revenue and usage statistics (2021)." BusinessofApps. 17.05.21. https://www.businessofapps.com/data/food-delivery-app-market/#2.1 (13.06.21).

THE GOOD

29   Hunt, Lindsey. "Biking for Your Brain: The Neurology of Cycling." Duvine. 05.06.18. https://www.duvine.com/blog/brain-biking-the-neurology-of-cycling/ (accessed 01.07.21).

30   Introducing distance-based fees." Deliveroo Rider Email. Deliveroo Team. 04.07.18. (14.08.21).

31   Witts, James. "How does hot weather affect your cycling performance?" Cyclist.21.07.21. https://www.cyclist.co.uk/in-depth/905/how-does-h ot-weather-affect-your- cycling-performance (10.08.21).

32   Long, Samantha. "Hot or cold shower after a bike ride?" Cycling Europe. 28.06.16. https://cyclingeurope.org/2016/06/28/hot-or-cold-shower- after-a-bike-ride/ (12.09.21).

33   Lindberg, Sara. "Cold showers vs. hot showers: Which one is better?" Healthline. 23.03.20. https://www.healthline.com/health/cold-shower- vs-hot-shower#So,-which-type-is-better? (12.09.21).

34   Walker, Peter. "The 'miracle pill': how cycling could save the NHS." The Guardian. 17.09.21. https://www.theguardian.com/environment/bike- blog/2017/sep/17/the-miracle- pill-how-cycling-could-save-the-nhs (18.08.21).

THE INTERLUDE

35   Adams, Richard. "Job prospects vary widely for graduates in England, data shows." The Guardian. 19.05.21. https://www.theguardian.com/e ducation/2021/may/19/job-prospects-vary-widely-for-graduates-in-e ngland-data-shows (02.08.21).

36   "Coronavirus: Restaurants are 'hurting', says Deliveroo boss." BBC News. 29.07.20. https://www.bbc.co.uk/news/business-53215411 (03.07.21).

37   Big 7 Travel Team. "Top 50 Friendliest Cities in the UK." Big 7 Travel. 26.09.19. https://bigseventravel.com/the-50-friendliest-cities-in-the-u k/ (18.08.21).

38   Finch, Isabel. "Manchester named most liveable city in the UK – again." BusinessLive. 06.09.19. https://www.business-live.co.uk/econo mic-development/manchester-named- most-liveable-city-16875221 (10.08.21).

39   Schmich, Mary. Wear Sunscreen: A primer for real life. Andrews McMeel Publishing, 2012.

THE BAD

40   Vita Student Accommodation Pricing. Manchester Circle Square 2021/2022. Ultimate Vita Room Apartments. https://www.vitastu dent.com/student-accommodation/manchester/circle-square/choose- your-room/?year_of_study=2021%20/%2022&term=51&floor_min=1

&floor_max=16&type=Ultimate%20Vita (18.08.21).

41　Reinberg, Steven. "Extreme exercise might dull the brain, study says." WebMD. 26.09.19. https://www.webmd.com/fitness-exercis e/news/20190926/extreme-exercise- might-dull-the-brain-study-says (19.08.21).

42　Yeager, Selene. "What happens to your stomach when you ride." Bicycling. 07.09.16. https://www.bicycling.com/training/g200472 84/what-happens-to-your-stomach-when- you-ride/ (10.08.21).

43　Hurford, Molly. "How to prevent stomach upset while riding." Bicycling. 03.09.15. https://www.bicycling.com/training/a20044837/how-to-pr event-stomach-upset-while- riding/ (10.08.21).

44　Zapata, Kimberly. "Bloated after your workout? Here's what might be causing it." Healthline. 28.05.21. https://www.healthline.com/health/fi tness/bloated-after-workout#causes (11.08.21).

THE UGLY

45　Blain, Bastien et al. "Neuro-computational impact of physical training overload on economic decision-making." Current Biology. Volume 29 Issue 19. 07.10.19. https://www.cell.com/current-biology/fulltext/S09 60-9822(19)31104-2 (17.08.21).

46　Lane, Barnaby. "Tyson Fury gave a bizarre interview ahead of his Deontay Wilder fight where he said he's masturbating 7 times a day to 'keep testosterone pumping.'" Business Insider. 15.01.2020. https://w ww.businessinsider.com/tyson-fury-interview-masturbating- seven-times-a-day-wilder-rematch-2020-1?r=US&IR=T (01.08.21).

47　Firth, Robert. "Deliveroo strike Manchester: the money we make per delivery is decreasing." The Meteor. 27.02.19. https://themeteor.org/2 019/02/27/deliveroo-strike-manchester-the-money-we-make-per-del ivery-is-decreasing/ (02.08.21).

THE PANDEMIC

48　McIntyre, Alex. "Lost deer spotted wandering the empty streets of Newcastle during the coronavirus lockdown." Chronicle Live. 19.05.20. https://www.chroniclelive.co.uk/news/ north-east-news/lost-deer-spotted-wandering-empty-18277951 (10.02.21).

49　Thomson, Helen & New Scientist. This Book Could Fix Your Life. John Murray Publishers Ltd, 2021.

50 Parsons, Guy. "London is among the loneliest cities in the world." TimeOut. 16.02.17. https://www.timeout.com/london/blog/londo n-is-among-the-loneliest-cities-in-the-world- 021617 (14.06.21).

51 Schwartz, Barry. The Paradox of Choice: Why More is Less. Harper Perennial, 2004.

52 Parker, George et al. "How two decades of EU migration went into reverse." Financial Times. 01.04.21. https://www.ft.com/content/de72 1f35-d228-48de-bd9f-d2168b16aba6 (04.08.21).

53 Molzner, Chrissy. "Urban loneliness & isolation: The dark side of living in a big city." The Roots of Loneliness Project. https://www.rootsoflon eliness.com/urban-loneliness-isolation (14.06.21).

54 Craille, Gillies. "What's the worlds loneliest city?" The Guardian. 07.04.16. https://www.theguardian.com/cities/2016/apr/07/loneli est-city-in-world (05.04.21).

55 Lilly, Chris. "Working from Home (WFH) Statistics 2021." Finder. 01.03.21. https://www.finder.com/uk/working-from-home-statistics. (01.10.21).

56 Lilly, Chris. "Working from Home (WFH) Statistics 2021." Finder. 01.03.21. https://www.finder.com/uk/working-from-home-statistics. (01.10.21).

57 Littlehales, Nick. Sleep: The Myth of 8 Hours Sleep, the power of naps... and the New Plan to Recharge your Body and Mind. Penguin Life, 2016.

58 Iddenden, George. "Food delivery app downloads boomed 33% during pandemic." Charged Retail. 11.05.21. https://www.chargedretail.co.uk /2021/05/11/food-delivery-app-downloads-boomed-33-during-pand emic/ (04.08.21).

59 The Business Research Company. "Online Food Delivery Services Global Market Report 2021: Covid-19 Growth and Change to 2030." Report Linker. April 2021. https://www.reportlinker.com/p06064489 /Online-Food-Delivery-Services-Global-Market-Report-COVID-19- Growth-And-Change-To.html (08.08.21).

60 Browne, Ryan. "Deliveroo doubled orders and trimmed losses in the first six months of 2021." CNBC. 11.08.21. https://www.cnbc.com/2021/0 8/11/deliveroo-doubles-orders-in- first-half-of-2021.html (20.08.21).

61 Migration Advisory Committee Report. "Impact of international students in the UK."Gov.uk. September 2018. https://assets.publis

hing.service.gov.uk/government/uploads/system/uploads/attachment
_data/file/739089/Impact_intl_students_report_published_v1.1.pdf
(26.06.21).

62   Summary Report for the Higher Education Policy Institute and
      Universities UK International.   "The costs and benefits of inter-
      national higher education students to the UK economy."   London
      Economics. September 2021. https://www.hepi.ac.uk/wp-content/
      uploads/2021/09/Summary-Report.pdf (23.09.2021).

63   Wong, Tessa. "Coronavirus: Why some countries wear face masks and
      other don't." BBC News. 12.05.20. https://www.bbc.co.uk/news/worl
      d-52015486 (04.06.21).

About the Author

Ryan was born in Ashington, Northumberland. He studied sports at Leeds Met, graduated and worked in the leisure industry for seven years. He went back into higher education to study international politics for a postgraduate degree at Newcastle University and has been a cycle courier ever since. He lives in Newcastle, and enjoys investing in his spare time, researching new energy and healthcare stocks. He also enjoys house music, politics, economics, coffee, whiskey, fitness and travelling when not out riding or in researching. He has been a beach lifeguard, multi-sports coach and DJ amongst many other jobs. He now spends the majority of the time in the saddle, behind a computer screen, or in bed sleeping.

You can connect with me on:

🌐 https://www.goodreads.com/user/show/134964255-ryan-murphy

🐦 https://twitter.com/ryanYGTGmurphy

🔗 https://www.mixcloud.com/bothalboy

Printed in Great Britain
by Amazon